Getting Started with Oracle Cloud Free Tier

Create Modern Web Applications Using Always Free Resources

Adrian Png
Luc Demanche

Apress®

Getting Started with Oracle Cloud Free Tier: Create Modern Web Applications Using Always Free Resources

Adrian Png
Vancouver, BC, Canada

Luc Demanche
Montreal, QC, Canada

ISBN-13 (pbk): 978-1-4842-6010-4
https://doi.org/10.1007/978-1-4842-6011-1

ISBN-13 (electronic): 978-1-4842-6011-1

Managing Director, Apress Media LLC: Welmoed Spahr
Acquisitions Editor: Jonathan Gennick
Development Editor: Laura Berendson
Coordinating Editor: Jill Balzano

Cover image designed by Freepik (www.freepik.com)

Distributed to the book trade worldwide by Springer Science+Business Media New York, 233 Spring Street, 6th Floor, New York, NY 10013. Phone 1-800-SPRINGER, fax (201) 348-4505, e-mail orders-ny@springer-sbm.com, or visit www.springeronline.com. Apress Media, LLC is a California LLC and the sole member (owner) is Springer Science + Business Media Finance Inc (SSBM Finance Inc). SSBM Finance Inc is a **Delaware** corporation.

For information on translations, please e-mail booktranslations@springernature.com; for reprint, paperback, or audio rights, please e-mail bookpermissions@springernature.com.

Apress titles may be purchased in bulk for academic, corporate, or promotional use. eBook versions and licenses are also available for most titles. For more information, reference our Print and eBook Bulk Sales web page at http://www.apress.com/bulk-sales.

Any source code or other supplementary material referenced by the author in this book is available to readers on GitHub via the book's product page, located at www.apress.com/9781484260104. For more detailed information, please visit http://www.apress.com/source-code.

Printed on acid-free paper

Dedicated especially to my wife. I would not have come this far without your love, support, and encouragement.
—Adrian Png

A special thank-you to my family, my kids and especially to my wife Marie-Eve, for their support, patience, and understanding during this project.
—Luc Demanche

Table of Contents

About the Authors

Adrian Png is Senior Consultant at Insum Solutions. He has over two decades of experience in designing and implementing software solutions using a wide variety of programming languages. Adrian has a deep passion for Oracle Application Express and has helped many organizations succeed in developing robust data management practices. As a full-stack developer, he also does double duty as a database and cloud administrator. "Design for the user" is his motto, and he continually seeks to optimize processes and adopt new strategies and technologies to improve how data is captured, integrated, and used effectively.

Luc Demanche is an Oracle DBA with 20 years of experience. His high-level expertise recently earned him the distinctions of Oracle Cloud Infrastructure 2019 Certified Architect Professional, Oracle Autonomous Database Cloud 2019 Certified Specialist, and Oracle Certified Professional 12c. His passion for the discipline has also led him to share his knowledge through a 2016 IOUG-published book titled *Oracle Application Express Administration*, which he co-authored with his colleague Francis Mignault, CTO at Insum. Luc specializes in Oracle Databases from 7.3 to 19c and is particularly knowledgeable about the numerous Oracle tools used on his projects. He is heavily involved in building the Oracle Cloud team at Insum and has several successfully completed cloud projects to his credit.

About the Technical Reviewer

Christoph Ruepprich has been working in various roles with Oracle since 2003. He has worked as a database administrator, developer, and software architect using various Oracle technologies. He has designed and implemented highly customized APEX applications, utilizing a variety of technologies including REST, Node.js, and so on. He has helped automate Oracle Cloud processes via Python and Terraform. He has also developed DevOps processes with Jenkins. Christoph is an Oracle ACE, Oracle Cloud and Google Cloud Certified, and an active presenter on Oracle-related topics at various user group meetings, such as RMOUG and KScope. He co-authored the book *Expert Oracle Application Express*.

Acknowledgments

We would like to thank Jonathan Gennick for involving us in this exciting project and for keeping us in pace throughout the journey. We are grateful to Jill Balzano for her guidance and for keeping us organized. Last but not least, our heartfelt thanks to the brilliant minds at Oracle who engineered the products we have written about. This book would be meaningless without your great work and dedication to the advancement of technology. Thank you!

—Adrian Png and Luc Demanche

I would like to thank Adrian for giving me the opportunity of writing this book with him. It has been a pleasure working with him on this project.

—Luc Demanche

Introduction

The Oracle Cloud Infrastructure (OCI) is Oracle's Infrastructure-as-a-Service (IaaS) offering. Like its competitors, the OCI offers customers a broad range of network, compute, database, and other supporting components needed to build a cloud-based computing infrastructure. By carefully designing and engineering your systems architecture, you can deploy, scale, and maintain a robust environment that supports from the simplest to the most complex computing workloads, such as web applications and even Machine Learning tasks!

In 2019, Oracle made a surprising announcement at its annual Oracle OpenWorld event. Mr. Larry Ellison, Oracle's Executive Chairman and Chief Technology Officer, announced the availability of the Oracle Cloud Free Tier. With it comes a suite of Always Free components that will allow anyone to deploy web applications using state-of-the-art technology such as the Oracle Autonomous Database.

This book is carefully divided into four parts. We begin by understanding how to obtain a free account and then set up the necessary credentials to access the OCI console and use its facilities. Next, we take a deep dive into all the Always Free components where you will understand what they are, how to create and use them, and any Always Free limitations that you need to be aware of. In Part 3, we will put on the web developer's hat and demonstrate how to create a multitiered web application environment using the Oracle Autonomous Database and a variety of programming languages and frameworks. Last but not least, we will cover some advanced topics on improving your efficiency as an OCI administrator as well as discuss next steps.

Whether you are a fresh graduate software programmer or an experienced database administrator, we hope that this book will provide a comprehensive guide to the Oracle Cloud's Free Tier offering and that the knowledge will enable you to fully utilize the technology and tools available to you and then use them to build a robust computing environment for supporting your web applications.

PART 1

Getting Started

CHAPTER 1

Create an Account

As with every online service that we use, the first step often involves creating an account to manage our activities, monitor costs, and make payments. While the process for registering an Oracle Cloud account has evolved over the last few years, this chapter provides guidance and explanations based on the most recent instructions from Oracle that, I am confident, will help you successfully set up your account.

The *Oracle Cloud Infrastructure* (OCI) console is the window to all your Oracle Cloud resources. To access the console, users will need either an Oracle *Identity Cloud Service* (IDCS) or OCI account. During registration, an Oracle IDCS account is created. It has full administrative access to your OCI console including managing billing information. Hence, great care must be taken to ensure that the credentials do not fall into the wrong hands. Choose a password that goes beyond the minimal requirements listed later in this chapter and store it securely.

Process

Signing up for an *Oracle Cloud Free Tier* account is simple. However, before you begin, ensure that you have the following:

1. An email address that has not previously been used to sign up for an Oracle Cloud account

2. A mobile number that you have access to

3. A valid credit card

Start by going to the URL *https://oracle.com/cloud/free* using your preferred web browser, and then click the *Start for free* button (Figure 1-1).

© Adrian Png and Luc Demanche 2020
A. Png and L. Demanche, *Getting Started with Oracle Cloud Free Tier*,
https://doi.org/10.1007/978-1-4842-6011-1_1

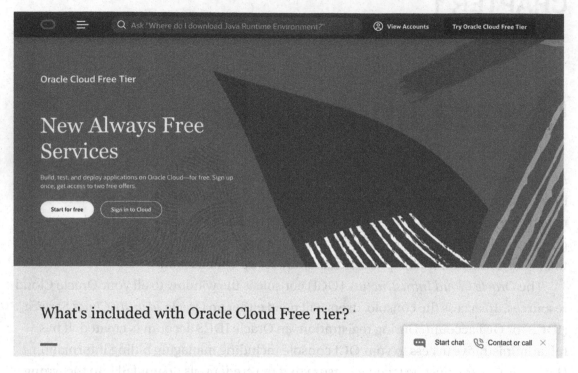

Figure 1-1. *Getting started*

The first step involves entering your email address and then selecting an appropriate country or territory that you are registering the account from (Figure 1-2).

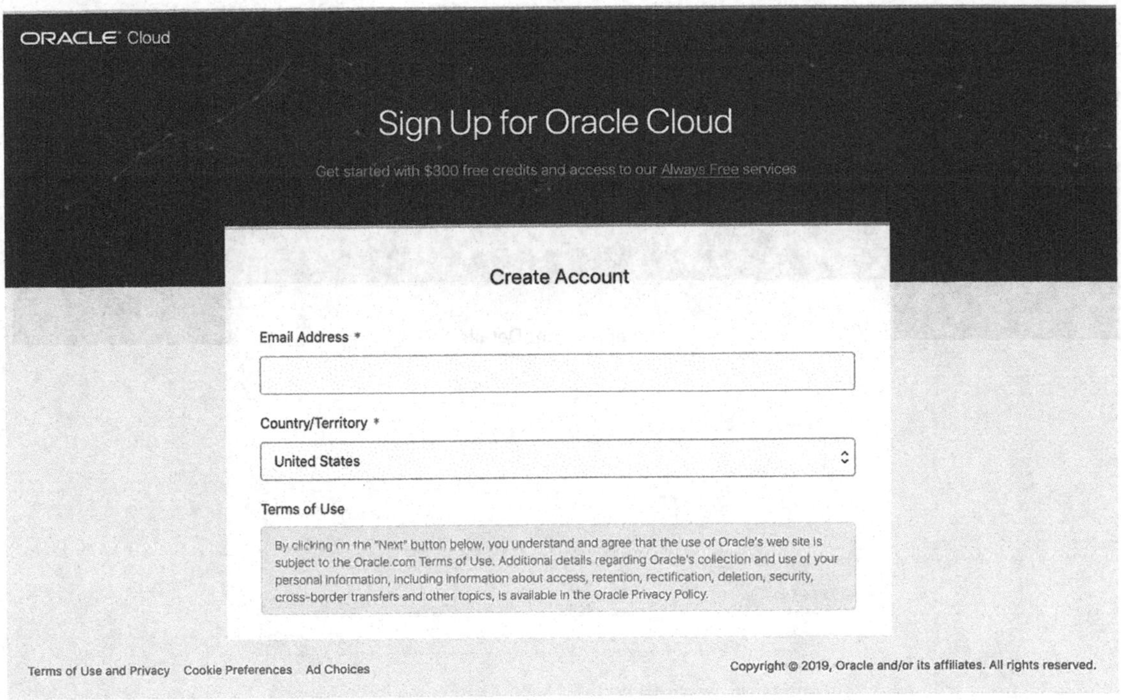

Figure 1-2. *Provide an email address and select the country/territory the account is registered from*

It is important that the email entered is not currently associated with an Oracle Cloud account, or an error will be triggered. After the country/territory is selected, the page is updated with the amount of free credits available for the 30-day trial in your local currency. The amount would be the equivalent of USD 300. Click *Next* to proceed to the next page.

Note   After entering your email address, a pop-up message may inform you that additional trial credits and/or terms are available to you. These additional credits and terms are preassigned by an authorized Oracle employee under special circumstances, for example, participation at an Oracle event. These credits will be available to you upon successful creation of the account.

Select the *Account Type,* whether the account is for company or personal use. Make sure to choose the appropriate account type as it helps Oracle determine how it is set up and assigned to the appropriate account managers for follow-up. It can be a lengthy process to convert account types after it has been created.

Next, enter an appropriate *Cloud Account Name* (Figure 1-3). The Cloud Account Name is immediately validated and checked that it is unique. If the validation fails, please try entering a new one or a variation of the original name proposed.

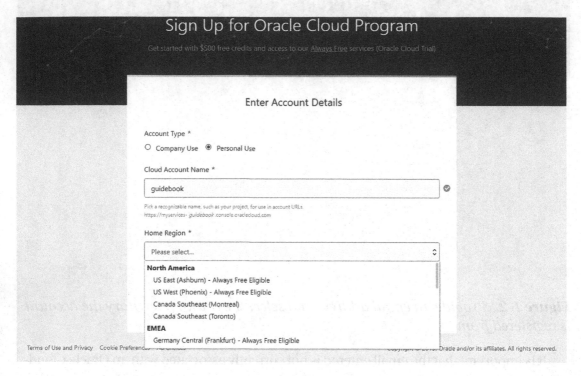

Figure 1-3. *Provide additional account details*

The field requires you to select your choice for *Home Region*. The next session explains what data regions are and how to select the Home Region from your account. If your goal is to utilize the *Always Free* services, then be sure to select regions that are tagged *Always Free Eligible*.

Regions and Home Region

Oracle has data regions located strategically all around the world. At the time of writing, the company has 15 data regions across North America, EMEA (Europe, the Middle East, and Africa), Asia-Pacific, and Latin America. It is anticipated that there will be up to 36 regions, including government regions, by the end of the year 2020.

Each data region has one or more availability domains that, in turn, have one or more data centers. Availability domains are designed to run independently of each other within and between regions. They do not share vital infrastructure resources, and hence, in well-architected systems, there should be little or no disruption to services, should an availability domain suffer an outage.

When signing up for an Oracle Cloud Free Tier account, it is important to consider that data region that you would like to use for your Home Region. *Always Free* resources, described in detail later in this chapter, can only be created in your Home Region.

As a rule of the thumb, consider the services that you require and then chose one that is closest to your users. There are also certain guidelines when choosing a region depending on where you live. Consult Oracle's website (*www.oracle.com/cloud/data-regions.html*) for guidance and up-to-date information on service availability in each data region.

At the time of writing this chapter, the following are the available regions and the region groupings that they belong to:

- North America

  - US East (Ashburn)

  - US West (Phoenix)

  - Canada Southeast (Montreal)

  - Canada Southeast (Toronto)

- EMEA

  - Germany Central (Frankfurt)

  - Netherlands Northwest (Amsterdam)

  - Saudi Arabia West (Jeddah)

  - Switzerland North (Zurich)

  - UK South (London)

- Asia-Pacific

  - Australia East (Sydney)

  - Australia Southeast (Melbourne)

  - India West (Mumbai)

- - Japan Central (Osaka)

  - Japan East (Tokyo)

  - South Korea Central (Seoul)

- Latin America

  - Brazil East (Sao Paulo)

Billing and Verifications

Once your choice for Home Region has been decided, continue filling out the billing information for the account and provide a mobile number (Figure 1-4). The latter is required for one of two verification methods used by Oracle Cloud.

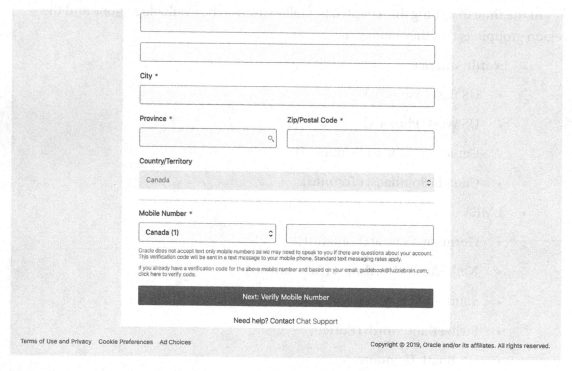

Figure 1-4. *Provide a mobile number for verification*

Once your billing information and mobile number have been submitted, wait for a verification code to be sent to your mobile phone as a text message. Enter the code received, and then click *Verify Code* to complete the first verification step (Figure 1-5).

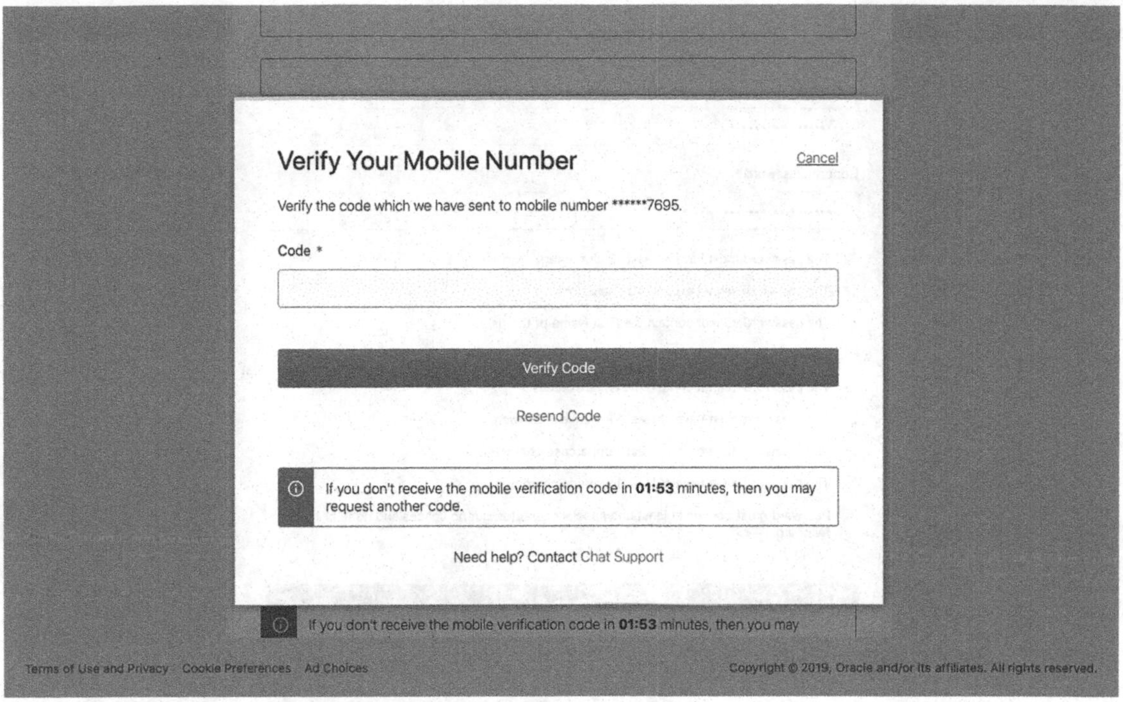

Verify Your Mobile Number   Cancel

Verify the code which we have sent to mobile number ******7695.

Code *

[   ]

[Verify Code   ]

Resend Code

ⓘ If you don't receive the mobile verification code in **01:53** minutes, then you may
   request another code.

Need help? **Contact** Chat Support

ⓘ If you don't receive the mobile verification code in **01:53** minutes, then you may

Figure 1-5. *Verify your mobile number*

If you do not receive the verification code within two minutes, click *Resend Code* to request a new one. You will not be able proceed beyond this point without completing this process.

Next, set the password for your Oracle IDCS account. The username for this account is the email address that you had provided earlier. It is the primary credential for managing your Oracle Cloud account, and hence there are strict requirements for setting a complex password (Figure 1-6).

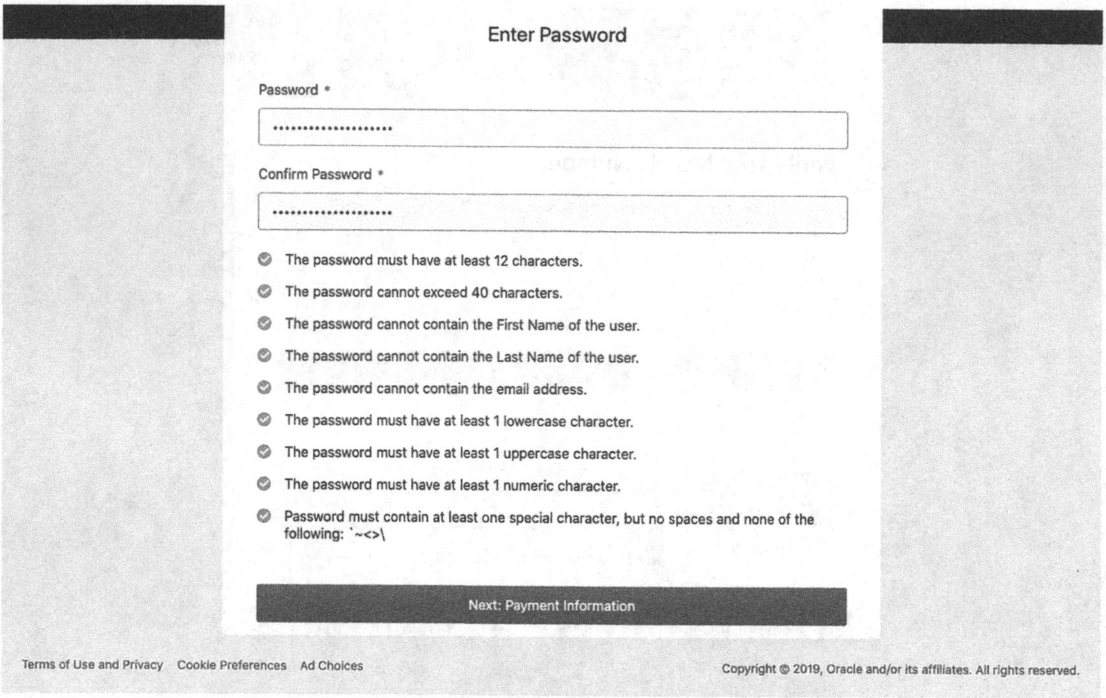

Figure 1-6. *Complexity requirements for account password*

Your password should meet the following criteria:

1. Between 12 and 40 characters long

2. Should not contain any part of the user's name or email address

3. Have at least a lowercased, uppercased, and numerical character

4. Have at least one special character that is not a space and **not** any of the following characters: `~<>\

Tip   Both Oracle IDCS and OCI console allow users to secure their accounts further with Multifactor Authentication (MFA). You are strongly encouraged to explore how this can be enabled for your account(s).

The final step involves providing Oracle with a valid credit card for the second verification step (Figure 1-7).

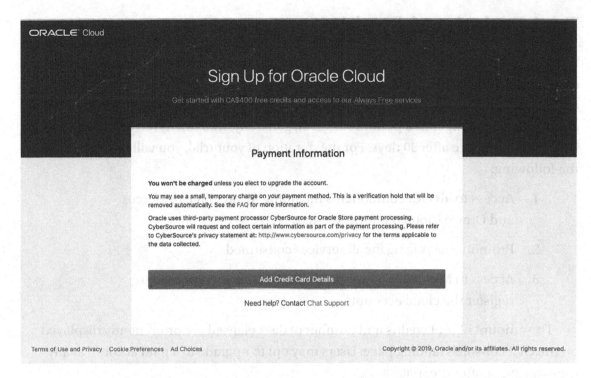

Figure 1-7. *Provide credit card information for additional verification*

Oracle assures us that the payment information provided is strictly for the purpose of verifying your account request. You will have an opportunity later to change the credit card information used when upgrading to a paid account.

Account Confirmation

Once your payment information has been successfully verified, Oracle will begin creating your account and an Oracle Support identifier. You should receive a few emails from Oracle once these have been completed. They include the following:

1. Acknowledgment and notice that your account has been created successfully. At this point, you have access to the OCI console, but there are additional provisioning tasks that are ongoing.

2. Notice that your account setup is completed. The email will also include information about how much trial credits are awarded to your account and their expiry.

3. Notice that an Oracle Support identifier has been assigned to your Oracle Cloud subscription/account.

11

Trial Period and Credits

The amount of trial credits and the length of the trial may be different in certain situations. For example, an Oracle representative might preregister you for a trial at an Oracle workshop, or you belong to a special program that entitles you to additional credits and/or a longer trial period. However, generally, trials are given the equivalent of USD 300 that expire after 30 days. For the duration of your trial, you will have access to the following:

1. Access to **all** OCI components including Always Free resources and Oracle Cloud platform services

2. Promotional pricing for all services consumed

3. Access to My Oracle Support using the email address used to register the cloud account

The amount of trial credits and number of days elapsed are prominently displayed on the OCI console's landing page. Users may opt to upgrade to a paid account at any time during or after the trial.

Promotional Pricing

For the duration of the trial, you are billed at a discounted rate when using Oracle Cloud services. The charges are deducted daily from your balance trial credits. Typically, users are only charged for the "physical" resources used, such as CPU, memory, and storage. You are not billed for any Oracle licenses required to run the service.

For example, suppose you provision an Oracle Database Standard Edition server using an *Oracle Database Cloud Service* (DBCS) virtual machine (VM) DB system with the *VM.Standard2.1* shape. A shape in OCI is a template that describes the number of CPUs and amount of memory allocated to the instance. The VM.Standard2.1 shape provides 1 Intel CPU core and 15 GB of memory. For storage, the smallest amount that one can allocate to a DB system is 256 GB.

Note   For a DB system, Oracle allocates additional storage for the database recovery files. A DB system with 256 GB assigned will consume up to 712 GB of block storage that is charged to the customer.

Based on the Oracle Cloud pricing (*www.oracle.com/database/vm-cloud-pricing.html*) web page, it is estimated that the DB system will cost about USD 0.4032 per hour. That works out to approximately USD 300 per month if the server is kept running 24x7. If Oracle were to charge trial users the full rate, you can appreciate how there is very little you can do with your account in 30 days.

Fortunately for us, during the trial period, users are only billed for any resources consumed by the instance. There are no charges for the Oracle Database Standard Edition license required. Based on current rates, a VM.Standard2.1 costs USD 0.0638 per hour to operate and, for *Block Volume Storage* with balanced performance, USD 0.0425 per GB per month. The estimated monthly cost works out to be:

```
$0.0638 x 24 hours x 31 days + $0.0425 x 712 GB = $77.73 monthly
```

This amount is significantly lower than what you would anticipate paying in the future, and thus, you should be careful not to make budget decisions based on the OCI *Cost Analysis* reports in your account during the trial period. For a more accurate evaluation of costs, always use the Oracle Cloud cost estimator tool, which you can access at *https://oracle.com/cloud/cost-estimator.html*.

My Oracle Support

For the duration of the trial, users will have access to My Oracle Support (MOS) and the ability to file Service Requests (SRs) should the need arises. MOS can be access at the URL *https://support.oracle.com/*. Within the web portal, users also have access to a wealth of technical information through its knowledge base and community forums. Searching through these resources often provides answers and solutions to technical challenges and problems that you might encounter with both systems and Oracle software.

After signing up successfully for your Oracle Cloud account, you will receive three emails, one of which contains information about your MOS support identifier. You are automatically enrolled to MOS using the email address provided during registration. Do **not** log in to MOS using any Oracle account previously created. You can associate any preexisting account with your support identifier once the MOS account setup is completed. Instead, click the *New User? Register Here* link at the top right of the support portal's home page (see Figure 1-8).

Figure 1-8. Oracle Support Portal Homepage

Fill up the required information, making sure to use the email address that was used to create the Oracle Cloud account. Once the form is submitted, an email will be sent to verify your email address and activate your account. The link expires with 24 hours, so do this as soon as you receive the verification email and then log in with your new credentials.

If the Oracle Cloud account is upgraded to a paid account, you will continue to have access to these support resources and features. If the account is not upgraded, then you will no longer have access to MOS after the trial ends. The only support available will be through community channels such as forums and social media.

Overview of Always Free Resources

On September 16, 2019, Larry Ellison, co-founder and Chief Technology Officer of Oracle, announced the Oracle Cloud Free Tier offering at his Oracle OpenWorld (OOW) keynote. Included is a suite of Always Free resources for both new and some existing customers. Used together, one can host a full-stack web application on an enterprise-grade platform.

Oracle is best known for its database platform and would be the cloud vendor most trusted to manage and optimize its product. Recently, the company has been aggressively marketing its *Autonomous Database* (ADB) technology, a managed Oracle Database that includes many of its enterprise features. Using machine learning (ML), the company also touts that the system can self-patch, self-optimize, and self-heal. With the Oracle Cloud Free Tier offering, users have access to not one, but **two** free ADBs. These can be configured for either transactional or data warehouse workload types.

Each ADB also comes with a suite of tools for database developers and data analysts, no installation required. These include *Oracle Application Express* (APEX), *SQL Developer* (SQLDEV) Web, and *Oracle Machine Learning* (OML) Notebooks. APEX is a low-code platform that allows both professional and citizen developers to create modern, functional, and secure web applications. Combined with SQLDEV Web, developers have access to all the necessary tools to model and manage data schemas for these applications. OML Notebooks is a web-based tool for data wranglers and ML specialists to access, analyze, and visualize data. They will also be able to use these tools to train and generate ML models using built-in Oracle Database PL/SQL packages. All these features will be discussed in depth in Part 4 of the book.

With so much functionality available for free, you might wonder, what's the catch? There are key limitations when using an Always Free ADBs, for example, instances have 1 OCPU and 20 GB storage cap. These instances will also stop automatically if usage is not detected after seven days. These restrictions will be discussed in greater detail in Chapter 7.

To complement the ADBs, Oracle also provides two *Compute* VMs, each with 1/8 OCPU and 1 GB memory. Users also have an option to distribute 100 GB of block storage volumes to use between these VMs. You will also have access to about 10 GB of *Object Storage* and 10 GB of *Archive Storage*. Compute instances are discussed in Chapter 5 and storage in Chapter 4.

Finally, the Oracle Cloud Free Tier offering also gives you access to some auxiliary services – a single *Load Balancer* for creating redundancy and failover for your web applications and Monitoring and Notifications features that will enable administrators to monitor the system metrics and be informed if they fall below user-specified thresholds. These topics will be discussed in Chapters 8 and 9.

Summary

Mr. Ellison's announcement of the Oracle Cloud Free Tier offering at OOW 2019 probably caught many by surprise. Though Oracle joined the cloud race a little later than some of her competitors, the current generation of the Oracle Cloud has much to offer and is probably the best cloud environment to host any Oracle Database.

Providing a complete stack of free resources will allow many new and old developers and database administrators to appreciate what it has to offer. This chapter not only outlines the steps needed to kick-start your adventure, but also ensures that you are equipped with enough background about what is available to you and what are the nuances of managing an Oracle Cloud account.

CHAPTER 2

Identity and Access Management

The purpose of this chapter is to provide a basic understanding of the *Oracle Cloud Infrastructure Identity and Access Management (IAM)*. Using this service, we are able to create users, groups, and policies that will be used to control the access to your cloud resources. This chapter will provide a brief description of the main IAM components and will give an example to demonstrate how this is working all together.

IAM Components

Home Region

As explained in Chapter 1, the *Home Region* is the region from where you have created your Oracle Cloud Infrastructure (OCI) account. You should always use the URL related to your Home Region to access the OCI console. The IAM entities' metadata (users, policies, groups, etc.) resides in your Home Region and the changes are automatically propagated to every other region.

Resource

Resources are the components you can manage in the cloud. These include compute instances, database instances, block volumes, load balancers, and so on. Using IAM, we will have to grant permissions to users in order for them to access these resources.

© Adrian Png and Luc Demanche 2020
A. Png and L. Demanche, *Getting Started with Oracle Cloud Free Tier*,
https://doi.org/10.1007/978-1-4842-6011-1_2

User

The tenancy provisioning process creates the first user as the default administrator for the tenancy. This user is automatically in the default group *Administrators*. Every individual or system that needs to interact with resources should have their own user account. For ease of governance, it is crucial to have dedicated users for individuals and systems that interact with the resources.

Note   By user, we are not referring to the application's users, but the individual or service that will connect to the OCI console or needs to interact with resources.

Group

A group is a set of users that require the same access and permissions on resources. During the tenancy provisioning process, a default group called *Administrators* is created and contains the initial user. This default group shouldn't be deleted and should always contain at least one user.

Policies

A policy specifies the type of access a user can have on a resource or a group of resources. The policy is assigned to a group and is set at the tenancy or compartment level. If the permission is granted at the tenancy level, the users in the group will get the same permissions for every compartment in this tenancy. During the tenancy provisioning process, a default policy is created that provides permissions on *all-resources* for the group *Administrators* which contains the initial user.

Compartment

The compartment is one of the fundamental components in OCI. It helps to group related Cloud resources. This is used for the purpose of segregation, isolation, and organization and also to easily get usage and cost information. When the tenancy is provisioned, we can see two different compartments, the main one called "accountname (root)" and another one called *ManagedCompartmentForPaaS*.

Note   The compartment "ManagedCompartmentForPaaS" is an internal compartment used to integrate Oracle PaaS services within the Oracle Cloud Infrastructure.

In order to help to regroup Cloud resources within a compartment, you are allowed to also create subcompartments within a compartment. The compartment will become the parent compartment and can have up to six levels of subcompartments. A good example of subcompartments could be to regroup resources in the compartment "IT". The following table represents an example of compartment hierarchy.

Parent Compartment	Subcompartment	Subcompartment	Description
IT	Finance	System A	Compartment hosting the systems A with sensitive data
		System B	Compartment hosting the systems B with sensitive data
IT	HR		Systems and application for HR
IT	Engineering		Systems and application for Engineering

Federation

Companies use an identity provider (IdP) to manage their user's credentials. This is also used to manage access to services and resources across the company. By default, Oracle Cloud Infrastructure provisioning process creates a federation with *Oracle Identity Cloud Service (IDCS)*. Federation is also supported with Microsoft Active Directory, Microsoft Azure Active Directory, Okta, and other providers that support the SAML2 protocol. The initial user created during the tenancy provisioning process is a federated user from IDCS.

Managing IAM Components

We would like to provide an example of an IAM strategy. Two departments of our company want to have their applications running on OCI. They have their own IT team that will manage the servers and the autonomous databases. They also want to have the ability to measure their own Cloud usage and cost. However, the IT department will take care of the virtual cloud network as well as the general management of the infrastructure. You can see in Figure 2-1 the IAM strategy.

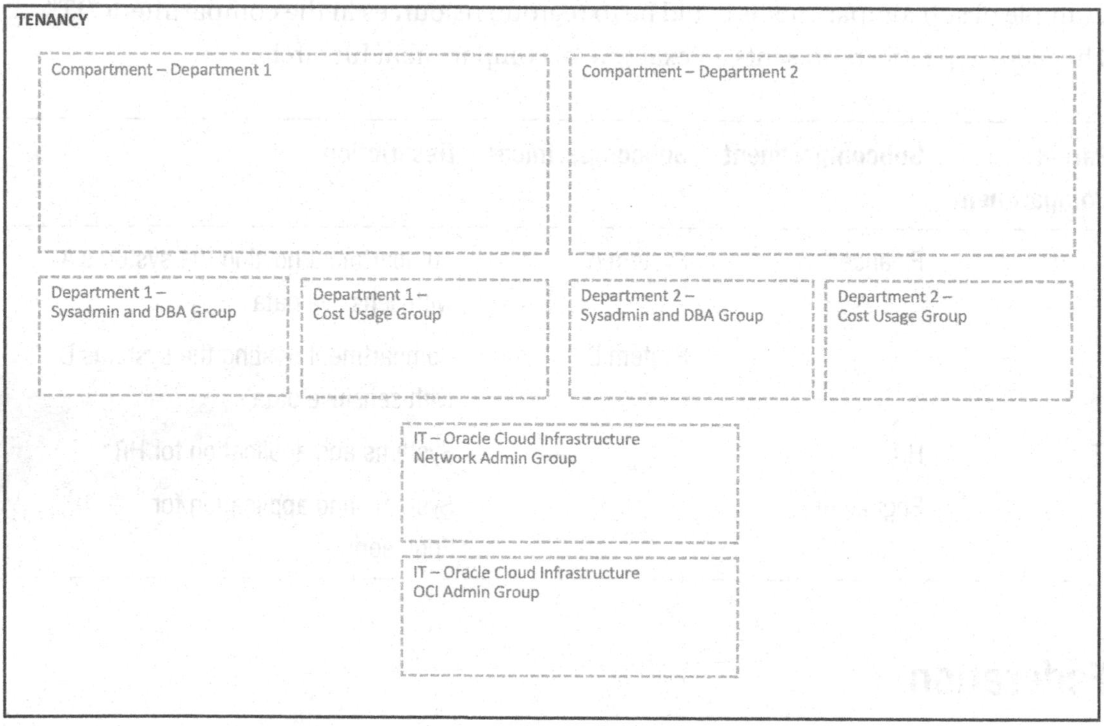

Figure 2-1. *Identity and Access Management Strategy*

In order to deploy this strategy, we will create the following:

- Two compartments

- Six groups

- Six policies

- Six users

For this exercise, we will not use any identity provider (IdP), and the entities will be created locally in Oracle Cloud Infrastructure IAM.

Managing Compartments

As mentioned earlier, the concept of compartment is fundamental to isolate resources. We can regroup resources per either application, team, department, and so on. In our case, we will group by department. Here is the process of creating the compartments:

From the Oracle Cloud Infrastructure console, click the navigation menu at the top left to open the menu, and select *Identity* and then *Compartments* as you can see in Figure 2-2.

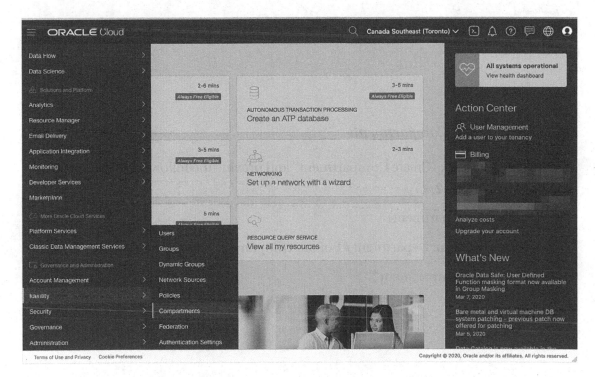

Figure 2-2. *Select Compartment*

As you can see in Figure 2-3, we have the two default compartments:

- Account name (root), which is the root compartment

- ManagedCompartmentForPaaS to integrate PaaS services to OCI

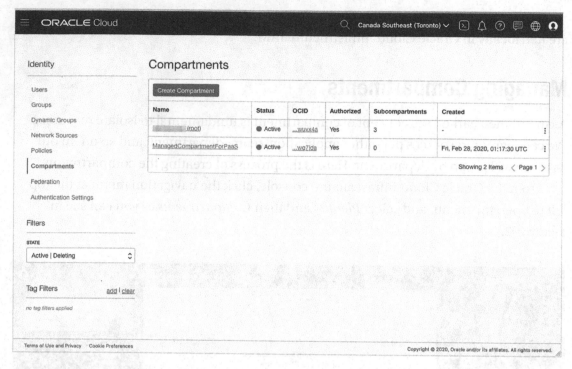

Figure 2-3. *List of Compartments*

You can now click "Create Compartment" and provide the following information as you can see in Figure 2-4 :

- **Name**: Department1

- **Description**: Department #1 of our company

Click "Create Compartment".

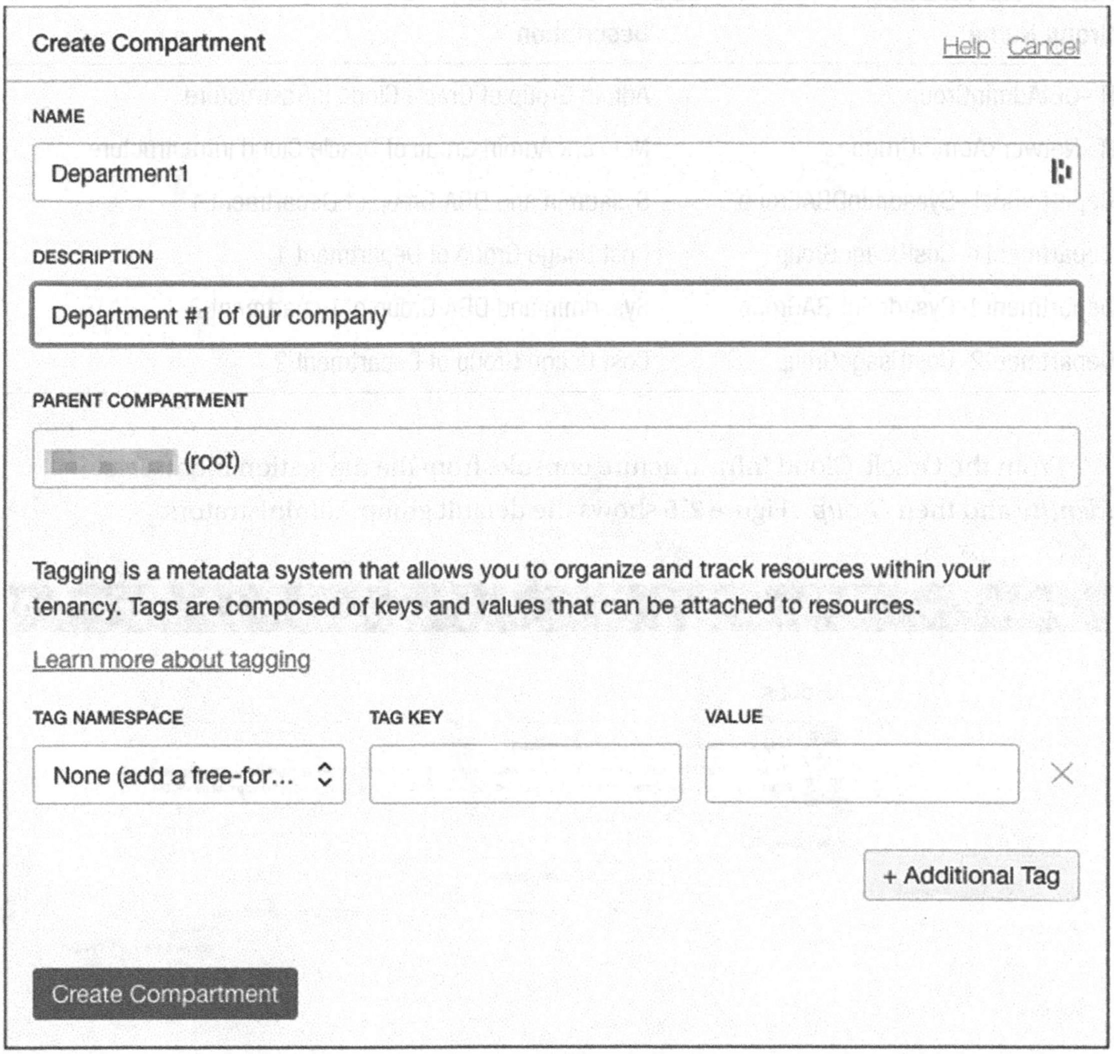

Figure 2-4. *Creation of the Compartment Department #1*

Perform the same steps for the creation of the compartment Department 2.

Managing Groups

Now that we have two compartments, we will create the groups. Through policies, these groups will have the required permissions to allow their users to perform their tasks. Here is the list of groups we have to create for our example:

Group Name	Description
IT–OCIAdminGroup	Admin Group of Oracle Cloud Infrastructure
IT–NetworkAdminGroup	Network Admin Group of Oracle Cloud Infrastructure
Department1–SysadminDBAGroup	Sysadmin and DBA Group of Department 1
Department1–CostUsageGroup	Cost Usage Group of Department 1
Department2–SysadminDBAGroup	Sysadmin and DBA Group of Department 2
Department2–CostUsageGroup	Cost Usage Group of Department 2

From the Oracle Cloud Infrastructure console, from the navigation menu select *Identity* and then *Groups*. Figure 2-5 shows the default group Administrators.

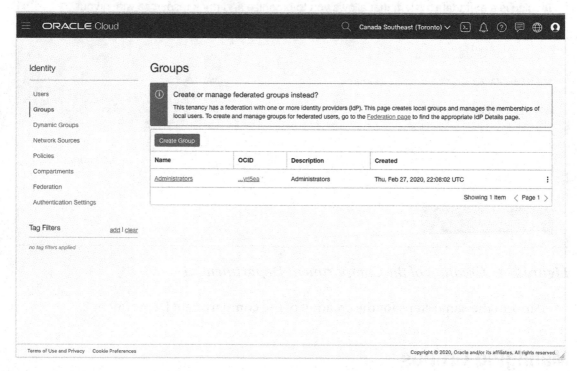

Figure 2-5. *List of Groups*

You can now click "Create Group" and provide the following information as you can see in Figure 2-6 and click "Create":

- **Name**: IT–OCIAdminGroup

- **Description**: Admin Group of Oracle Cloud Infrastructure

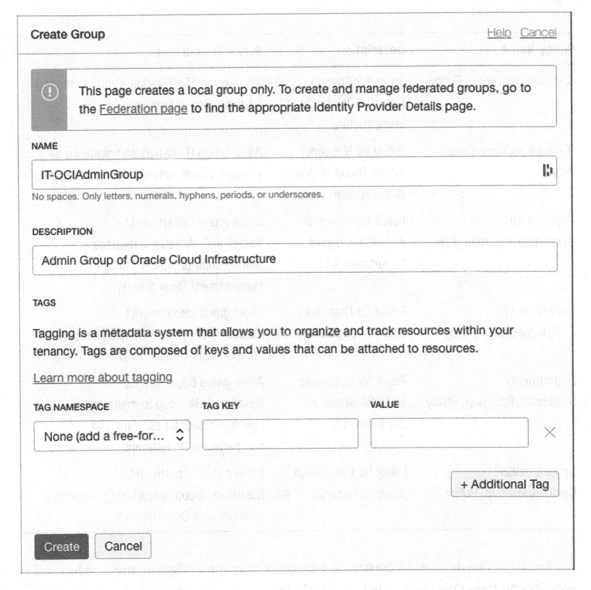

Figure 2-6. *Creation of a Group*

Perform the same steps for the creation of the other groups.

Managing Policies

Now that we have the required groups, depending on the tasks users will have to perform, we will create corresponding policies. The policies will give the required permissions to the groups. For our example, here is a table with the policies to be created.

Policy Name	Description	Policy Statements
IT–OCIAdminGroup_Policy	Policy for Admin Group of Oracle Cloud Infrastructure	Allow group IT–OCIAdminGroup to manage all-resources in tenancy
IT–NetworkAdminGroup_Policy	Policy for Network Admin Group of Oracle Cloud Infrastructure	Allow group IT–NetworkAdminGroup to manage virtual-network-family in tenancy
Department1–SysadminDBAGroup_Policy	Policy for Sysadmin and DBA Group of Department #1	Allow group Department1–SysadminDBAGroup to manage autonomous-database-family in compartment Department1
Department1–CostUsageGroup_Policy	Policy for Cost Usage Group of Department #1	Allow group Department1–CostUsageGroup to read usage-reports in compartment Department1
Department2–SysadminDBAGroup_Policy	Policy for Sysadmin and DBA Group of Department #2	Allow group Department2–SysadminDBAGroup to manage autonomous-database-family in compartment Department2
Department2–CostUsageGroup_Policy	Policy for Cost Usage Group of Department #2	Allow group Department2–CostUsageGroup to read usage-reports in compartment Department2

From the Oracle Cloud Infrastructure console, from the navigation menu select *Identity* and then *Policies* and click "Create Policy".

Provide the following information as you can see in Figure 2-7 and click "Create":

- **Name**: IT–OCIAdminGroup_Policy

- **Description**: Policy for Admin Group of Oracle Cloud Infrastructure

- **Statement 1**: Allow group IT-OCIAdminGroup to manage all-resources in tenancy

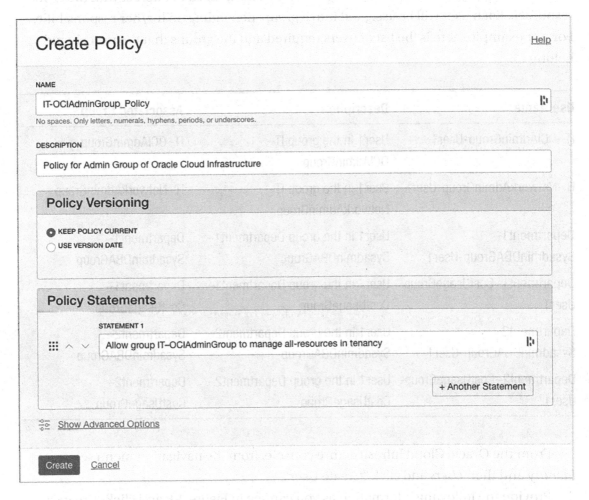

Figure 2-7.   Creation of a Policy

Perform the same steps for the creation of the other policies.

An important aspect of security is the principle of least privilege (POLP). We should always limit user access to the minimum required to perform their tasks. This principle becomes one of the more important policies when it comes to data security, protection against malicious activities, and fault tolerance.

Note   Always ensure you are respecting the principle of least privilege.

Managing Users

We are now ready to create the individual users that will need to interact with the Cloud resources. Each user will be assigned into a group, depending on his/her responsibility. For our example, here is the list of users required and the groups that the user should belong to:

Username	Description	Associated Group
IT–OCIAdminGroup-User1	User1 in the group IT–OCIAdminGroup	IT–OCIAdminGroup
IT–NetworkAdminGroup-User1	User1 in the group IT–NetworkAdminGroup	IT–NetworkAdminGroup
Department1–SysadminDBAGroup-User1	User1 in the group Department1–SysadminDBAGroup	Department1–SysadminDBAGroup
Department1–CostUsageGroup-User1	User1 in the group Department1–CostUsageGroup	Department1–CostUsageGroup
Department2–SysadminDBAGroup-User1	User1 in the group Department2–SysadminDBAGroup	Department2–SysadminDBAGroup
Department2–CostUsageGroup-User1	User1 in the group Department2–CostUsageGroup	Department2–CostUsageGroup

From the Oracle Cloud Infrastructure console, from the navigation menu select *Identity* and then *Users* and click "Create User".

Provide the following information as you can see in Figure 2-8 and click "Create":

- **Name**: IT–OCIAdminGroup-User1
- **Description**: User1 in the group IT–OCIAdminGroup

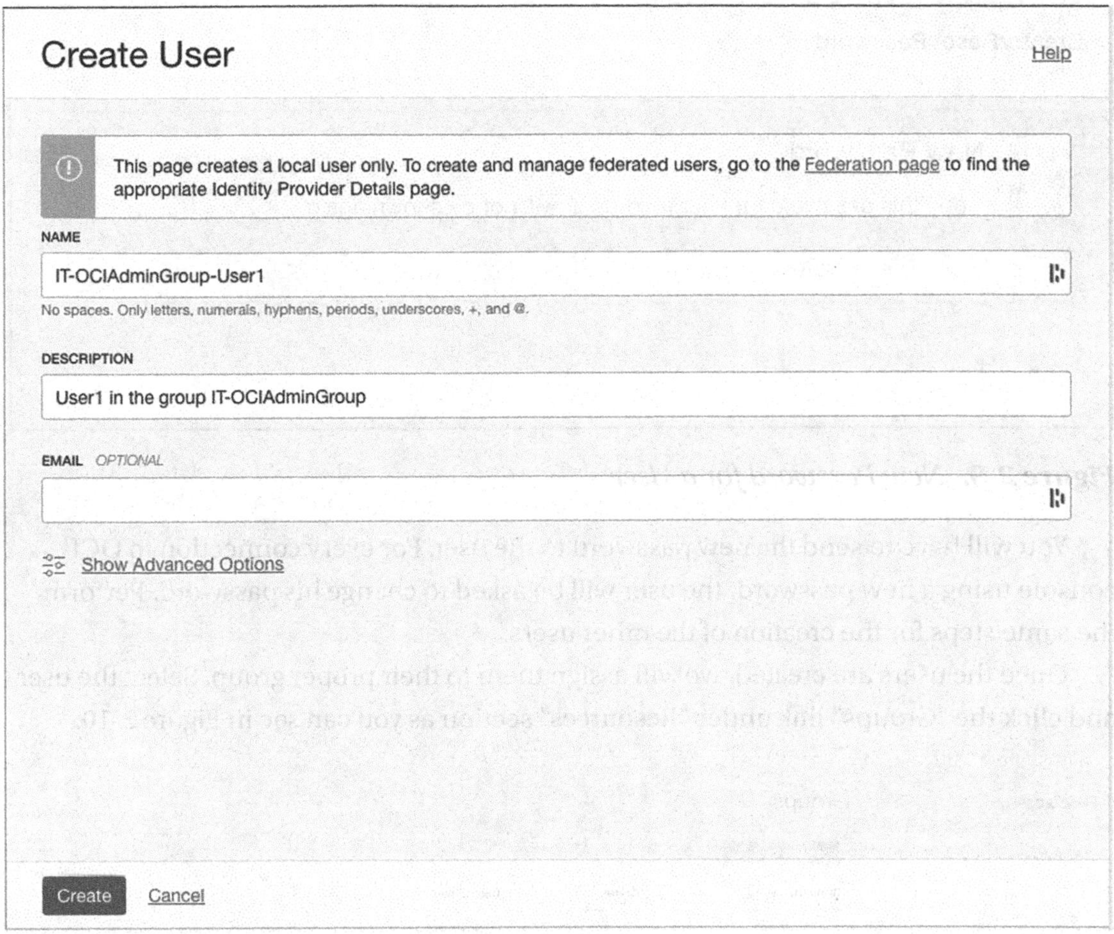

Create User

> ⓘ   This page creates a local user only. To create and manage federated users, go to the Federation page to find the appropriate Identity Provider Details page.

NAME

IT-OCIAdminGroup-User1

No spaces. Only letters, numerals, hyphens, periods, underscores, +, and @.

DESCRIPTION

User1 in the group IT-OCIAdminGroup

EMAIL *OPTIONAL*

⸬ Show Advanced Options

Create   Cancel

Figure 2-8. *Creation of a User*

Once a user is created, you will have to create his first password. To do so, select the newly created user and click "Create/Reset Password". It will ask you for a confirmation and then you will see this page (Figure 2-9).

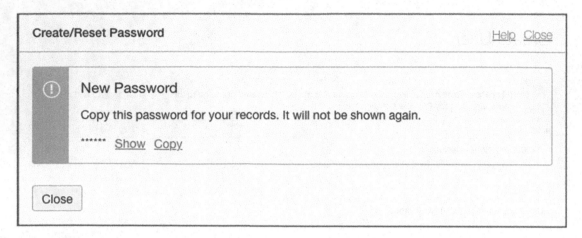

Figure 2-9. *New Password for a User*

You will have to send the new password to the user. For every connection to OCI console using a new password, the user will be asked to change his password. Perform the same steps for the creation of the other users.

Once the users are created, we will assign them to their proper group. Select the user and click the "Groups" link under "Resources" section as you can see in Figure 2-10.

Resources	Groups		
API Keys	Add User to Group		
Auth Tokens	**Group Name**	**Status**	**Description**
SMTP Credentials			
Customer Secret Keys	No items found.		
Groups			Showing 0 Items
Terms of Use and Privacy Cookie Preferences			Copyright © 2020, Oracle and/or its affiliates. All rights reserved.

Figure 2-10. *Groups Link*

You can now click "Add User to Group" and select the group you want this user to belong to. When selected, click "Add". Your user is now part of this group.

Perform the same steps to assign the users to their respective groups. We have now completed the configuration of the IAM strategy we have designed at the beginning of this section. Here are the key concepts of this strategy:

- Department's applications are isolated into their own compartment.

- Segregation of roles using IAM groups and policies.

Authentication Settings

We can customize the authentication settings for nonfederated users in the tenancy, by having control on some password's attributes. From the Oracle Cloud Infrastructure console, from the navigation menu select *Identity* and then *Authentication Settings* and click "Edit". As you can see in Figure 2-11, here are the default values of the attributes.

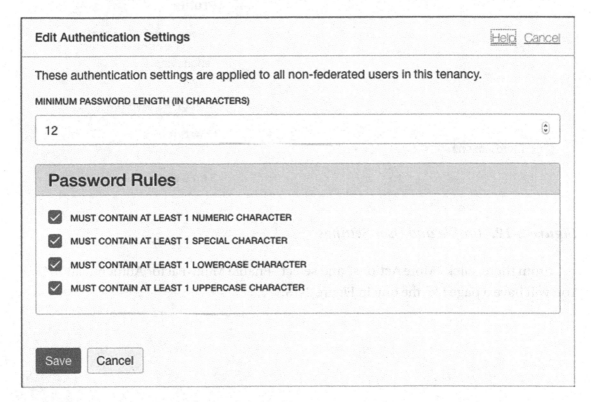

Edit Authentication Settings   Help Cancel

These authentication settings are applied to all non-federated users in this tenancy.

MINIMUM PASSWORD LENGTH (IN CHARACTERS)

12

Password Rules

☑ MUST CONTAIN AT LEAST 1 NUMERIC CHARACTER

☑ MUST CONTAIN AT LEAST 1 SPECIAL CHARACTER

☑ MUST CONTAIN AT LEAST 1 LOWERCASE CHARACTER

☑ MUST CONTAIN AT LEAST 1 UPPERCASE CHARACTER

Save   Cancel

Figure 2-11. *Authentication Settings*

You can then modify some values to respect your enterprise's password policy.

Multifactor Authentication

Multifactor authentication (MFA) is a method in which a user is asked to provide multiple credentials. The first factor of authentication will be the IAM user's password and the second factor would be a verification code coming from an authenticator app device like "Oracle Mobile Authenticator" and "Google Authenticator" running on iPhone or Android.

To enable the MFA, log in to the OCI console and click the "Profile" icon and select "User Settings" as we can see in Figure 2-12.

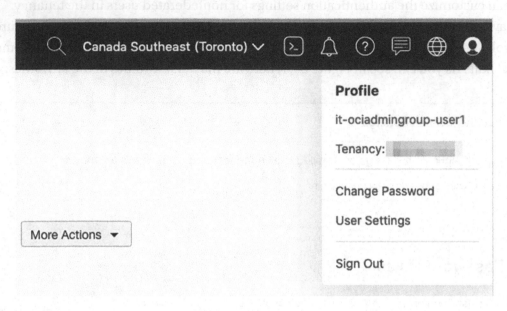

Figure 2-12. *Profile and User Settings*

From there, click "More Actions" and select "Enable Multi-Factor Authentication". You will have a page like the one in Figure 2-13.

Figure 2-13. *Enable MFA*

Using your favorite authenticator app, scan the QR code and you will have to complete the verification process by using the verification code coming from the app. From there, every time you will be logging in to the OCI console, you will have to provide the code from the authenticator app.

You can disable MFA by clicking "More Actions" and "Disable Multi-Factor Authentication" or ask your administrator if you don't have access to the console.

I would like to bring to your attention some important points:

- We can enable MFA on local IAM users and not on federated users.

- User must enable MFA for themselves.

Summary

In this chapter we have covered the Oracle Cloud Infrastructure Identity and Access Management service. This service is crucial to control the access to cloud resources. We have explained the main concepts as well as how to use IAM users, groups, and policies to control the permissions on resources. Throughout the chapter, we have built a real example, so we were able to demonstrate how these concepts are working together.

PART 2

Infrastructure and Operations

CHAPTER 3

Basic Networking

The purpose of this chapter is to provide a basic understanding of the *Oracle Cloud Infrastructure* (OCI) *Networking* service. This chapter will be divided into three main sections. The first section will explain the general concepts and components of a network. The second will explain the concepts and components of an Oracle Cloud *Virtual Cloud Network* (VCN) and how we can relate to the on-premise network. In the third section, we will conclude with an example of a network topology and the way to create this VCN using the "Networking Quickstart" wizard.

Networking Concepts

A network is defined as a group of nodes (computers and devices) connecting in a way that they can communicate with each other, sending and receiving data over the network. Each node is uniquely identified across the network by its own IP address. A router is used to manage and route the traffic within a network. In order to secure the traffic, the concept of network segmentation and firewall are used. All of this will be explained in this section.

IP Address

As we have mentioned, the IP address uniquely identified a node within a network. The common type of IP address is the IPv4, for example, 10.0.0.0. Each of the four numbers can range from 0 to 255. As you can imagine, IPv4 has a limit in terms of available IP addresses, considering the explosion of new devices around the world.

IPv6 is another type of IP that provides a much larger number of IP addresses for the future. An IPv6 address is composed of eight groups of four hexadecimal digits; here is an example: 2002:0db7:15a3:0000:0000:8b3r:0456:1234.

37

© Adrian Png and Luc Demanche 2020
A. Png and L. Demanche, *Getting Started with Oracle Cloud Free Tier*,
https://doi.org/10.1007/978-1-4842-6011-1_3

> **Note**   IPv4 supports a maximum of 4.3 billion of IP addresses. IPv6, in theory, will never run out.

Router

A router is used to route the data packets from a source to a destination, using route rules. Source and destination are usually other networks (on-premise or virtual networks) or gateways. Routers inspect the destination IP addresses of a network request. If it matches a route rule, it will forward the data packet to the destination. If no route rule matches the source and the destination, the packet will simply be dropped. A route rule is a destination and a target that instructs the packet where and how to transmit. For example, in Table 3-1 we have a route rule to allow the traffic to access the Internet through the Internet Gateway.

Table 3-1. *Route rule*

Destination	Target
0.0.0.0/0	Internet Gateway vcn-20200614-0910

> **Note**   Route tables contain the route rules.

Firewall

The Internet eases the day-to-day communication, but it also has security and vulnerability issues. Firewalls were introduced in order to secure the traffic between various networks and devices. A firewall examines the flow of data from the source and either permits or blocks the packet based on security rules. Firewalls shouldn't only examine traffic from external sources but should also validate traffic within the network as the threats can be coming from external as well as internal systems.

Network Segmentation

One of the main reasons for doing network segmentation is to reduce the attack surface for hackers. A zone is a segment of your network that groups resources. Typically, you can group data and resources, based on their sensitivity, into different zones. For example, you can have an Internet-facing zone that groups load balancers, which receive traffic from the Internet. Based on security rules, the traffic can then go into another zone that has a group of application servers. From there, the traffic can be redirected into the zone with database servers. Using this approach, firewalls and zones can secure the application servers and database servers from Internet attacks.

Virtual Cloud Network

A Virtual Cloud Network (VCN) is a private virtual network that is running in one of the Oracle Cloud Infrastructure regions. Planning your virtual network topology is a crucial task. A VCN serves as a foundation onto which you will be able to easily deploy your application servers, databases, load balancers, and any other cloud services, taking into account concepts like redundancy, high availability, scalability, security, and so on.

We will be listing the main VCN components, with a brief explanation of the components.

IP Address Range

The IP CIDR block is the first decision you have to make during the planning phase for the VCN.

Note   To help you with the calculation of your CIDR blocks, you can use this link
`https://tinyurl.com/yy98hu7h`.

The VCN network range should be anything between /16 and /30, for example, 10.0.0.0/16. A network range of /16 means that your VCN will have a total of 65,536 available IP addresses and /30 will have 4 available IP addresses. You have to properly size the VCN and subnet in order to host all the Cloud resources you would like to create. If your VCN network range is too small, you will not have enough IP addresses and you will need to create another VCN and peer them together.

Note   Oracle recommends using one of the private IP address ranges specified by RFC 1918 (10.0.0.0/8, 172.16/12, and 192.168/16) or a publicly routable range.

We would like to bring to your attention few important points:

1. You cannot change the VCN and subnet sizes after their creation.

2. IP range must not overlap with any network or VCN you want to peer with.

3. Subnets within a VCN must not overlap with each other.

4. Networking service reserves the two IP addresses, the first and the last.

Notes   The VCN is using a contiguous IPv4 CIDR block. IPv6 is supported in Government Cloud only.

In the example at the end of the chapter, we will use the following information:

VCN Name	IP CIDR Block
VirtualCloudNetwork_Book01	10.100.0.0/21

Throughout the chapter, we will be building an example of a network topology. Here is the first diagram (Figure 3-1), showing the VCN in the region Ashburn.

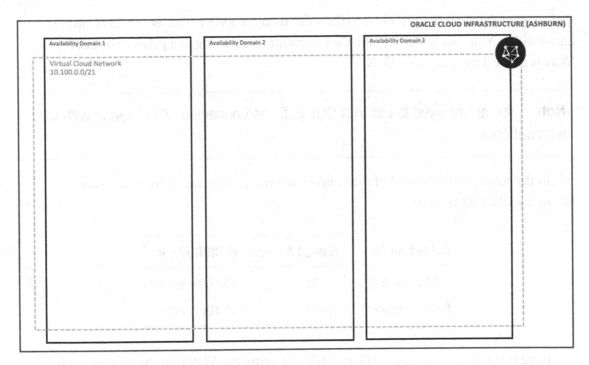

Figure 3-1. Virtual Cloud Network

We can identify in the diagram three Availability Domains (ADs) running in the Ashburn region. ADs are physical, totally segregated data centers. The four first regions (Ashburn, Phoenix, London, and Frankfurt) have three ADs each. The other new regions have only one AD. In our example, the VCN covers all three ADs. The next section will explain what a subnet is and how it will be deployed in a VCN.

Subnet

A subnet is a subdivision within your VCN using a contiguous IP range. A subnet is like a zone; it serves to group resources. Subnets can be local to a single Availability Domain (AD), or regional, spanning all three ADs. Regional subnets are the recommended configuration.

During the subnet creation process, we have to designate the subnet to be either a public or private subnet. A Cloud resource created in a public subnet will have a private IP address and, optionally, a public IP address and, therefore, will be Internet facing. On the other hand, Cloud resources created in a private subnet will only have a private IP address and will be reachable by other resources in the same VCN or from the on-premise network attached to the VCN using the VPN Connect or FastConnect capabilities. You can also reach the Cloud resources running in a private subnet if your VCN is peered with another VCN.

Note   You are allowed to use VPN Connect, FastConnect, or VCN peering with paid account only.

In the example at the end of the chapter, we will create two subnets with the following IP CIDR blocks:

Subnet Name	Subnet Access	IP CIDR Block
Public_Subnet01	Public	10.100.0.0/24
Private_Subnet01	Private	10.100.1.0/24

Here is the second diagram (Figure 3-2), showing the VCN and the two regional subnets.

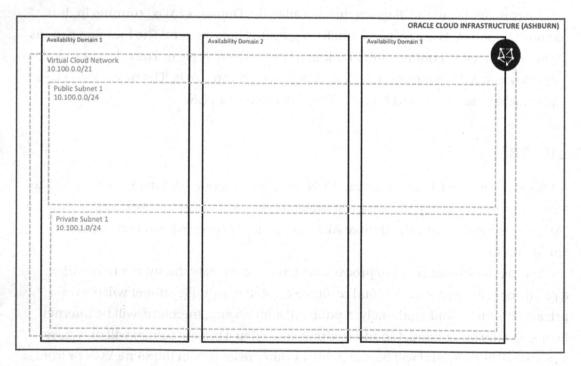

Figure 3-2. *Subnets*

Now that we understand the concepts of subnets in a VCN, the next section will describe the concept of Route Tables.

Route Table

A Route Table contains rules to route traffic out of your virtual cloud network (VCN). It allows the traffic from your VCN to reach destinations like

- The Internet

- An on-premise network

- A peered VCN

When we manually create a VCN, a default Route Table is automatically created.

Note   When using the wizard, the default Route Table contains a rule using the Internet Gateway.

We prefer not to use this default Route Table and rather create a dedicated Route Table for every subnet. This way, we can easily manage the route rules depending on the subnet traffic requirements. For example, the public subnet will need a rule routing traffic to the Internet Gateway with the destination 0.0.0.0/0.

Note   The CIDR block 0.0.0.0/0 matches all the address in the IPv4 address space.

A private subnet doesn't need that same rule. In order to reach the public Internet, a private subnet will need to have a rule routing traffic to a NAT Gateway with the destination 0.0.0.0/0.

Additional points:

- Traffic within a VCN is not governed by the Route Table.

- In case of overlapping rules, OCI uses the more specific rule.

- Traffic is dropped if there is no rule that matches the request.

Every rule has a target, which can be

- Dynamic Routing Gateway (DRG)

- Internet Gateway (IG)

- NAT Gateway

- Service Gateway

- Local Peering Gateway (LPG)

- Private IP, routing traffic to a specific instance in the VCN

Some of these targets will be explained later in this chapter.

In the example at the end of the chapter, we will create two Route Tables (one per subnet) with the following information:

Subnet	Route Table	Target
Public_Subnet01	Route_Table_Public_Subnet01	Internet Gateway
Private_Subnet01	Route_Table_Private_Subnet01	NAT Gateway

The next section will be describing the concept of security rules using either Security Lists or Network Security Groups.

Security List and Network Security Group

Security Lists and Network Security Groups are acting like firewalls in an on-premise network. OCI offers two different security rule features to control traffic between subnets at the packet level:

- **Security Lists**: Act as regular firewalls for subnets

- **Network Security Groups**: Act as firewalls for groups of instances across subnets

You can use a Security List to define the rules that apply to all inbound (ingress) and outbound (egress) traffic of a subnet. You can associate up to five Security Lists per subnet. Similar to Route Tables, for easier management we recommend dedicated Security Lists for subnets.

Network Security Groups (NSGs) allow us to build rules for groups of instances, even if these instances are in different subnets, for example, NSGs specific for the application servers running a particular application, or for the database servers. After you create the NSGs, you have to add the appropriate instances to the newly created NSGs.

If you decide to use both Security List and Network Security Groups, the rules that apply to a VNIC are the union of the rules from the Security List and the rules specific for this VNIC on the NSG.

When using the console wizard for the creation of a VCN, a default Security List with three ingress rules and one egress rule is created.

In the example at the end of the chapter, we will create two Security Lists (one per subnet) with these rules:

Subnet	Security List	Rule
Public_Subnet01	Security_List_Public_Subnet01	TCP - 22 from the Internet
		TCP - 443 from the Internet
		ICMP – type 3, 4, 8 from the Internet
Private_Subnet01	Security_List_Private_Subnet02	TCP - 22 from Public_Subnet01
		TCP - 1521 from Public_Subnet01
		ICMP – type 3, 4, 8 from Public_Subnet01

Operating System Firewall

It is important to validate that your OS firewall rules match your Security Lists and Network Security Groups rules. If you are running Linux 7.x, you will use the utility *firewalld* to manage the local firewall. Using the root user, here are some useful commands.

To stop, start, and get the status of the firewall:

```
# systemctl stop firewalld
# systemctl start firewalld
# systemctl status firewalld
```

The following command is giving you the current firewall settings:

```
# firewall-cmd --list-all
```

You will see a list of services and ports allowed. In the following example, services *dhcpv6* and *ssh* are allowed through the local firewall:

```
  services: dhcpv6-client ssh
  ports:
```

If I have Apache running on this server, I would need to add other services in order for the traffic to go through the ports 80 and 443 to Apache. Using this command, I'm adding the services *http* and *https* in the list of allowed services.

```
# firewall-cmd --zone=public --permanent --add-service=http
# firewall-cmd --zone=public --permanent --add-service=https
# firewall-cmd –reload
# firewall-cmd --list-all
```

Once executed, I will have the following list of services allowed by the firewall, and we can confirm that *http* and *https* traffic will be able to reach Apache.

```
  services: dhcpv6-client http https ssh
  ports:
```

Internet Gateway

An Internet Gateway (IG) is a virtual router to get direct access to and from the public Internet. If your instance has a public IP, and the public subnet in which the instance runs has a route rule to the associated IG, then your instance can be directly accessed from the public Internet. Such a configuration would be used by a web server that needs to be accessible on the Internet.

In the example at the end of the chapter, we create an Internet Gateway attached to the VCN.

Figure 3-3 shows the VCN with the Internet Gateway attached.

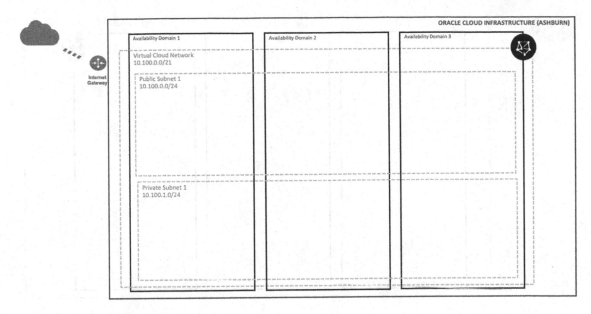

Figure 3-3. *Internet Gateway*

NAT Gateway

Network Address Translation (NAT) Gateway is a virtual router that allows outbound traffic to the Internet. An instance without a public IP address can use a NAT for software updates. NATs do not expose instances for inbound Internet traffic.

In the example at the end of the chapter, we create a NAT Gateway attached to the VCN.

Figure 3-4 shows the VCN with the NAT Gateway attached.

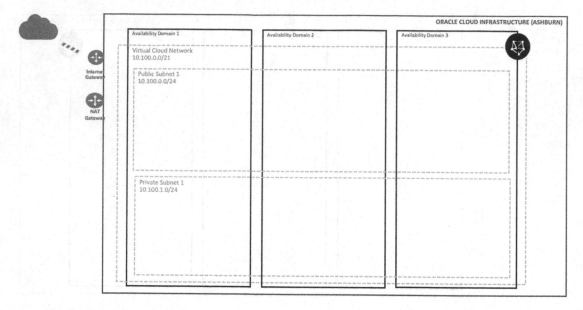

Figure 3-4. *NAT Gateway*

Service Gateway

A Service Gateway (SG) is a virtual router that allows resources without a public IP address to access supported services in the Oracle Service Network. A good example is the access to the Cloud service Object Storage. Using the SG, a database running in a private subnet is able to send the database backups to Object Storage over the Oracle network fabric, never traversing the Internet.

In the example at the end of the chapter, we will create a Service Gateway attached to the VCN.

Figure 3-5 shows, on the right side of the topology, the VCN with the Service Gateway attached to it. The SG will provide private access to the Object Storage Cloud service.

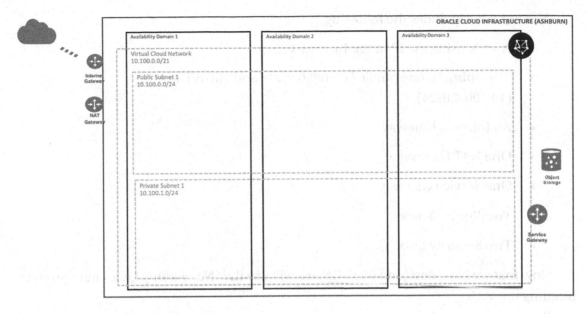

Figure 3-5. *Service Gateway*

Simple Network Topology

Figure 3-6 shows an example of a Virtual Cloud Network topology that includes the components mentioned earlier.

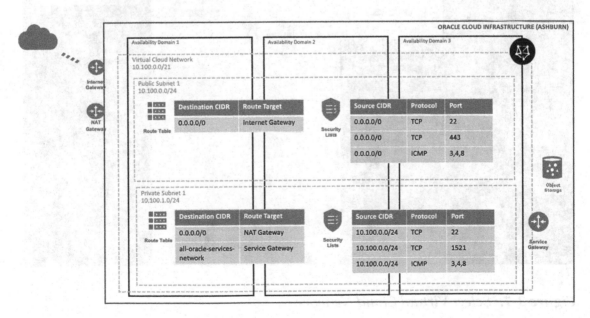

Figure 3-6. *Simple Network Topology*

The topology includes the following:

- A VCN using the IP range 10.100.0.0/21

- Two subnets, one public (10.100.0.0/24) and one private (10.100.1.0/24)

- An Internet Gateway

- One NAT Gateway

- One Service Gateway

- Two Route Tables

- Two Security Lists

Now that we have designed our VCN, we will use the "Networking Quickstart" to start building the VCN.

From the Oracle Cloud Infrastructure console, from the navigation menu select *Networking* and then *Virtual Cloud Network* as shown in Figure 3-7.

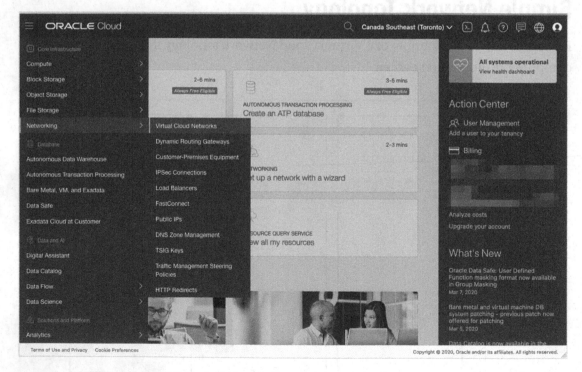

Figure 3-7. *Select Virtual Cloud Network*

On the Virtual Cloud Network main page, click the "Networking Quickstart" button shown in Figure 3-8.

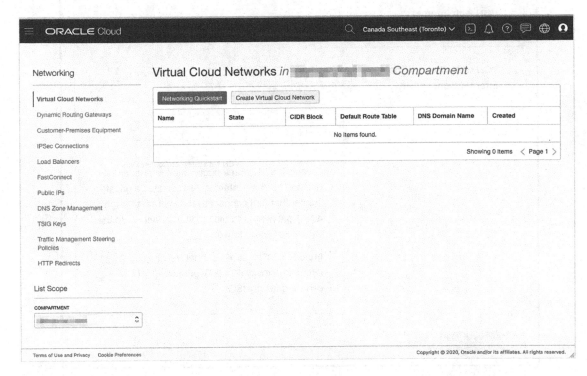

Figure 3-8. *Virtual Cloud Network main page*

On the first page of the wizard, select "VCN with Internet Connectivity" and click the "Start Workflow" button (Figure 3-9).

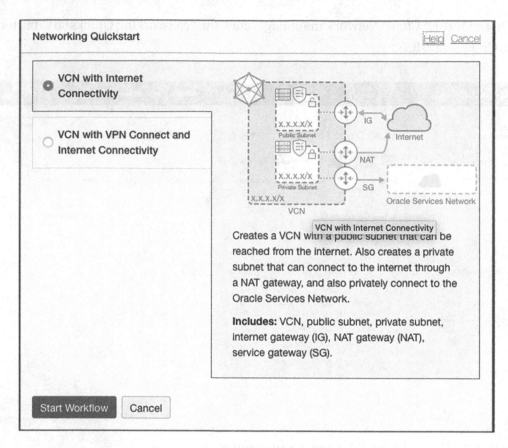

Figure 3-9. *First page of the wizard, select "VCN with Internet Connectivity" and click on "Start Workflow"*

On the next page of the wizard, provide the requested information:

- **VCN Name**: VirtualCloudNetwork_Book01

- **Compartment**: compartment of your choice

- **VCN CIDR Block**: 10.100.0.0/21

- **Public Subnet CIDR Block**: 10.100.0.0/24

- **Private Subnet CIDR Block**: 10.100.1.0/24

- **Use DNS Hostnames in This VCN**: Checked

Figure 3-10 shows an example of the requested information. You have to scroll down the page in order to provide all the information. When it is complete, click "Next".

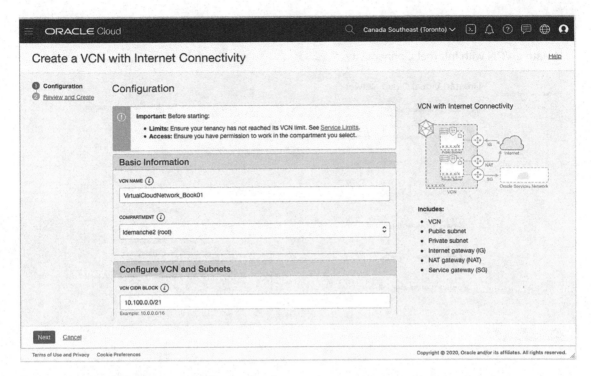

Figure 3-10. *Main page of the wizard*

After the values are reviewed, click "Create", and the VCN will be provisioned. Figure 3-11 shows the status of the provisioning process. You can click "View Virtual Cloud Network" to go into the VCN main page.

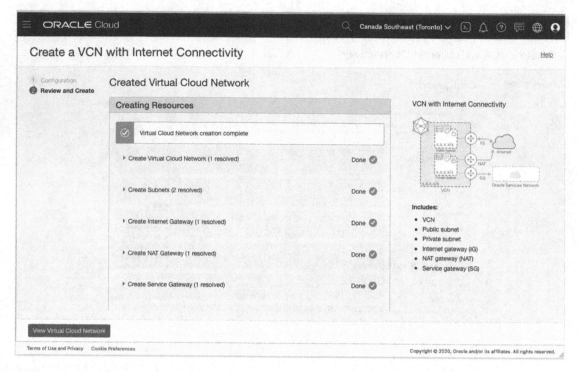

Figure 3-11. *Status of the provisioning process*

Congratulations, we have now created your first Virtual Cloud Network. This topology is enough to start building Cloud resources like compute instances, Database Cloud Services, load balancers, respecting concepts like high availability, scalability, security, and so on.

Click "View Virtual Cloud Network" to see the VCN details (Figure 3-12).

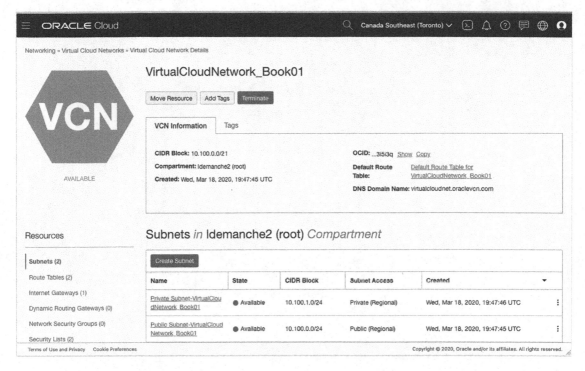

Figure 3-12. *VCN details*

Now that your foundation is in place, you can navigate and explore the different components of your Virtual Cloud Network and start building Cloud components.

Summary

In this chapter we have covered the basic cloud networking concepts. We have described the main Virtual Cloud Network components, provided a brief description of these components, and finally integrated these components into a simple Virtual Cloud Network. We concluded this chapter by giving an example of the "Networking Quickstart" wizard which simplifies VCN creation.

CHAPTER 4

Compute Instance

The purpose of this chapter is to provide a basic understanding of the *Oracle Cloud Infrastructure (OCI) Compute* service. The OCI compute service is an important cloud service that is used to provision virtual or "bare-metal" instances.

Compute instances can be used for different purposes, such as running an Apache Tomcat web server, a Docker engine, a manually installed Oracle Database, or any other application that you would install on your on-premise servers.

Before launching a Compute Instance, you will need to have a virtual cloud network (VCN), an SSH key (for Linux), and other information like availability domain, software image, and the instance shape you would like to use.

An image is a predefined set of software applications including the operating system and other applications packaged together. There are a variety of images to choose from:

- Platform images (Linux, Windows)

- Oracle images

- Partner images

- Custom images, including "bring your own" images

Images are discussed in the following section.

The shape determines the type of the machine (bare metal or virtual machine), type of processor, the number of CPU, RAM, type of storage, and networking information associated with the new instance. The various shapes will be described later in this chapter.

Images

A virtual machine image is a single file that contains a bootable operating system. The simplest image is the operating system only, which we will refer to as a *platform image*. We also have access to more complex images that contain the operating system along with a set of applications.

57

© Adrian Png and Luc Demanche 2020
A. Png and L. Demanche, *Getting Started with Oracle Cloud Free Tier*,
https://doi.org/10.1007/978-1-4842-6011-1_4

Oracle Platform Images

Oracle has a list of *platform images* that use different operating systems such as Oracle Linux, CentOS, Ubuntu, and Windows Server.

At the time of writing this book, Oracle published the following platform images:

Image	Operating System Version	Description
Oracle Autonomous Linux	Oracle Linux 7	Autonomous Linux automates live patching using Ksplice. This operating system is highly secure and reliable.
Oracle Linux Unbreakable Linux	Oracle Linux 6, 7 and 8	Unbreakable Enterprise Kernel (UEK) is an optimal kernel for Oracle workload.
CentOS	6 and 7	A free, open source Linux distribution.
Ubuntu	16.04, 18.04 and 20.04	A free, open source Linux distribution. Uses smaller boot volume, boots faster.
Windows Server	Windows 2012 R2 Windows 2016 and Windows 2019	Windows 2012 R2, 2016 and 2019 are supported to run production workload on OCI.

Note   Oracle updates their images every month to include new patches and software fixes.

Windows Server images are not "Always Free Eligible".

Oracle Images

Oracle also publishes more complex images that contain more than just the operating systems. These are prebuilt enterprise images and solutions. For example, you can provision a new instance using an image that runs "Oracle Enterprise Manager (OEM)". Once the Compute Instance is provisioned, you will have a new OEM instance already configured ready for use. Oracle is constantly adding more images to their catalog. Here is a list of some interesting free images:

- Oracle Cloud Developer Image

- Oracle E-Business Suite Demo Install Image

- Oracle Linux KVM Image

Other images require licenses to be used. For example:

- JD Edwards EnterpriseOne

- Oracle Key Vault

- PeopleSoft

- Siebel

Partner Images

Third-party vendors have prepared and published their own images on Oracle Cloud Infrastructure. Vendors like Check Point Software, Fortinet, IBM, and OpenVPN have made their images available so we can easily provision a new Compute Instance using them.

In the context of the Oracle Cloud Free Tier, not every partner image is eligible to be used with *Always Free* resources. The only way to validate whether you can use the image in the context of Oracle Cloud Free Tier is to select the image and see if the *Always Free* eligible compute shape is available for this image.

Custom Images

The Oracle or Partner images might not be as complete as you wish. Imagine a situation where you provision a new instance using the Autonomous Linux image and you install some applications required for your system. Now you have an instance that contains everything you need, and you can create a custom image from it. Now you can provision identical new instances using this custom image.

The custom image that you create includes the installed software, customization, configuration, and any data stored in the boot volume. Attached block volumes will not be part of the custom image. If you have user data on the boot volume, make sure to clean up the volume before creating a custom image. Usually we try not to have user data on the boot volume, but on attached block volumes.

Note   Backup of user data will be discussed in Chapter 5.

This *custom image* feature is very useful when you have to provision multiple, identical customized instances. Here are the steps for the creation of a custom image. From the list of available compute instances, select the instance you would like to create a custom image from. From the Instance Details page, click "Actions" and "Create Custom Image" as you can see in Figure 4-1.

Note   Your Compute Instance will be taken offline during this process.

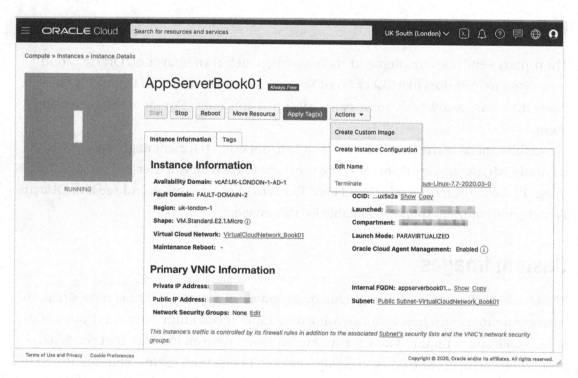

Figure 4-1. *Instance Details page*

Provide a name for the new custom image and click "Create Custom Image" as you can see in Figure 4-2.

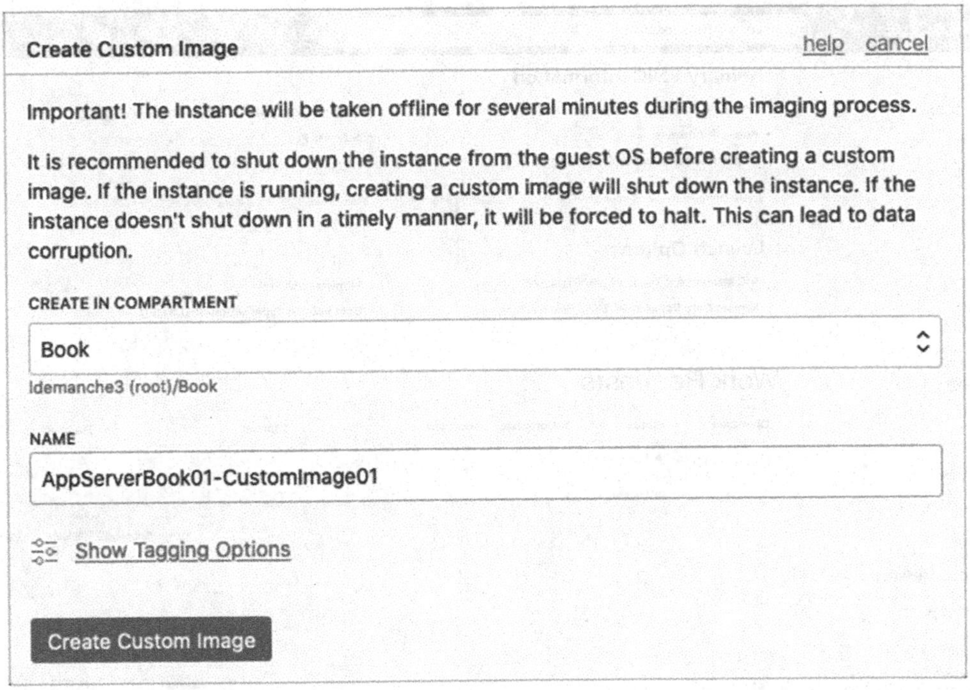

Create Custom Image   help   cancel

Important! The Instance will be taken offline for several minutes during the imaging process.

It is recommended to shut down the instance from the guest OS before creating a custom image. If the instance is running, creating a custom image will shut down the instance. If the instance doesn't shut down in a timely manner, it will be forced to halt. This can lead to data corruption.

CREATE IN COMPARTMENT

| Book | ⌄ |

Idemanche3 (root)/Book

NAME

AppServerBook01-CustomImage01

⇅ Show Tagging Options

Create Custom Image

Figure 4-2. *Create Custom Image*

From this page, we have access to a work requests page where we can see the status of the operation. Under the "Resources" section, you can click the "Work Requests" link, and you will have the page in Figure 4-3.

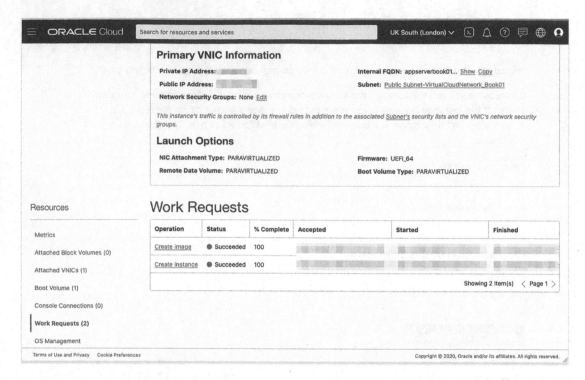

Figure 4-3. *Instance Work Requests page*

You have all the operations that occur on the instance since the initial provisioning. You can see the "Create image" operation status is "Succeeded". For curiosity, click the "Create image" link to see all the details, from shutting down the instance up to powering on the instance.

Export and Import Images

A custom image is specific to a region, so in order to share this custom image between regions and/or tenancies, we will use the export and import process. To perform this operation, you have to follow these steps.

First of all, you have to create a bucket in the *Object Storage* service. This is covered in Chapter 5. When the bucket is created, click the navigation menu, and under "Compute" select "Custom Images". Make sure you select the right compartment, and then you will see the list of custom images created. Select the custom image you would like to export to the *Object Storage*. Figure 4-4 shows the page with the custom image information.

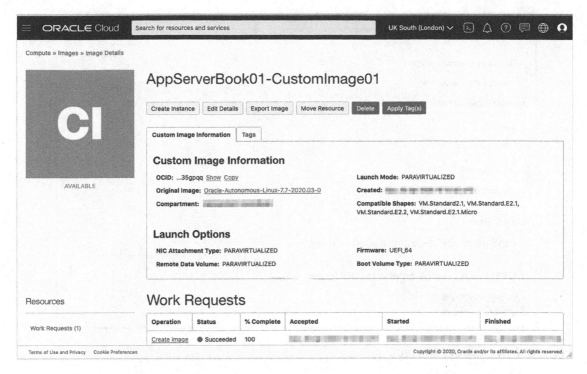

Figure 4-4. *Image Details page*

In this page you see the detailed information of the custom image. You can also see the compatible shapes that you can use to provision new instances from this custom image. In this example, this custom image can be used to provision a new instance using the shapes VM.Standard2.1, VM.Standard.E2.1, VM.Standard.E2.2, and VM.Standard. E2.1.Micro.

From this page you can do multiple actions. First, you can directly provision a new instance by clicking "Create Instance"; you can edit the details or delete this custom image. If you want to export the image, click "Export Image", and you will get a new page as you can see in Figure 4-5.

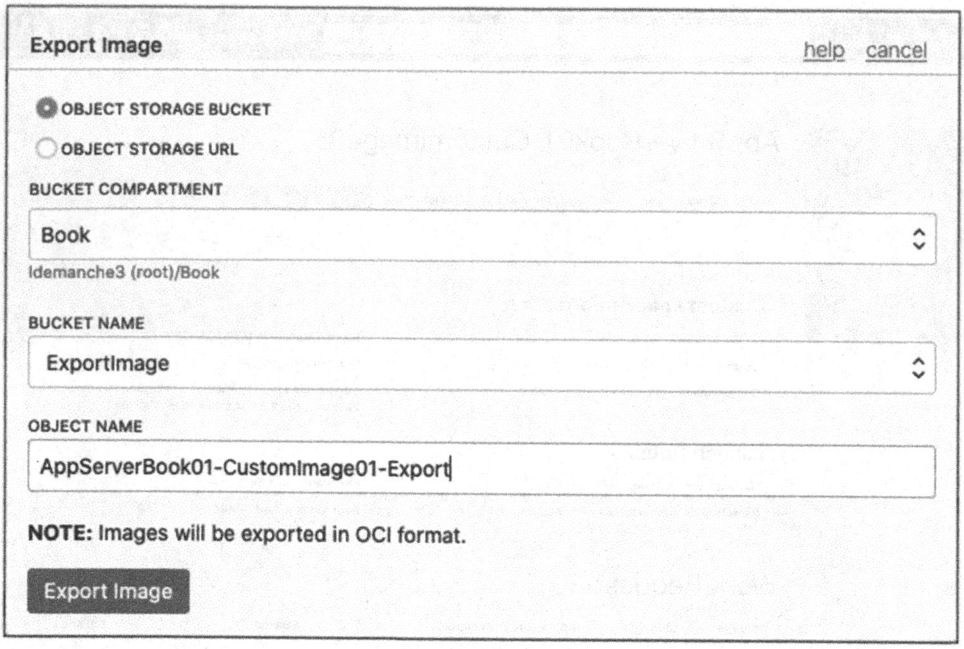

Figure 4-5. *Export Image*

You have to provide the compartment name, bucket name, and a name for the object. Then click "Export Image".

Under the "Resources" menu, click "Work Requests" where you can see the progress of the "Export Image" operation (Figure 4-6).

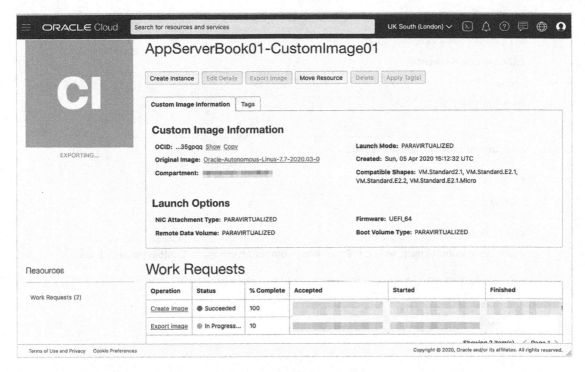

Figure 4-6. *Progression of "Export Image" Process*

Note   The file format of an exported custom image is ".oci".

Once the custom image is exported into a bucket in *Object Storage* service, this image is available to be sent. Chapter 5 explains how to send an object from the *Object Storage* to another region or tenancy.

To import an exported custom image from a bucket in *Object Storage*, click the navigation menu, and under "Compute", select "Custom Images", and then click the "Import Image" button. You have to provide the compartment name, the name of the new custom image, the source operating system, the Object Storage URL (provided by the person that exported the custom image), and the image type. In the case where the source instance is coming from Oracle Cloud Infrastructure, you select "OCI". You then click "Import Image".

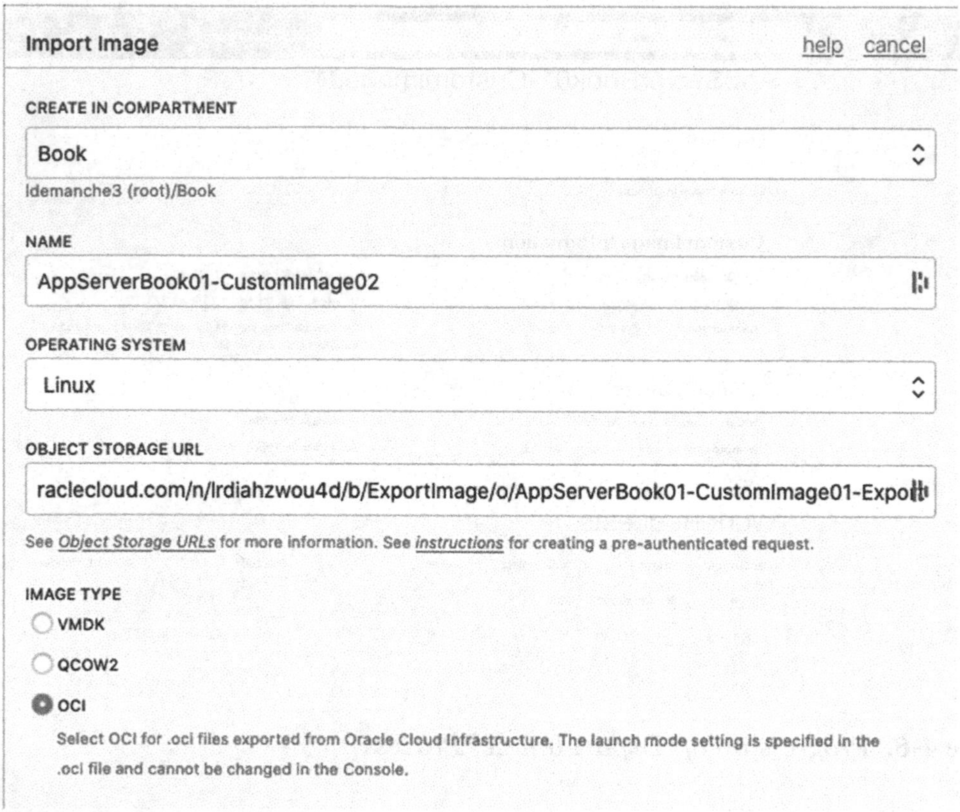

Figure 4-7. *Import an Exported Custom Image*

You will be redirected to the "Image Details" page where you can follow the progress of the import process.

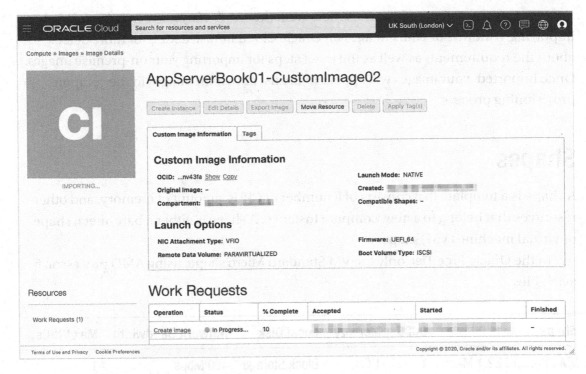

Figure 4-8. *Import Process Progession*

As you have seen, we can import other types of custom images, VMDK or QCOW2. We will discuss the other types in the next section.

Bring Your Own Images

Oracle Cloud Infrastructure Compute service allows you to "Bring Your Own Images (BYOI)" in order to import images from different sources, such as on-premise infrastructure. This feature is essential to enable *lift-and-shift cloud migration* projects and also allows the use of older operating systems.

There is a list of requirements that an on-premise Windows or Linux system must fulfill before an image that would be imported in OCI can be created. These include the following:

- Maximum image size is 400 GB.

- Image must be set up for BIOS boot.

- Disk image cannot be encrypted.

- Network interface must be DHCP.

67

I encourage you to read the documentation (https://tinyurl.com/yd6yzqlb) about importing Windows or Linux images on Oracle Cloud Infrastructure for more details about the requirements as well as the exact steps for importing your on-premise images. Once imported, your images will appear in the list of custom images in the compute provisioning process.

Shapes

A shape is a template that consists of a number of CPUs, amount of memory, and other resources that belong to a new Compute Instance. A shape is either a bare-metal shape or virtual machine (VM) shape.

In the Oracle Free Tier, only the VM Standard Micro shape, using AMD processor, is available:

Shape	OCPU	Memory	Local Disk	Network Bandwidth	Max VNICs
VM.Standard.E2.1.Micro	1	1 GB	Block Storage	480 Mbps	1

If you decide to upgrade to a paid account, you will have access to more shapes:

- Bare-metal shapes, using Intel or AMD processors, with 36, 44, 52, or 64 OCPU

- Virtual machine shapes, using Intel processors, AMD processors, Dense I/O shapes, and GPU shapes

- Dense I/O shapes using NVMe-based SSD using Intel processors, with 36 or 52 OCPU

- GPU shapes designed for hardware-accelerated workload, using Intel processors with 28 or 52 OCPU

- HPC shapes designed for high-performance workloads using Intel processor with 36 OCPU

Note   Oracle will soon allow the dynamic change of the number of CPU and RAM for virtual machines.

How to Create a Compute Instance

Now that we understand the concepts of images and shapes, we are ready to provision a new Compute Instance. From the navigation menu, navigate to Compute and then Instances. Click the "Create Compute Instance" button. Fill out the form with the values provided in Figure 4-9.

- **Instance Name**: AppServerBook02.

- **Image or Operating System**: Click "Change Image".

Figure 4-9. *Create Compute Instance*

Figure 4-10 shows a list of "Platform Images". Select "Oracle Autonomous Linux 7.7" and click "Select Image".

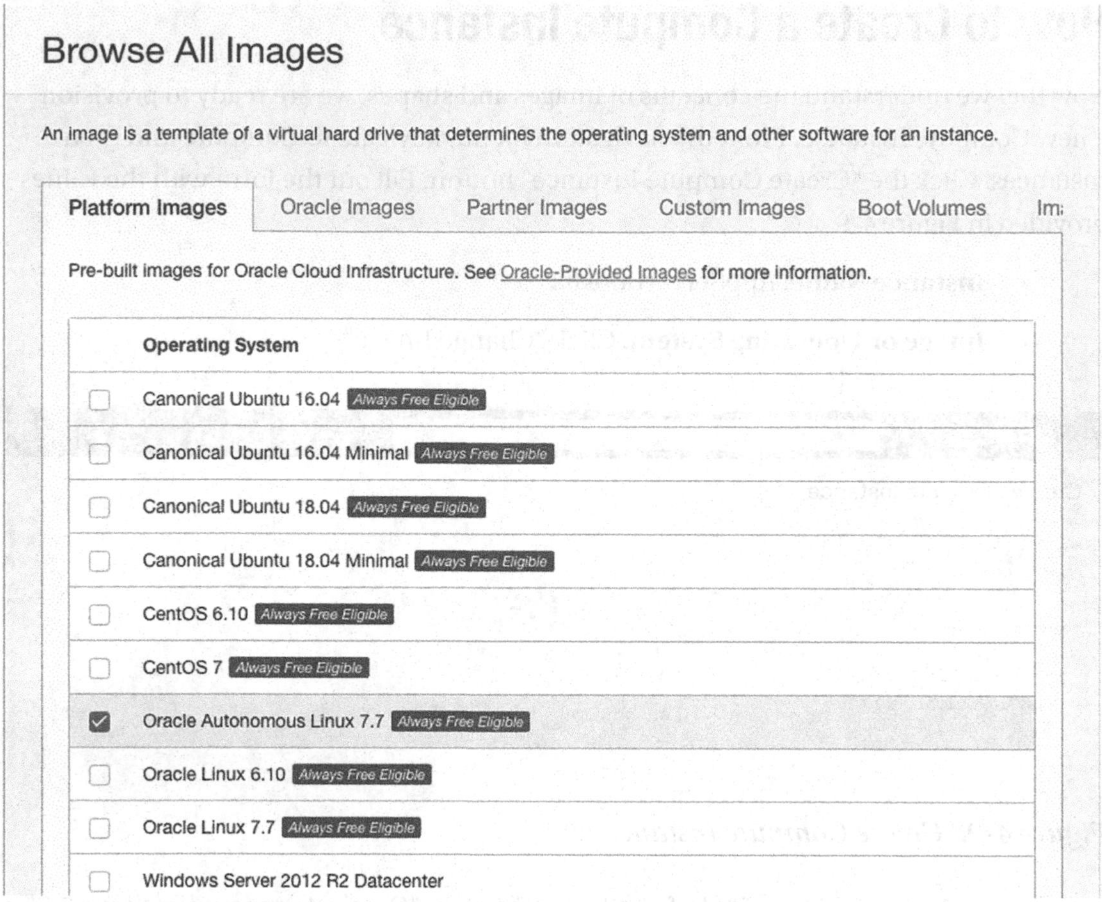

Figure 4-10. *Select the image*

You can navigate into the different tabs, Oracle Images, Partner Images, Custom Images, Boot Volumes, and Image OCID to see all the available images. The custom image we have created earlier is under the Custom Images tab.

On the Create Compute Instance page, you can click "Show Shape, Network and Storage Options" in order to modify the default selections proposed for availability domain, shape and type, boot volume size, and network.

Upload a public SSH key file (Figure 4-11).

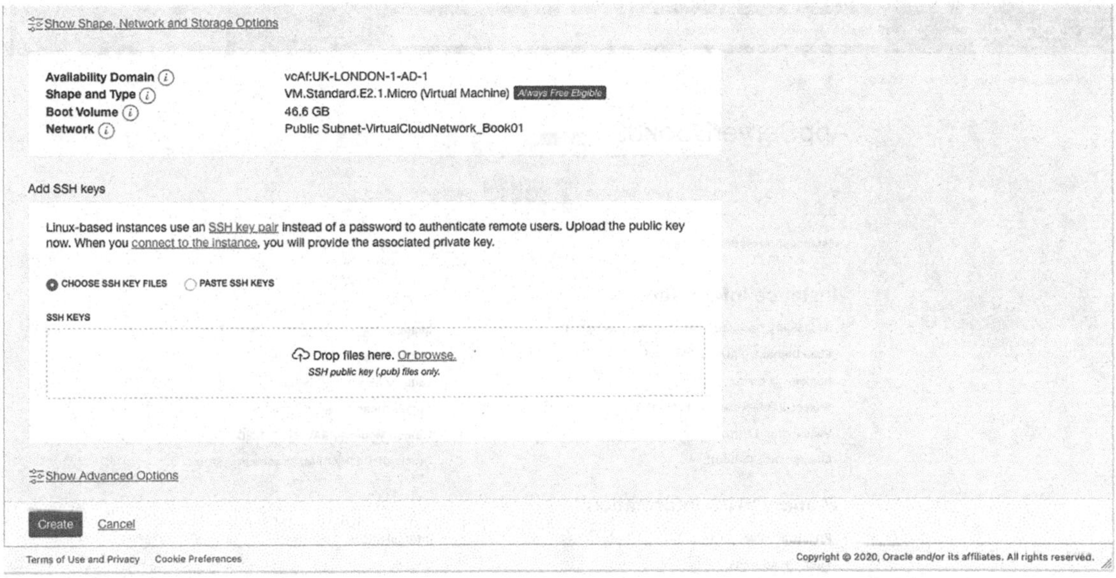

Figure 4-11. *SSH public key*

The "Show Advanced Options" allows us to change default values like

- Compartment

- Fault domain

- Execution of an initialization script

- Provide a private IP address

- Provide a different hostname

- Networking type

Once you click the "Create" button, you will be redirected to the "Instance Details" page where can see the progress of the instance provisioning process (Figure 4-12).

71

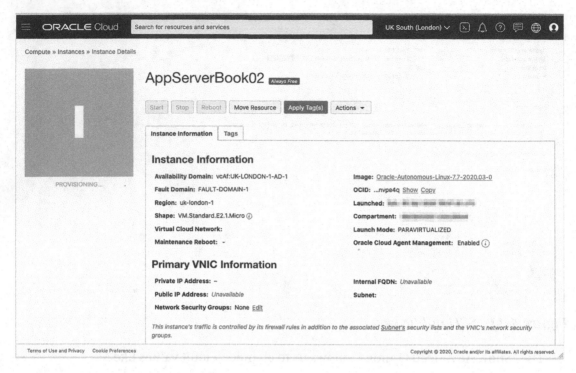

Figure 4-12. *Instance provisioning process*

After a few minutes, we have a new Compute Instance using the Oracle Autonomous Linux 7.7 image.

After provisioning a new instance, we have some post-provisioning steps to perform. OCI uses high-quality Sun servers, but you have to make sure your system is as resilient as possible. For a system that has to be highly available, you must plan resiliency and failover components.

For non-Autonomous Linux instances, you should also use Ksplice to apply important security and critical kernel updates without rebooting the instance. Ksplice is available on Oracle Linux instances. To connect on your new instance using SSH, use your private SSH key and the public IP address of your instance.

```
$ ssh -i my_private_key opc@xxx.xxx.xxx.x
```

If this instance doesn't have a public IP address, you have to connect on a bastion server that has a public IP address first and then on the instance using this private address.

Note   You have to use the OS user *opc*. Once connected, you can switch on the root user using *sudo su -*

You can configure the automatic updates by changing the value of autoinstall to yes in the file "/etc/uptrack/uptrack.conf".

To manually update your kernel using Ksplice, you can run

```
[root@appserverbook02 ~]# uptrack-upgrade
Nothing to be done.
Your kernel is fully up to date.
Effective kernel version is 4.14.35-1902.300.11.el7uek
[root@appserverbook02 ~]#
```

Note   You are responsible for applying OS security updates for instance running non-Autonomous Linux.

Limitations

The Oracle Cloud Infrastructure Compute service in the Oracle Cloud Free Tier has a number of limitations:

- Maximum of two *Always Free* compute instances.

- *Always Free* compute instances must be created in the Home Region.

- **Shape Limits**:

  - **Shape**: VM.Standard.E2.1.Micro

  - **Processor**: 1/8th of an OCPU

  - **Memory**: 1 GB

  - **Networking**: One VNIC with one public IP address and up to 480 Mbps network bandwidth

- **Image Limits**:

  - **Operating System**: Oracle Linux, Ubuntu Linux, or CentOS Linux

Summary

In this chapter we have discovered the Oracle Cloud Infrastructure Compute service. We have seen what information was required to provision a new instance. We saw the different types of images: platform images, Oracle images, Partner images, as well as custom images. We have explained the different shapes: bare-metal and virtual machine shapes. We have created a new Linux instance by going through the provisioning process using the console. We concluded by providing the limitation of the Oracle Cloud Infrastructure Compute service in the context of Oracle Free Tier.

CHAPTER 5

Storage

We have discussed compute instances in Chapter 4. We have seen how to create a new Compute Instance, using one of the images provided by Oracle or Partner-provided images. Now that we have a Compute Instance, we will see in this chapter what the *Oracle Cloud Infrastructure Storage* service is, how a Compute Instance uses the boot volume, and how it can use a newly provisioned block volume to store application data.

This chapter will also explore the *Object Storage* service and how we can manage different types of objects stored using this service. Many features are also available to manage the objects in Object Storage service, like lifecycle policy rule, replication, and retention rules.

Block and Boot Volume

Since you have your compute, you will need to install your application and have a location to store the data. The Compute Instance will need to have access to persistent, secure, durable, and very performant storage, comparable to your on-premise storage network area (SAN). Also like your SAN, boot and block volume life span is independent of your Compute Instance; you can terminate your Compute Instance and decide to keep the volumes for future use. This cloud service allows you to provision, attach, connect, and move your storage depending on your needs. We describe all these steps.

Let's take the Compute Instance created in Chapter 4, which comes with a boot volume. The boot volume is, first of all, a detachable volume device that contains the image used to boot the instance. By default, the size of the boot volume is 46.6 GB which you can change during the compute provisioning process. We recommend keeping the boot volume for the OS only and not installing any applications or not storing any data on it. Applications and data should reside on dedicated block volumes so that they are completely isolated from the boot volume. We can see a couple of advantages by doing so; first, you will be able to detach the application and data block volume to

© Adrian Png and Luc Demanche 2020
A. Png and L. Demanche, *Getting Started with Oracle Cloud Free Tier*,
https://doi.org/10.1007/978-1-4842-6011-1_5

attach it onto another Compute Instance. This could be useful if you want to move that application and its data to another instance, using a different shape or different processors. Second of all, if you have an issue with your instance and the boot volume is no longer responding, your application and the data are securely stored on the block volume, and you can easily attach the volume to another instance.

As you have to install your application on a dedicated volume, you will need to first create the block volume. From the navigation menu, select "Block Storage" and "Block Volumes", and you will be in the Block Volumes page as you can see in Figure 5-1.

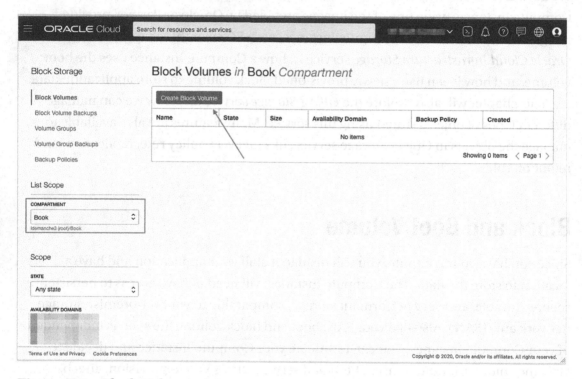

Figure 5-1. *Block Volumes page*

From this page, make sure you are in the right compartment, and click "Create Block Volume". You will have to provide some information in order to create the block volume as you can see in Figures 5-2 and 5-3.

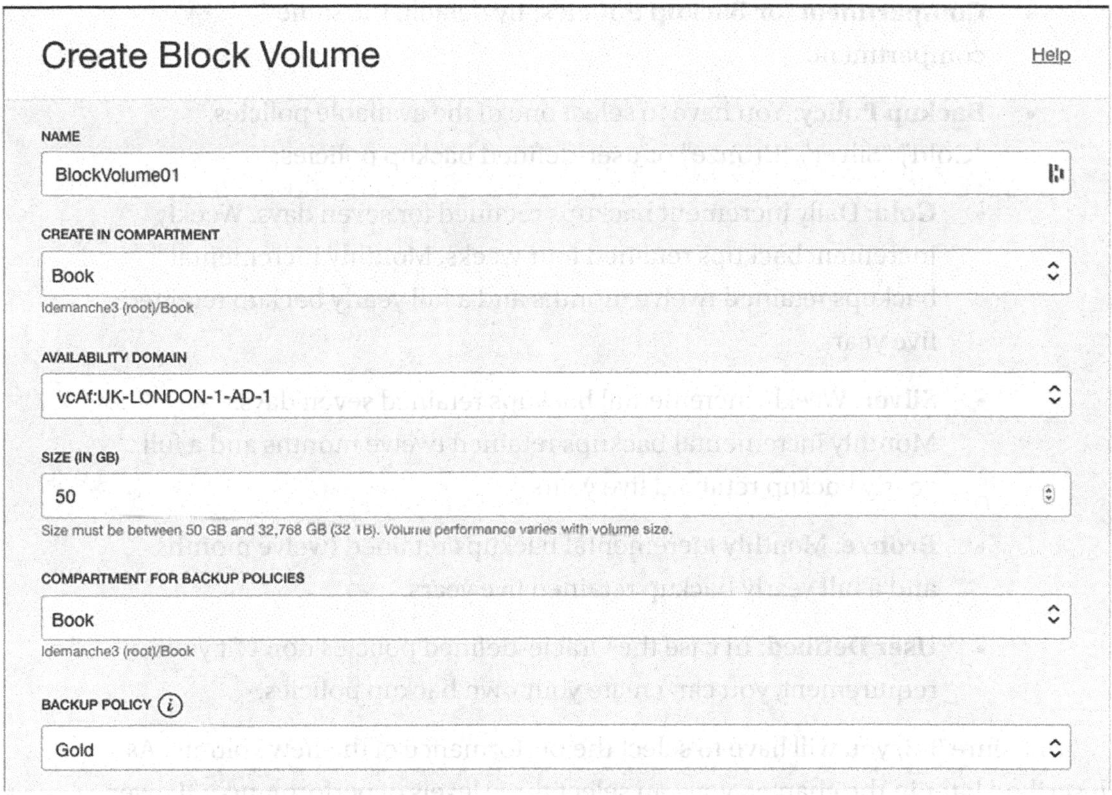

Create Block Volume

NAME

BlockVolume01

CREATE IN COMPARTMENT

Book

ldemanche3 (root)/Book

AVAILABILITY DOMAIN

vcAf:UK-LONDON-1-AD-1

SIZE (IN GB)

50

Size must be between 50 GB and 32,768 GB (32 TB). Volume performance varies with volume size.

COMPARTMENT FOR BACKUP POLICIES

Book

ldemanche3 (root)/Book

BACKUP POLICY ⓘ

Gold

Figure 5-2. *Section 1 of the creation of Block Volume*

You will have to provide the following information:

- **Name**: Name of the block volume.

- **Create in Compartment**: Select the right compartment.

- **Availability Domain**: Select the same availability domain as the one for the Compute Instance.

- **Size**: From 50 GB to 32 TB.

Note   Oracle Cloud Always Free allows you to have a total of 100 GB of storage only, including boot volumes.

- **Compartment for Backup Policies**: By default, the same compartment.

- **Backup Policy**: You have to select one of the available policies, "Gold", "Silver", "Bronze", or user-defined backup policies:

  - **Gold**: Daily increment backups retained for seven days. Weekly increment backups retained four weeks. Monthly incremental backups retained twelve months and a full yearly backup retained five years.

  - **Silver**: Weekly incremental backups retained seven days. Monthly incremental backups retained twelve months and a full yearly backup retained five years.

  - **Bronze**: Monthly incremental backups retained twelve months and a full yearly backup retained five years.

  - **User Defined**: In case the Oracle-defined policies don't fit your requirement, you can create your own backup policies.

In Figure 5-3, you will have to select the performance of the new volume. As described later in the chapter, you can select three levels of performance, "Lower Cost", "Balanced", and "Higher Performance". For this example, we will keep the default selection. For the encryption, you can either use "Oracle-Managed keys" or your own keys. You can click "Create Block Volume" to start the process of provisioning.

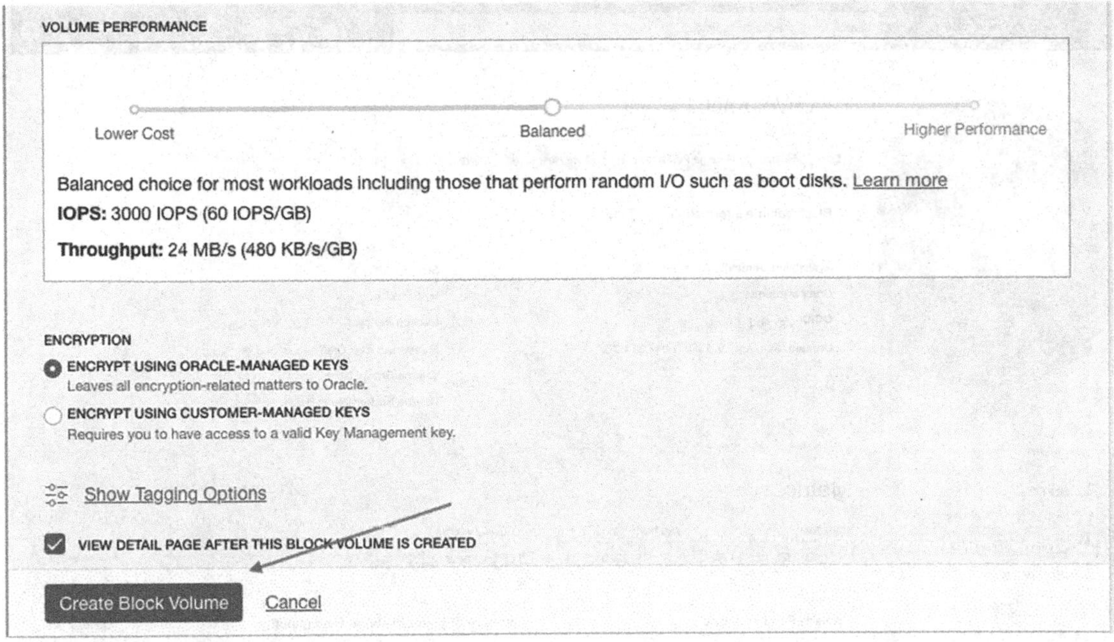

Figure 5-3. *Section 2 of the creation of Block Volume*

Once the provisioning process is completed, you will be on the newly created block volume page. Figure 5-4 shows the block volume page summarizing the information.

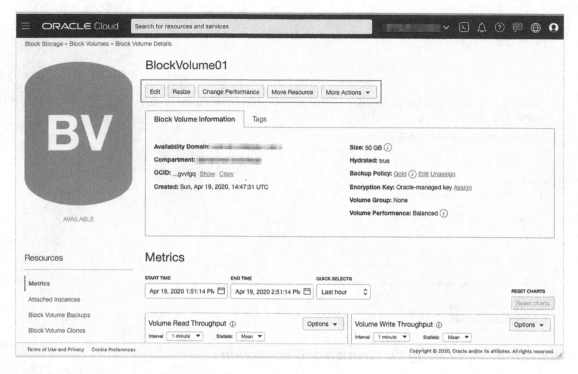

Figure 5-4. *Newly created Block Volume page*

At the beginning of the page, you have five different buttons:

- **Edit**: You can change the name or label of the block volume.

- **Resize**: Once detached from the Compute Instance, you can resize it using this button.

- **Change Performance**: You can dynamically change the performance of the block volume. This will be discussed later in the chapter.

- **Move Resource**: You can move this resource under a new compartment within the same tenancy.

- **More Actions**: You can add tags or terminate this block volume.

Note   Terminating a block volume will not delete the backups or clones created from this block volume.

If you click "Attached Instances" under the "Resources" menu, you will see this block volume is not yet attached to a Compute Instance. This will be the next step.

Let's now attach the block volume to our Compute Instance, running Oracle Autonomous Linux 7.7. Go back in the block volume page and click "Attached Instances" under the "Resources" menu. As you can see in Figure 5-5, this block volume is not attached to any Compute Instance.

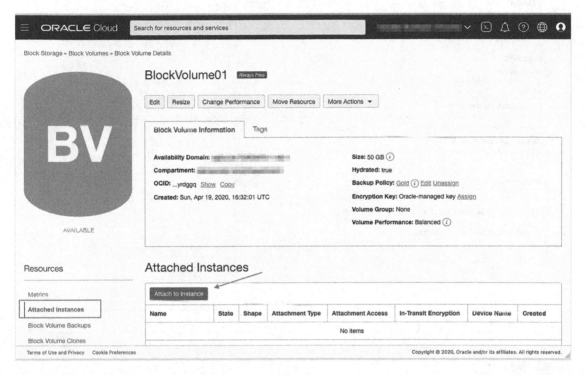

Figure 5-5. *Attached Instances*

Click "Attach to Instance" so we will identify on which Compute Instance we would like this block volume to be attached on. We have to provide information in order to attach a block volume to a Compute Instance.

- **Attachment Type**: For simplicity, select "Paravirtualized".

- **Access Type**: Read/Write.

- **Choose Instance**: Select the instance name.

- **Device Name**: Select the device name to be used.

In Figure 5-6 we will see the necessary information in order to attach the block volume to the Compute Instance.

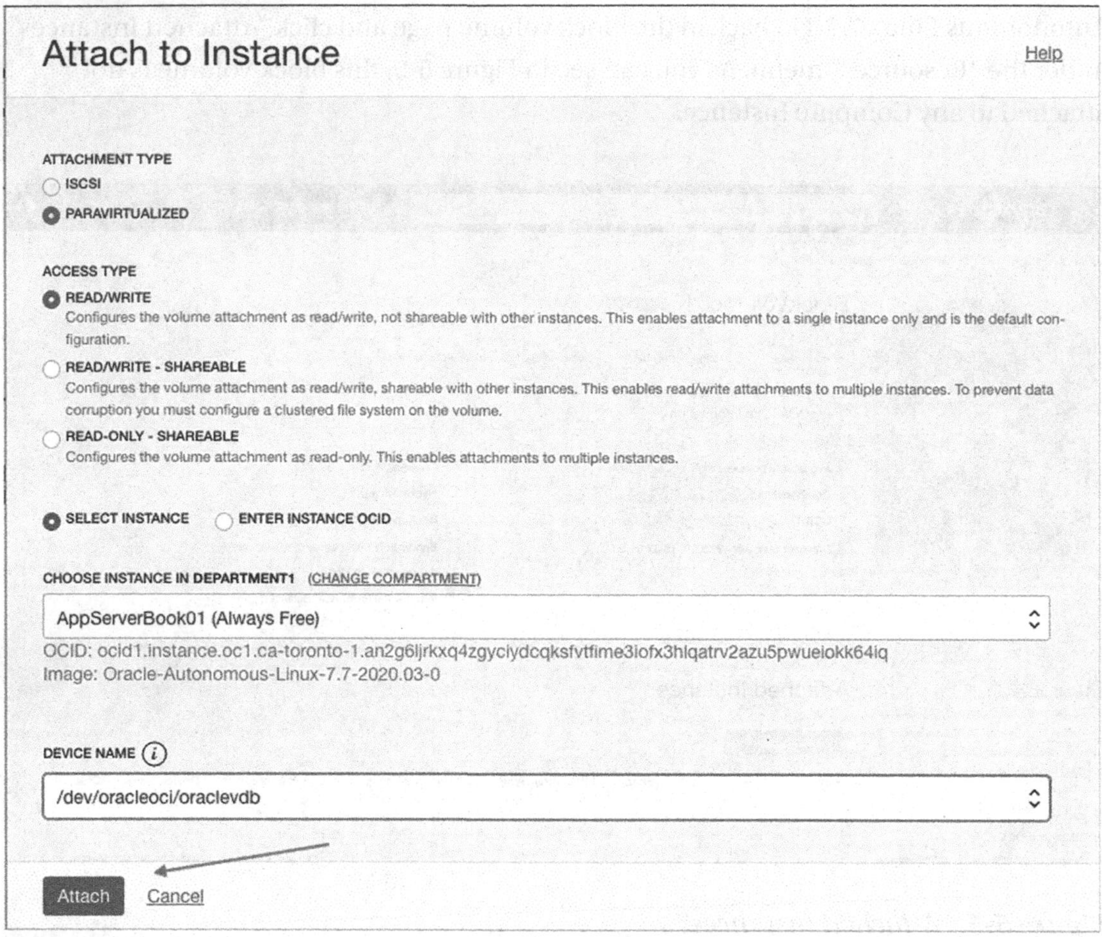

Figure 5-6. *Attaching to an instance*

You have to click "Attach" and the volume will be attached to the Compute Instance. At the end of the process, you will see Figure 5-7, the page with information such as follows:

- **Attachment Type**: Paravirtualized

- **Attachment Access**: Read/Write

- **Device Name**: /dev/oracleoci/oracledb

Attached Instances

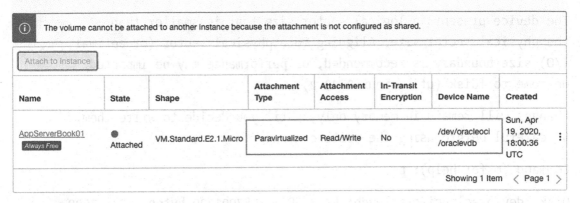

ⓘ   The volume cannot be attached to another instance because the attachment is not configured as shared.

Attach to Instance

Name	State	Shape	Attachment Type	Attachment Access	In-Transit Encryption	Device Name	Created
AppServerBook01 Always Free	● Attached	VM.Standard.E2.1.Micro	Paravirtualized	Read/Write	No	/dev/oracleoci /oraclevdb	Sun, Apr 19, 2020, 18:00:36 UTC

Showing 1 Item   ⟨ Page 1 ⟩

Figure 5-7. *Attachment information*

We now have to connect, using an SSH connection, to the Compute Instance and perform some steps in order to configure the volume. Once connected on the instance, you have to sudo to *root*, then validate if the volume is properly attached to the instance using this command:

```
$ sudo su -
Last login: Sun Apr 19 18:25:45 GMT 2020 on pts/0
# cd /dev/oracleoci/
# ls -l
total 0
lrwxrwxrwx. 1 root root 6 Apr 19 17:57 oraclevda -> ../sda
lrwxrwxrwx. 1 root root 7 Apr 19 17:57 oraclevda1 -> ../sda1
lrwxrwxrwx. 1 root root 7 Apr 19 17:57 oraclevda2 -> ../sda2
lrwxrwxrwx. 1 root root 7 Apr 19 17:57 oraclevda3 -> ../sda3
lrwxrwxrwx. 1 root root 6 Apr 19 18:22 oraclevdb -> ../sdb
#
```

The */dev/oracleoci/oraclevdb* represents the device name of the block volume we have previously attached. A symbolic link (e.g., oraclevdb) provides the operating system an interface to the device that it represents. Before going further, we need to create a least one partition on the device. To manage the partitions, we will use the Linux utility *fdisk*. Launch *fdisk* with the device we want to partition and using the command **p** to print the current partition table:

```
# fdisk /dev/oracleoci/oraclevdb
```

The device presents a logical sector size that is smaller than the physical sector size. Aligning to a physical sector (or optimal I/O) size boundary is recommended, or performance may be impacted. Welcome to fdisk (util-linux 2.23.2).

Changes will remain in memory only, until you decide to write them. Be careful before using the write command.

Command (m for help): **p**

Disk /dev/oracleoci/oraclevdb: 53.7 GB, 53687091200 bytes, 104857600 sectors
Units = sectors of 1 * 512 = 512 bytes
Sector size (logical/physical): 512 bytes / 4096 bytes
I/O size (minimum/optimal): 4096 bytes / 1048576 bytes
Disk label type: dos
Disk identifier: 0xbe8a9ac8

Device Boot	Start	End	Blocks	Id	System

Command (m for help):

You can see an empty partition table. We will now create a partition on the entire device, using the command **n**. We will create a primary partition that will be identified with the number 1, using the sector 2048 as the first sector and the default for the last sector. The partition will then be on the entire device. If you want to create a smaller partition, you can specify a partition size with this format *size{K,M,G}* for the last sector. Once the creation is completed, we will use the command **p** to print the partition table.

Command (m for help): **n**
Partition type:
   p   primary (0 primary, 0 extended, 4 free)
   e   extended
Select (default p): **p**
Partition number (1-4, default 1):
First sector (2048-104857599, **default 2048**):
Using default value 2048

Last sector, +sectors or +size{K,M,G} (2048-104857599, **default 104857599**):
Using default value 104857599
Partition 1 of type Linux and of size 50 GiB is set

Command (m for help): **p**

Disk /dev/oracleoci/oraclevdb: 53.7 GB, 53687091200 bytes, 104857600
sectors
Units = sectors of 1 * 512 = 512 bytes
Sector size (logical/physical): 512 bytes / 4096 bytes
I/O size (minimum/optimal): 4096 bytes / 1048576 bytes
Disk label type: dos
Disk identifier: 0xbe8a9ac8

```
                      Device
Boot      Start       End      Blocks   Id  System
/dev/oracleoci/oraclevdb1       2048   104857599
52427776   83   Linux
```

Command (m for help):

We can see during the creation process that partition 1 has been created with a size of 50 GB. Using the print command, we can confirm the partition name, */dev/oracleoci/oraclevdb1*, which we will format later. To confirm the creation and write into the partition table, we use the command **w**, and we quit the utility *fdisk*. From the OS point of view, we can confirm the creation of the partition using two different ways, listing the devices (as we have done earlier) and using *lsblk*.

The first method is to list the devices from the */dev/oracleoci* folder.

```
# cd /dev/oracleoci/
# ls -l
total 0
lrwxrwxrwx. 1 root root 6 Apr 19 17:57 oraclevda -> ../sda
lrwxrwxrwx. 1 root root 7 Apr 19 17:57 oraclevda1 -> ../sda1
lrwxrwxrwx. 1 root root 7 Apr 19 17:57 oraclevda2 -> ../sda2
lrwxrwxrwx. 1 root root 7 Apr 19 17:57 oraclevda3 -> ../sda3
lrwxrwxrwx. 1 root root 6 Apr 19 18:22 oraclevdb -> ../sdb
lrwxrwxrwx. 1 root root 6 Apr 19 18:45 oraclevdb1 -> ../sdb1
#
```

We can confirm the creation of the partition through */dev/oracleoci/oraclevdb1*.

We can also use the Linux utility *lsblk*. This utility lists information about the block devices.

```
# lsblk
NAME    MAJ:MIN RM  SIZE RO TYPE MOUNTPOINT
sdb       8:16   0   50G  0 disk
└─sdb1    8:17   0   50G  0 part
sda       8:0    0 46.6G  0 disk
├─sda2    8:2    0    8G  0 part [SWAP]
├─sda3    8:3    0 38.4G  0 part /
└─sda1    8:1    0  200M  0 part /boot/efi
```

Using this command, we can see the device (disk) *sdb* as well as the partition (part) we have just created, *sdb1*. Now that we have our device, with a partition, it is now time to format this partition. We will now format the device using

```
# mkfs -t ext4 /dev/oracleoci/oraclevdb1
```

Before mounting the device and to be usable at the OS level, we will create a folder:

```
# mkdir /mnt/disk1
# mount /dev/oracleoci/oraclevdb1 /mnt/disk1
# df -h
Filesystem      Size  Used Avail Use% Mounted on
devtmpfs        458M     0  458M   0% /dev
tmpfs           486M     0  486M   0% /dev/shm
tmpfs           486M   17M  470M   4% /run
tmpfs           486M     0  486M   0% /sys/fs/cgroup
/dev/sda3        39G  2.1G   37G   6% /
/dev/sda1       200M  9.7M  191M   5% /boot/efi
tmpfs            98M     0   98M   0% /run/user/1000
/dev/sdb         50G   53M   47G   1% /mnt/disk1
```

We can see the filesystem */mnt/disk1* which is the filesystem using the volume attached earlier.

In order to automatically mount this filesystem on reboot, you will have to add a line in */etc/fstab*. Here is the line that we have to add into:

```
/dev/oracleoci/oraclevdb1 /mnt/disk1 ext4 defaults,_netdev,nofail 0 2
```

The NFS options "**_netdev**" and "**nofail**" are strongly recommended by Oracle. The "**_netdev**" is used to configure the mount process to initiate before the volumes are mounted. Using the option "**nofail**" will allow an instance to boot even though a block volume is not accessible.

Note   For a paid account, the maximum number of block volumes attached to a compute is 32.

Security

Security is often a concern when using cloud services. Boot and block volumes (and their backups) are encrypted at rest using *Advanced Encryption Standard* (AES) algorithm with 256-bit key. The data is also secure when transiting over an internal secure network. But if you have more specific requirements in terms of data security in transit, you can enable encryption when data is transferring between volumes and computes. This is possible for compute instances only, not for bare-metal instances. This feature requires the use of paravirtualized volume attachments, not iSCSI attachments.

Performance

Oracle Cloud Infrastructure Storage uses NVMe-based (nonvolatile memory express) storage infrastructure for better performance. As we have seen during the creation process, we have the choice between three performance tiers, "Lower Cost", "Balanced", and "Higher Performance", and this tier can dynamically be changed after the creation. The "Elastic Performance" allows you to purchase more *volume performance units* (VPU) and allocate more resources to a specific boot of block volume. Augmenting the resource will increase IOPS/GB and throughput per GB. In contrast, you can purchase less VPU and then decrease the performance of the volume. This is a perfect example of cost saving.

We have the choice between three elastic performance configurations.

Performance Level	Description	Max IOPS/ Volume	Max Throughput/GB	VPU/ GB
Low Cost	Intensive workload with large sequential I/O.	3000	Up to 480	0
Balanced	Default setting. Good balance between performance and cost for random I/O.	25,000	480	10
Higher Performance	Highest I/O requirements.	35,000	480	20

To change the performance tier, you have to select the volume, and as we can see in Figure 5-8, you have to click "Change Performance".

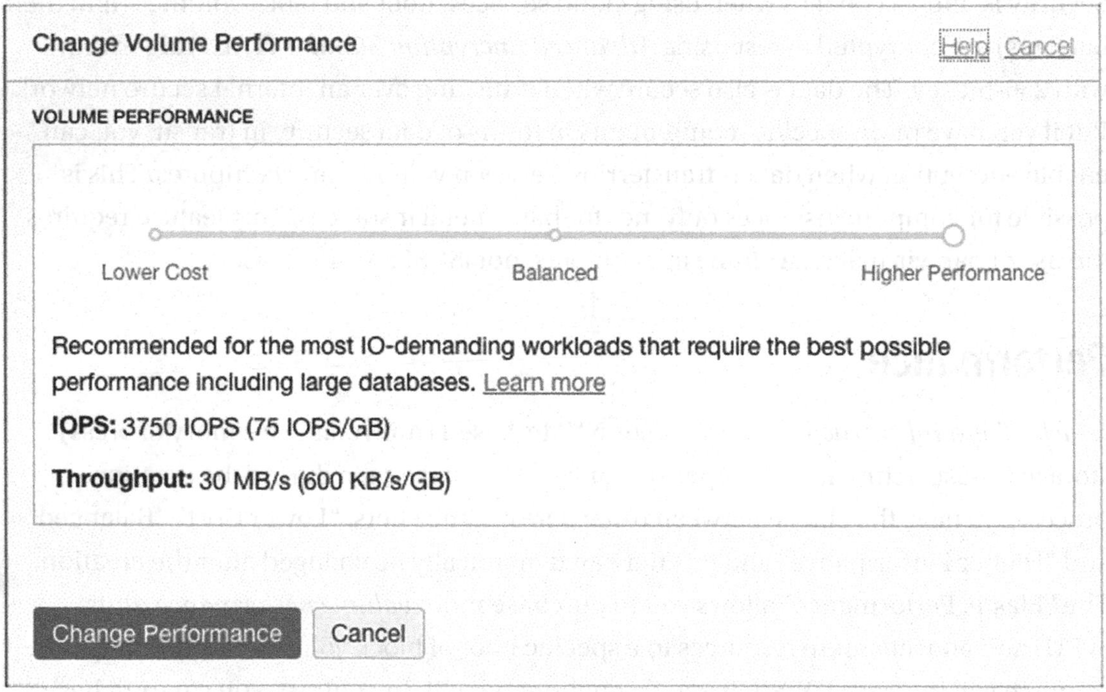

Figure 5-8. *Change Block Volume Performance*

You simply have to select the desired performance tier and click "Change Performance". The volume will now be using the new setting, and this will instantly have an impact on the cost. If you increase the performance, the service will be more expensive. If you decrease the performance, you will be saving some cost.

Backup

Using the console, you can create backups of your boot and block volumes. First, navigate to the volume page and click the "Block Volume Backups" (or "BootVolumes Backups" in case of boot volume) link under the "Resources" menu item. As you can see in Figure 5-9, there is no backup of this volume.

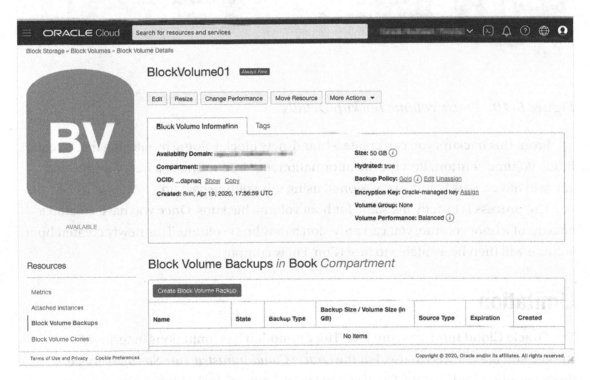

Figure 5-9. *No backup for this volume*

Click "Create Block Volume Backup" and provide a name and the type of backup, either "Full Backup" or "Incremental Backup". Backups contain records of all the changes from the creation of the block volume (full backup) or a record of all the changes from the last backup (incremental backup). These backups are stored and use resources in *Object Storage* service.

Once the backup is completed, navigate to the "Block Volume Backup" page. Click the navigation menu, and select "Block Storage" and "Block Volume Backup". You will see the details of the volume backup as you can see in Figure 5-10.

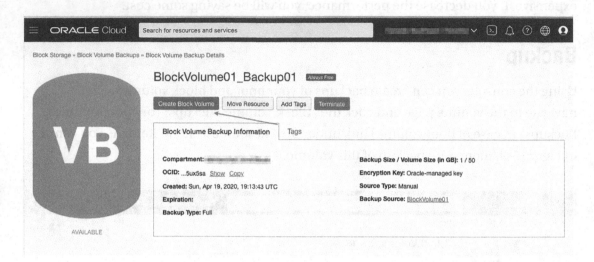

Figure 5-10. *Block Volume Backup Details*

From this backup, you can create a brand-new block volume by clicking the "Create Block Volume" button. Provide the information required to create a new volume, and you will have a new volume provisioned using this volume backup.

The process is exactly the same for boot volume backups. Once you have created a backup of a boot volume, you can provision a new boot volume. This newly created boot volume will then be available to provision a new compute.

Limitation

The Oracle Cloud Infrastructure Free Tier promotion has limitations in terms of storage you are allowed to use. For the *Oracle Cloud Infrastructure Storage* service, this promotion limits to 100 GB of storage total, boot or block volumes. Knowing the minimum size of a volume is 50 GB, you are allowed to provision a total of two volumes.

In terms of volume backups, you are allowed to have five backups of either boot or block volumes.

Object Storage

Oracle Cloud Infrastructure Object Storage service is fully programmable (using APIs), scalable, secure (encrypted at rest), and a very reliable cloud storage service. It offers two different tiers of storage. The first tier, *Object Storage*, is considered as a "hot" tier, and the second one, *Archive Storage*, is considered a "cold" tier.

The less expensive Archive Storage is used for infrequently accessed data. Long-term backups should be stored in this tier, for example.

There are three core components in this service, "Objects", "Bucket", and "Namespace". "Objects" is the data itself. An object could be a log file, an image, a video, or any other file that will be stored as an object. The "Bucket" is the container where the objects are stored. A bucket can be *private* or *public*. A tenant is associated with a *Namespace*, and every bucket is unique into a namespace. The namespace can be seen as the parent entity of the buckets.

Note   We can interact with Object Storage using APIs, command-line interface (CLI), Software Development Kits (SDK), and the console. Available SDKs for now are Java, Python, Ruby, and Go.

How to Create a Bucket

Let's start by creating the bucket. Click the navigation menu and select "Object Storage". Make sure you are in the right compartment and click "Create Bucket" as you can see in Figure 5-11.

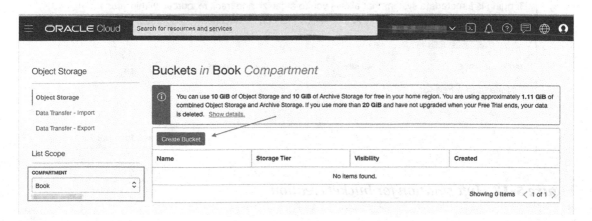

Figure 5-11. *Bucket creation*

You will have to provide information, as we can see in Figure 5-12:

- **Bucket Name:** Name of the bucket

- **Storage Tier:** Standard or Archive tier

- **Object Events:** To create events to be used with the Events service

- **Encryption:** Either use "Oracle-Managed keys" or you own keys

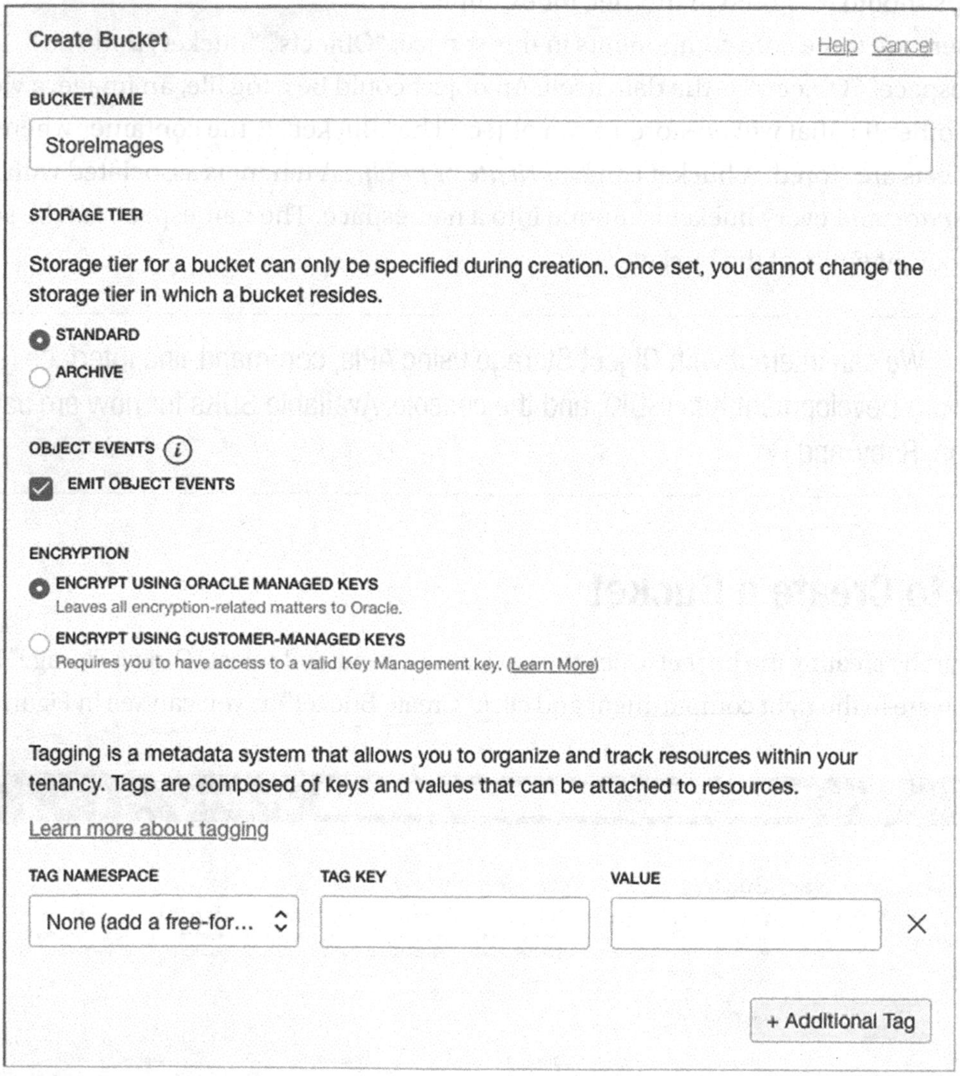

Create Bucket   Help Cancel

BUCKET NAME

StoreImages

STORAGE TIER

Storage tier for a bucket can only be specified during creation. Once set, you cannot change the storage tier in which a bucket resides.

- ● STANDARD
- ○ ARCHIVE

OBJECT EVENTS ⓘ

- ☑ EMIT OBJECT EVENTS

ENCRYPTION

- ● ENCRYPT USING ORACLE MANAGED KEYS
  Leaves all encryption-related matters to Oracle.
- ○ ENCRYPT USING CUSTOMER-MANAGED KEYS
  Requires you to have access to a valid Key Management key. (Learn More)

Tagging is a metadata system that allows you to organize and track resources within your tenancy. Tags are composed of keys and values that can be attached to resources.

Learn more about tagging

TAG NAMESPACE	TAG KEY	VALUE	
None (add a free-for... ⇕			✕

+ Additional Tag

Figure 5-12. *Information for bucket creation*

Click "Create Bucket" and the private bucket "StoreImages" will be created and ready to store objects. Navigate to the newly created bucket to see all the details of this bucket. In Figure 5-13 we have the detailed information and a list of actions we can perform on the bucket.

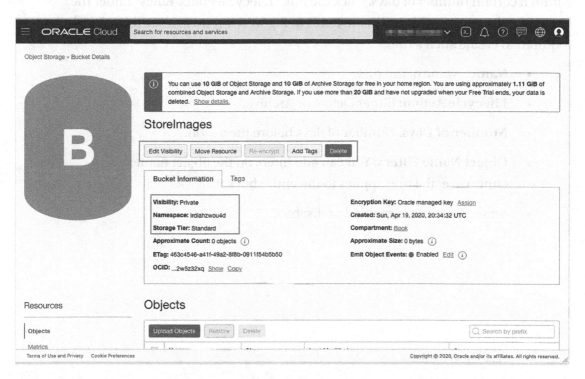

Figure 5-13. *Detailed information of the bucket*

First of all, we can see the visibility of this bucket, which is in this case a private bucket. We can see the namespace and also the bucket tier, which is a standard tier. If you click "Edit Visibility", you can switch the visibility from private to public and vice versa. The "Move Resource" button will be used to move this bucket to another compartment within the same tenancy. The "Add Tags" button will be used to add tags to this bucket, to track the cost, for example. And we have the "Delete" button to remove the bucket.

Note   The bucket needs to be empty in order to delete it.

Lifecycle Policy Rules

A very interesting feature is the ability to use a lifecycle rule on the objects in a bucket. We can create a rule saying that the objects will be automatically archived or deleted within a certain number of days. Click the link "Lifecycle Policy Rules" under the "Resources" menu and click "Create Rule". In Figure 5-14, we can see the information required to create such a rule.

- **Name**: Name of the rule.

- **Lifecycle Action**: Either Delete or Archive.

- **Number of Days**: Number of days before the action.

- **Object Name Filters**: You can add filters on the object names. Otherwise, the rule applies to the entire bucket.

- **State**: This rule is enabled or disabled.

Figure 5-14. *Creation of a lifecycle rule*

Click "Create" to complete the creation of the lifecycle rule. After the creation, you can modify all of these parameters as required.

You will have to create a policy to allow the service to manage the objects on your behalf. This policy must be created in the *root* compartment. Refer to Chapter 2 for the creation of a policy.

```
Allow service objectstorage-<region_identifier> to manage object-family in
compartment <compartment_name>
```

How to Upload an Object

Let's upload an object into the bucket we have created. From the bucket page, click "Upload Objects" as we can see in Figure 5-15.

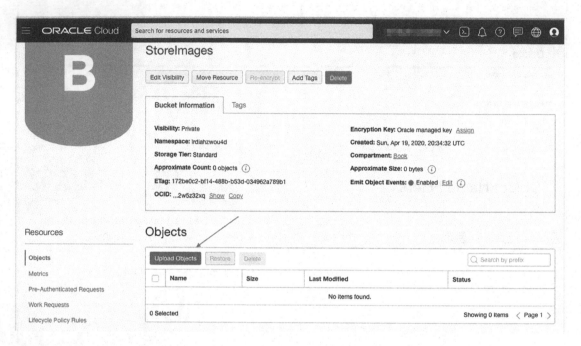

Figure 5-15. *To upload objects*

From the "Upload Objects" page, you can either drop files or select files. Once your files are selected, you have the ability to add "Response Header" and/or "Metadata". In my example, I have added the response header "Cache-Control" with a value of "no-cache". This doesn't have any effect on the Object Storage but can be used by the application that downloads or reads this object. Figure 5-16 is what we are seeing in the "Upload Objects" page.

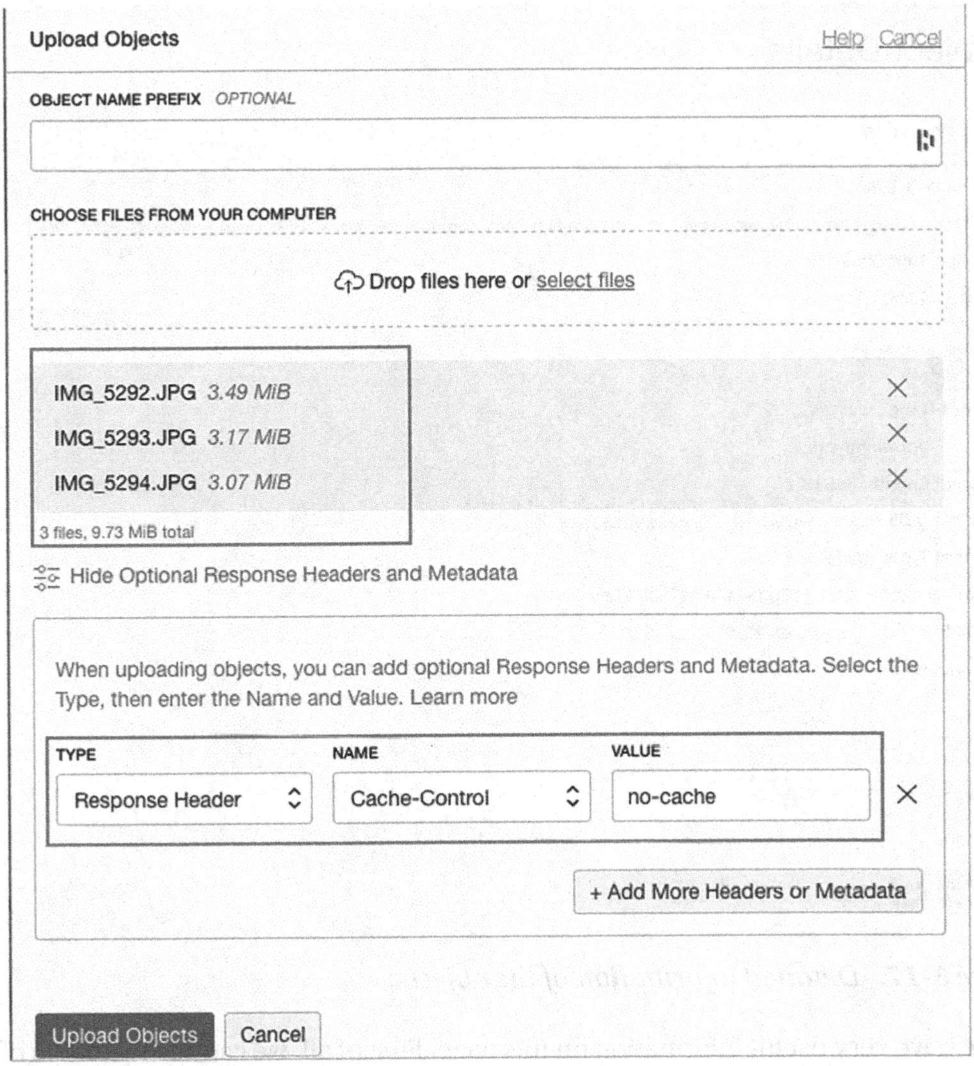

Upload Objects   Help Cancel

OBJECT NAME PREFIX *OPTIONAL*

CHOOSE FILES FROM YOUR COMPUTER

Drop files here or select files

IMG_5292.JPG *3.49 MiB*   ✕
IMG_5293.JPG *3.17 MiB*   ✕
IMG_5294.JPG *3.07 MiB*   ✕

3 files, 9.73 MiB total

Hide Optional Response Headers and Metadata

When uploading objects, you can add optional Response Headers and Metadata. Select the Type, then enter the Name and Value. Learn more

TYPE	NAME	VALUE
Response Header	Cache-Control	no-cache	✕

+ Add More Headers or Metadata

Upload Objects   Cancel

Figure 5-16. *Upload Objects page*

Once you click "Upload Objects", the files will be uploaded into the bucket. The console will be using multipart uploads for a file larger than 64 MB. Once the upload is completed, you will see the objects from the bucket page. To have detailed information for an object, click the three dots (":") on the right and to "View Object Details". Figure 5-17 shows the detailed information of an object.

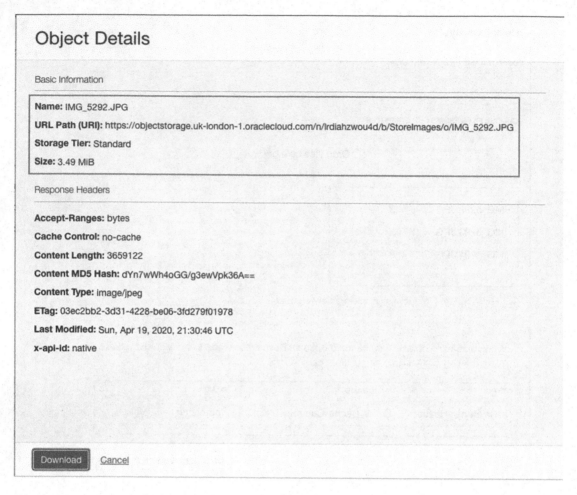

Figure 5-17. *Detailed information of the object*

We have very useful information on this page. First of all, we can see the name of the object, the storage tier, and the size. The URL Path (URI) will be needed to get the object using APIs, SDKs, and command line. You can quickly test this URL by having your bucket as public and use this URL in a browser. You can also click the "Download" button to get the object.

How to Delete an Object

Deleting an object is pretty simple from the console. Navigate to the bucket page. From the "Objects" menu under "Resources", select the objects to be deleted and click "Delete".

How to Replicate a Bucket

This replication feature replicates all the objects in the source bucket into a read-only destination bucket. The destination bucket can reside in the same or another region. You have to select the region, the compartment, and the destination bucket, and the replication process will start automatically. This is necessary to protect your objects from an outage or for your disaster recovery strategy. This feature is useful if you need to have a copy of these objects for the use of another application in the region or elsewhere in another region, to reduce latency.

In order to use the replication feature, you must have access to both buckets. You might have to create a policy in the *root* compartment. This policy will allow a group to manage the object in the entire tenancy. Refer to Chapter 2 on how to create a policy.

```
Allow group <group> to manage object-family in tenancy
```

You can also create less-permissive policies like this:

```
Allow group <group> to manage buckets in compartment <objectstore>
Allow group <group> to manage objects in compartment <objectstore>
```

How to Prevent the Object Modification

You can create a "Retention Rule" that prevents objects from being modified or deleted. The retention rule is created using a time-bound type (provide a duration in days or years) or could be indefinite, until the object is deleted. Figure 5-18 shows the error message when deleting an object protected by a retention rule.

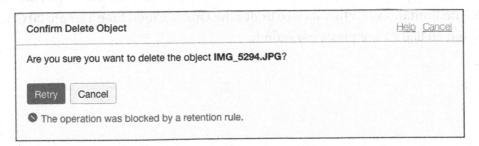

Figure 5-18. *Object protected by a retention rule*

Limitation

The Oracle Cloud Infrastructure Free Tier promotion has limitations in terms of storage and request you are allowed to use in Object Storage. This promotion limits to 20 GB of storage for both standard and archive tiers. You are limited to 50,000 Object Storage API requests per month as well. The Object Storage API is used to manage buckets, objects, and related resources.

If you are running Oracle Cloud Infrastructure using a trial account, you are allowed to exceed the above limits. If you don't upgrade your account before the trial ends, and you are using more than 20 GB of storage, all of your objects will be deleted. You will have to upload your objects again until you reach the limits.

Summary

In this chapter, we have discovered the Oracle Cloud Infrastructure Storage service. We have divided this service into two subjects, Block Volumes and Object Storage. As we have seen, the Block Volume service is used to provision boot and block volumes. The boot volume contains the image required to boot a Compute Instance. The block volume is persistent storage used to install applications and store the data. For Oracle Cloud Free Tier, we can use up to 100 GB of block volumes and a maximum of five backups per volume. Since the minimum size of a block volume is 50 GB, the free tier is limited to two block volumes.

The Object Storage service is used to store any type of object. It uses two types of buckets: standard buckets for "hot" objects and archive buckets for "cold" objects. We can use the console, APIs, SDKs, or command line to interact with the Object Storage service. The limitations for this service under the Oracle Cloud Free Tier are 20 GB of objects and 50,000 API requests per month.

CHAPTER 6

Oracle Autonomous Linux

In 2006, with the objective of proposing a more complete end-to-end software stack along with their database, Oracle decided to have their own distribution of Linux by modifying and compiling the Red Hat Enterprise Linux binaries. This new distribution is now called Oracle Linux and it's the operating system (OS) of choice for Oracle Cloud Infrastructure, Oracle Cloud at Customer, Oracle Engineered Systems like Exadata, and others. For your on-premise needs, you can also download this product for free from Oracle Software Delivery Cloud.

During Oracle OpenWorld in 2019, Larry Ellison, Oracle co-founder and CTO, announced the first autonomous operating system, Oracle Autonomous Linux. This version of Linux provisions itself, tunes itself, and also patches itself.

In this chapter, we will discover the benefits of using this new Autonomous Linux and why this should be used as much as possible.

What Autonomous Means

Oracle's first automated product was the database. Autonomous Database handles all the manual tasks that database administrators (DBA) were used to be responsible for, from the creation, patching process, backups, and tuning. Oracle wanted to come up with an operating system that would also reduce the day-to-day tasks that system administrators were responsible for.

Autonomous Linux with the new service Oracle OS Management Service (OS Management Service can be used on non-Autonomous Linux as well) handles the day-to-day, common management tasks like patching, package management, compliance reporting, and configuration management. The Oracle *Ksplice* feature enables the system to keep the kernel up to date with the latest critical fixes, minimizing the maintenance cost and planned downtime.

© Adrian Png and Luc Demanche 2020
A. Png and L. Demanche, *Getting Started with Oracle Cloud Free Tier*,
https://doi.org/10.1007/978-1-4842-6011-1_6

> **Note**   *Ksplice* requires Internet access. You have to add and configure the *NAT Gateway* or *Internet Gateway* to your VCN.

How to Provision Autonomous Linux

Creation of the Notification Topic

Before we create the new Autonomous Linux, we have to have a notification topic which will be used by Autonomous Linux to send notifications. I invite you to follow the instruction in Chapter 9 which covers this topic. We will create a topic called "AutonomousLinux" and subscribe to this topic. We will need the "Notification Topic Oracle Identifier (OCID)" during the provisioning process of the Autonomous Linux Compute Instance.

Creation of the Compute Instance

You can refer to Chapter 4 where we explain how to provision a new Compute Instance. During the provisioning process, make sure to select one of the available images "Oracle Autonomous Linux". During the process, we will have to provide the Notification Topic OCID we would like the Autonomous Linux to use to send notifications.

During the provisioning process, make sure to click "Show Advanced Options" where we see instructions to configure Autonomous Linux to use the desired Notification Topic. As you can see in Figure 6-1, we have to

- Select "Paste Cloud-Init Script"
- Add these instructions in the CLOUD-INIT SCRIPT section

```
#!/bin/bash
al-config -T ocid1.onstopic.oc1.uk-london-1.
aaaaaaaahy3dtqx7aofgcfswyd54ja3hebvntbcks62zhyjceax4v2jszh6a
```

where ocid is the Oracle Cloud Identifier of the Notification Topic.

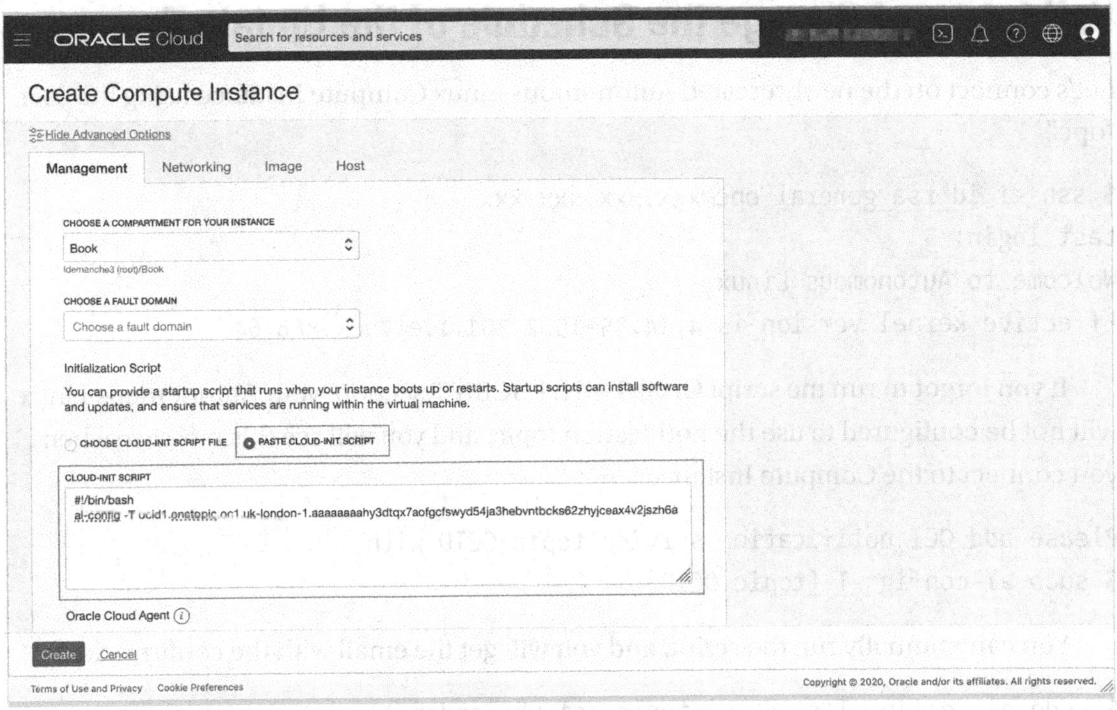

Figure 6-1. Notification Topic

The script will be executed at the end of the provisioning process. Click the "Create" button to launch the provisioning process of the Compute Instance.

Once provisioned, you should get a message (using the destination you have selected in your subscription to the notification topic) that confirms the new Autonomous Linux Compute Instance uses the notification topic mentioned in the cloud-init script section. In this example I configured my subscription to get an email that will contain something like this:

```
Configured OCI notification service topic OCID on instance AppServerBook01:
  ocid1.onstopic.oc1.uk-london-1.
  aaaaaaaahy3dtqx7aofgcfswyd54ja3hebvntbcks62zhyjceax4v2jszh6a
```

Validate and Change the Schedule of the Update Process

Let's connect on the newly created Autonomous Linux Compute Instance using the user "opc".

```
$ ssh -i id_rsa_general opc@xxx.xxx.xxx.xxx
Last login:
Welcome to Autonomous Linux
Effective kernel version is 4.14.35-1902.301.1.el7uek.x86_64
```

If you forgot to run the script CLOUD-INIT SCRIPT section, your Autonomous Linux will not be configured to use the notification topic, and you will see this message when you connect to the Compute Instance:

```
Please add OCI notification service topic OCID with
$ sudo al-config -T [topic OCID]
```

You can manually run the script, and you will get the email with the confirmation:

```
$ sudo al-config -T ocid1.onstopic.oc1.uk-london-1.
aaaaaaaahy3dtqx7aofgcfswyd54ja3hebvntbcks62zhyjceax4v2jszh6a
Configured OCI notification service topic OCID.
Publishing message 'AL: Notification enabled on instance AppServerBook01'
Published message 'AL: Notification enabled on instance AppServerBook01'
```

Now that we know the configuration is properly done, we can validate and change the schedule of the automatic update:

```
$ sudo al-config -s
Current daily auto update time window(24-hour): 21-1
Current daily auto update time(24-hour): 23:41
```

For a reason, you might want to change the schedule of the automatic update. You can change it by running the command. In this example, I will change the schedule to make sure the update process will run between 2AM and 4AM.

```
al-config -w [time window].
      where time-window
      format: <start_hour>-<end_hour>
              <start_hour> and <end_hour> must be integers between 0
              and 23.
              Minimum window is 2 hours, maximum window is 6 hours.
```

```
$ sudo al-config -w 2-4
Configured daily auto update time window(24-hour): 2-4
Configured daily auto update time(24-hour): 03:41
Created cron job file /etc/cron.d/al-update .
```

This script is updating the cron file "/etc/cron.d/al-update", which looks like this:

```
# Daily cron job for AL auto updates.
# Created by al-config, do not modify this file.
# If you want to change update time, use
# 'sudo al-config -w <time window>' to set auto update time window
41 3 * * * root /usr/sbin/al-update >/dev/null
```

As you can see, this cron is running the script "/usr/sbin/alupdate", and the script is doing the following:

```
# al-update:
# - ksplice upgrade
# - yum-cron - yum upgrade
# - report exploit attemp(s) if detected
# - report ksplice show
# - report needs-restarting
# - send notification if needed
```

Manually Run the Update Process

As we have seen, the update process is scheduled to run every day. If for any reason you would like to run it manually, you simply have to run the script mentioned in the cron file.

Here is how you can run that job and we can see the first part of the output:

```
$ sudo /usr/sbin/al-update
Starting upgrade.
+-------------------------------------------------------------------+
|  Ksplice upgrade report                                           |
+-------------------------------------------------------------------+
Running 'ksplice -y all upgrade'.
```

If the process is updating any components, it will send a message through the notification topic and then you will get notified.

Summary

Oracle Autonomous Linux performs automatic tasks that were under the responsibilities of the system administrators. The system is patching, securing, and tuning itself without human intervention. This allows IT staff to perform more efficient activities for the business than these day-to-day tasks. Also, Oracle Linux (not only the Autonomous) is using the feature *Ksplice* that allows the daily update process to be done online, without any outages.

This is dramatically decreasing the risks of attacks and data breaches and, by using Ksplice, minimizes the outages and, so, the impact on the business.

CHAPTER 7

Autonomous Databases

As you know already, Oracle has delivered a few decades of data management systems and innovation for on-premise, cloud, and hybrid type of deployment. The latest cloud version of the database is called the *Autonomous Database* (ADB). This system combines concepts like self-driving, self-securing, and self-repairing by redefining the database management tasks using machine learning and automation. This dramatically reduces the needs of human labor, costs, and manual tuning and then reduces the risk and human errors. This way, your system is more stable, more efficient in terms of performance but also in terms of cost.

What Is Autonomous Database

Oracle wanted to have an autonomous system that will take care of databases and the underlying infrastructure, as well as tuning and monitoring. Oracle came up with the Autonomous Database, a fully managed service that handles the operation like the creation of the database, the backup of the database, patching, upgrade, as well as the scaling of the database. Every DBA knows pretty well these activities as all of these tasks were manually done by them in the past. In fact, some of them like patching and upgrade were probably not done as they should have been done by lack of time and resources, which ended up with vulnerable systems.

By *self-driving*, Oracle is providing the capabilities of provisioning, automate patching, and upgrade and is able to tune itself. Scaling capabilities also allows the database to scale up/down the resources to automatically adjust with the workload.

By *self-securing*, Oracle is providing the capabilities of automatically applying security patches, protecting against know cyberattacks. Free of charge, the database is encrypted at rest and, in transit, can use Oracle Data Safe to mask sensitive data and also to alert suspicious data access.

107

© Adrian Png and Luc Demanche 2020
A. Png and L. Demanche, *Getting Started with Oracle Cloud Free Tier*,
https://doi.org/10.1007/978-1-4842-6011-1_7

By *self-repairing*, Oracle is providing the capabilities of protecting against all sorts of issues, system failures, user errors, and so on.

By using Autonomous Database, we know that important tasks like patching and upgrade have been taken care of automatically by Oracle. So, this eliminates the vulnerabilities of your system, with less administration efforts.

Difference Between ATP and ADW

Autonomous Database comes in two different flavors, *Autonomous Transaction Processing* (ATP) and *Autonomous Data Warehouse* (ADW) – two different configurations to meet specific requirements for online processing and data warehousing.

To help you determine which would be the better fit for your needs between ATP and ADW, let's start with differentiating two workloads, OLTP and *Data Warehousing* (DW). OLTP stands for *Online Transactional Processing,* and this type of application mainly deals with large numbers of transactions by a large number of users. You can imagine an application that executed hundreds of small transactions per second, like online banking type of application. ATP corresponds to this type of needs. Data warehousing is the concept behind many *Business Intelligence* (BI) application where it has to deal with large reports, complex analytic calculations, predictive scenario, ad hoc queries, and so on. This type of application is executing the smallest number of requests, but larger joins, more complex aggregations compare to the OLTP type of application. ADW corresponds to this type of needs.

More technically, ATP will not be configured the same as the ADW. First of all, ATP and ADW will not use the memory in the same way. ATP requires a very quick access to the data, so we will use a bigger memory area to hold more data in memory. This memory structure is called System Global Area (SGA). To help the ADW with the bigger and more complex joins and aggregations, Oracle will use another memory structure called Program Global Area (PGA). Second of all, query optimization is also different between ATP and ADW. ATP tries to use more indexes and ADW is doing more parallelized operations. Another important difference between ATP and ADW is the predefined database services or consumer groups. Consumer groups control the priority and parallelism used by the user's sessions when the system is under resource pressure. ATP has consumer groups that are able to deal with large numbers of small transactions and allow a high level of concurrency. On the other hand, ADW allows the highest level of CPU and I/O resources but allows a minimum number of concurrent sessions.

ADB Provisioning

It is now time to demonstrate how to provision a new ADB. From the console, click the navigation menu, and under *Database* section, select either *Autonomous Data Warehouse* if you want an ADW or *Autonomous Transaction Processing* for an ATP. Click "Create Autonomous Database", and you will have to provide this information:

- **Compartment**: Name of your compartment.

- **Display Name**: Name that will be displayed in the console.

- **Database Name**: Maximum of 14 characters, only letters and numbers.

- **Workload Type**: Either ADW or ATP.

- **Deployment Type**: For Always Free ADB, the only option is Shared Infra.

- **Configure the Database Section**:

  - Make sure to slide *Always Free.*

  - Select the desired database version.

  - **OCPU Count**: For Always Free ADB, it will be 1.

  - **Storage**: For Always Free ADB, it will be 0.02 TB.

  - Auto Scaling feature is not available.

- **Password for ADMIN**: 12 to 30 characters with lowercase, uppercase and a number.

- **Choose Network Access**: For Always Free, only "Allow secure access from everywhere" is available.

- **Configure Access Control Rules**: Leave unchecked.

- **Choose a License Type**: License Included is the only option.

Click *Create Autonomous Database* to launch the provisioning process.

Once the process is completed, you will be redirected to the Autonomous Database Details page, as you can see in Figure 7-1.

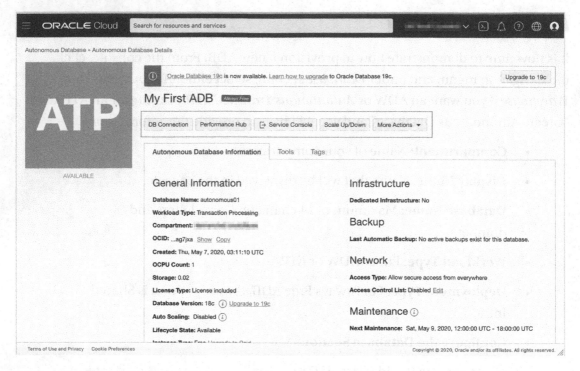

Figure 7-1. Autonomous Database Details

The first piece of information we are seeing is the name of the Autonomous Database, *My First ADB*. Just below, we have a series of buttons:

- **DB Connection**: From this menu, you will be able to perform two things:

  Download Wallet: Select the Wallet Type and click Download. You will be asked to create a password to protect the wallet. Here are the two wallet types:

  - **Instance Wallet**: Wallet for a single ADB

  - **Regional Wallet**: Wallet for every ADB within this tenancy and a region

  Rotate Wallet: This feature is for invalidating instance or regional wallet. Rotating an instance wallet is not affecting the regional wallet. Existing connections on the ADB will remain but will disconnect after a certain period. They will have to be reestablished using the new wallet.

110

- **Performance Hub**: This button will bring you to the Performance Hub page that we will discuss later.

- **Service Console**: This page will be discussed later in this chapter.

- **Scale Up/Down**: This menu is used to increase or decrease the number of OCPU and storage.

Note   The Always Free Autonomous Database is limited to 1 OCPU and 20 GB of storage.

- **More Actions**: This menu allows you to perform multiple tasks, like

  - **Stop/Restart/Start the ADB**.

  - **Restore/Create Clone**: This will be discussed later in the chapter.

  - **Access Control List**: To edit the access list by adding IP addresses or VCN.

  - **Admin Password**: To change the password of the user ADMIN.

  - **Update License Type**: Modify the license type between Bring Your Own License (BYOL) and License Included.

  - **Upgrade Database Instance to Paid**.

  - **Move Resource**: Move this ADB to another compartment.

  - **Add Tags**: Associate tags to the ADB.

  - **Terminate**: Stop and delete the ADB.

Pause reading now, and download your wallet as described in the preceding list. Select the Wallet Type, click Download, and choose a password. Save the wallet somewhere on your local drive. You can choose either wallet type, and choosing Instance Wallet is a good way to keep things simple.

Below the buttons, you will have three tabs, the default selected tab, *Autonomous Database Information*; *Tools*; and *Tags*. In the default tab, you will find a lot of important information; we will not go through all of them, but I would like to mention few items:

- **Database Name**: The name of the Autonomous Database.

- **Workload Type**: ATP or ADW.

- **Database Version**: The current database version.

- **Dedicated Infrastructure**: "No" means we are using shared Exadata infrastructure.

- **Backup – Last Automatic Backup**: "No active backups". No backup has been done yet. We will discuss about backups later in this chapter.

- **Network – Access Control List**: Disabled. The ATP is accessible from everywhere by default.

- **Maintenance – Next Maintenance**: This is the predefined maintenance windows to automatically patch your system. The database should remain available during that period. You might get disconnected, but you should be able to reconnect immediately.

If you select the tab *Tools*, you will have access to four tools, as you can see in Figure 7-2.

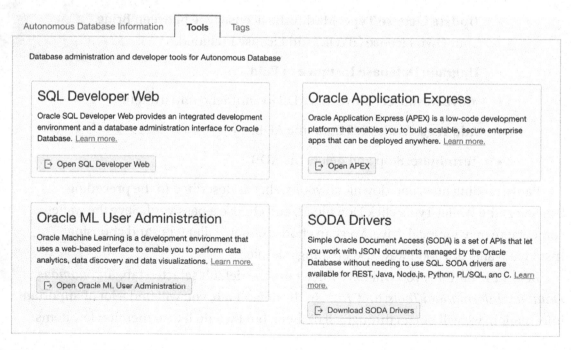

Figure 7-2. Tab Tools

The four tools that you'll have access to are the following:

- **SQL Developer Web**: Chapter 10 covers this tool in detail.

- **Oracle Application Express**: I invite you to read Chapter 11 for a detailed explanation of this tool.

- **Oracle ML User Administration**: Chapter 14 provides an introduction to machine learning.

- **SODA Drivers**: A set of APIs to develop an application that stores the data in JavaScript Object Notation (JSON) documents, managed by Oracle Database. This subject will not be covered in the book.

If you select the last tab *Tags,* you will see any current tags as shown in Figure 7-3.

| Autonomous Database Information | Tools | **Tags** |

Defined Tags (2)

Oracle-Tags.**CreatedBy:** oracleidentitycloudservice/ ▓▓▓▓▓▓▓▓▓
Oracle-Tags.**CreatedOn:** 2020-05-07T03:11:10.303Z

Figure 7-3. Tab Tags

If you have created your tenancy after December 17, 2019, your tenancy has one default Tag Namespace in the root compartment. The Tag Namespace is called *Oracle-Tags* with two tag keys:

- **CreatedBy:** Contains the name of the principal that created the resource

- **CreatedOn:** Date of the creation of the resource

Later in Chapter 16, we will see how to use these tags in the "Cost Analysis" section. Now let's explore the menu on the left side, under *Resources.* If you click the menu *Metrics,* you will have six interesting metrics. Figure 7-4 shows the selected period and the first four metrics:

- **CPU Utilization:** A percentage that shows the CPU usage aggregated across all consumer groups

- **Storage Utilization:** The percentage of the storage capacity currently in use

- **Sessions**: The number of sessions in the database during that period

- **Execute Count**: The number of user and recursive calls that executed SQL statements during that period

- **Running Statements**: The number of running statements during that period, aggregated across all consumer groups

- **Queued Statements**: The number of queued statements during that period, aggregated across all consumer groups

---

Note   The last two metrics are not shown in the figure.

Figure 7-4. *First four metrics*

Chapter 9 will cover in more detail the monitoring and metrics.

Connecting to ADB

Now that we have downloaded the wallet, we will configure SQL Developer for the connection to the ADB as well and demonstrate how to connect using SQLcl.

CHAPTER 7   AUTONOMOUS DATABASES

Note   If you haven't downloaded your wallet yet, then do so now as described in the preceding section. Chose Instance Wallet as your wallet type.

Launch your SQL Developer, click the new connection icon (✛), and select *New Database Connection*. You will have to provide the following information:

- **Name**: Name of the connection.

- **Username**: admin (or any other user).

- **Password**: Password of this user.

- **Connection Type**: Cloud Wallet.

- **Configuration File**: Select the wallet zip file previously downloaded.

- **Service**: Select the appropriate service.

You can see in Figure 7-5 the information.

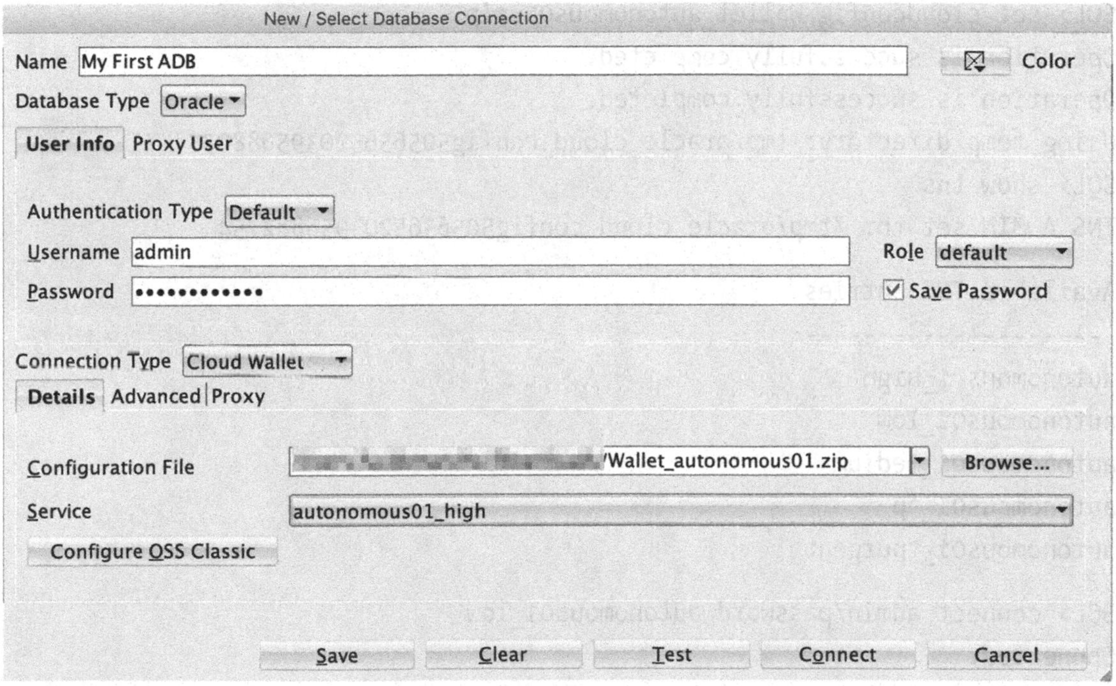

Figure 7-5. *Creation of the connection*

Click *Test* to validate the information. If the validation is successful, you can click *Connect*. The new connection will be saved and will appear in the Oracle Connections list (the left panel), and you will also have a new connection established to your Autonomous Database. You can then run SQL statement against your database.

Now we will demonstrate how to use SQLcl and the wallet to connect on the Autonomous Database. First of all, you have to install SQLcl on your Compute Instance using the user root:

```
[root@appserverbook02 ~]# yum install sqlcl
```

Transfer the wallet zip file on the Linux server. You can create a folder "wallet" under /root to store this file. From this location, we will launch SQLcl, set the location of the wallet file, and create a connection.

```
[root@appserverbook02 wallets]# /opt/oracle/sqlcl/bin/sql /nolog

SQLcl: Release 19.4 Production on Wed May 13 19:39:33 2020

Copyright (c) 1982, 2020, Oracle.  All rights reserved.

SQL> set cloudconfig Wallet_autonomous01.zip
Operation is successfully completed.
Operation is successfully completed.
Using temp directory:/tmp/oracle_cloud_config5056565203956882754
SQL> show tns
TNS_ADMIN set to: /tmp/oracle_cloud_config5056565203956882754

Available TNS Entries
---------------------
autonomous01_high
autonomous01_low
autonomous01_medium
autonomous01_tp
autonomous01_tpurgent

SQL> connect admin/password@autonomous01_low
Connected.
SQL> select instance_name from v$instance;
```

```
INSTANCE_NAME
----------------
fepe1pod2
```

We can confirm that both connections from SQL Developer and SQLcl work using the wallet zip file we have previously downloaded.

Service Console

The next page we will discuss is the *Service Console* that you can reach by clicking the *Service Console* button. This will open up a new browser tab with four menus.

The Overview Menu

The Overview menu provides for real-time information on the utilization of ADB. Figure 7-6 shows the Overview page. We can quickly see the information in regard to the current storage used as well as some other metrics.

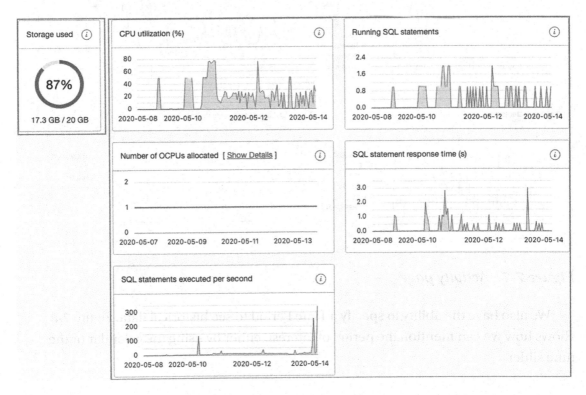

Figure 7-6. *Overview page*

We can see the system is using 87% of the allocated storage. In terms of metrics, we can see the real-time utilization of CPU, average number of running SQL, current number of OCPU, average SQL response time, and the number of executed SQL statements per second for this period.

The Activity Menu

The Activity menu provides real-time and historical information on utilization. You have two main views, **Monitor** and **Monitored SQL**. By default, the view **Monitor** is selected. In Figure 7-7, we are seeing four metrics, first of all the average number of sessions using CPU or waiting on a wait event, CPU utilization per consumer group, average number of running statements, and average number of queued statements per consumer group as well.

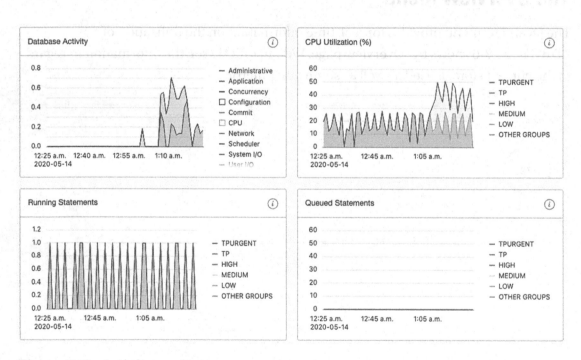

Figure 7-7. *Activity page*

We also have the ability to specify a Time Period to see historical data. Figure 7-8 shows how we can mention the period of interest, either by using the calendar or the time slider.

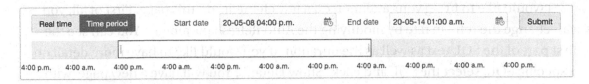

Figure 7-8. *Time period*

You can change the start date and end date using the calendar and click Submit. The metrics will get updated based on your selection. Using the time slider, the metrics will change automatically.

The default retention period is 8 days. To change the retention period, you have to use the Automatic Workload Repository (AWR) PL/SQL procedure. The value for the retention is in minutes. The code in the following example changes the retention period to 30 days:

```
BEGIN
DBMS_WORKLOAD_REPOSITORY.MODIFY_SNAPSHOT_SETTING (retention => 43200);
END;
/
```

Still under the menu *Activity*, select the view **Monitored SQL** on the top of this page. You will then have, as you can see in Figure 7-9, a view of the current and past monitored SQL.

	STATUS	SQL TEXT	DURATION
	Show Details Download Report	Cancel Execution	Auto Refresh 5 seconds ▼
1	✓ DONE (ALL ROWS)	SELECT NVL(MAX(CARD_ID),0) FROM CARD_DETAILS	6 s
2	✓ DONE	begin declare cust_count number :=0; order_count number :=0; add_count number :=	10 s
3	✓ DONE	CREATE INDEX carddetails_cust_ix ON card_details(customer_id) tablespace DATA p	8 s
4	✓ DONE	CREATE INDEX cust_func_lower_name_ix ON customers (lower(cust_last_name), low(	8 s
5	✓ DONE	CREATE INDEX cust_email_ix ON customers (cust_email) tablespace DATA parallel 4	8 s
6	✓ DONE	CREATE INDEX cust_dob_ix ON customers (dob) tablespace DATA parallel 4 nologgin	6 s
7	✓ DONE	CREATE INDEX cust_account_manager_ix ON customers (account_mgr_id) tablespac	7 s
8	✓ DONE	CREATE INDEX ord_warehouse_ix ON orders (warehouse_id, order_status) tablespac(	10 s
9	✓ DONE	CREATE INDEX ord_order_date_ix ON orders (order_date) REVERSE tablespace DAT/	8 s
10	✓ DONE	CREATE INDEX ord_customer_ix ON orders (customer_id) REVERSE tablespace DAT/	7 s
11	✓ DONE	CREATE INDEX ord_sales_rep_ix ON orders (sales_rep_id) REVERSE tablespace DAT/	8 s
12	✓ DONE	CREATE INDEX item_product_ix ON order_items (product_id) REVERSE tablespace D	29 s
13	✓ DONE	CREATE INDEX item_order_ix ON order_items (order_id) REVERSE tablespace DATA [	36 s

Figure 7-9. *Current and past monitored SQL*

I would like to bring your attention on a few elements on this page. First of all, you can change the refresh rate by modifying the Auto Refresh parameter. You can see the first part of the SQL text as well as the duration. If you would like to have more detail on a specific SQL, select the SQL and click "Show Details". You will have a new page, with three new tabs, Overview, Plan Statistics, and Metrics (Figure 7-10).

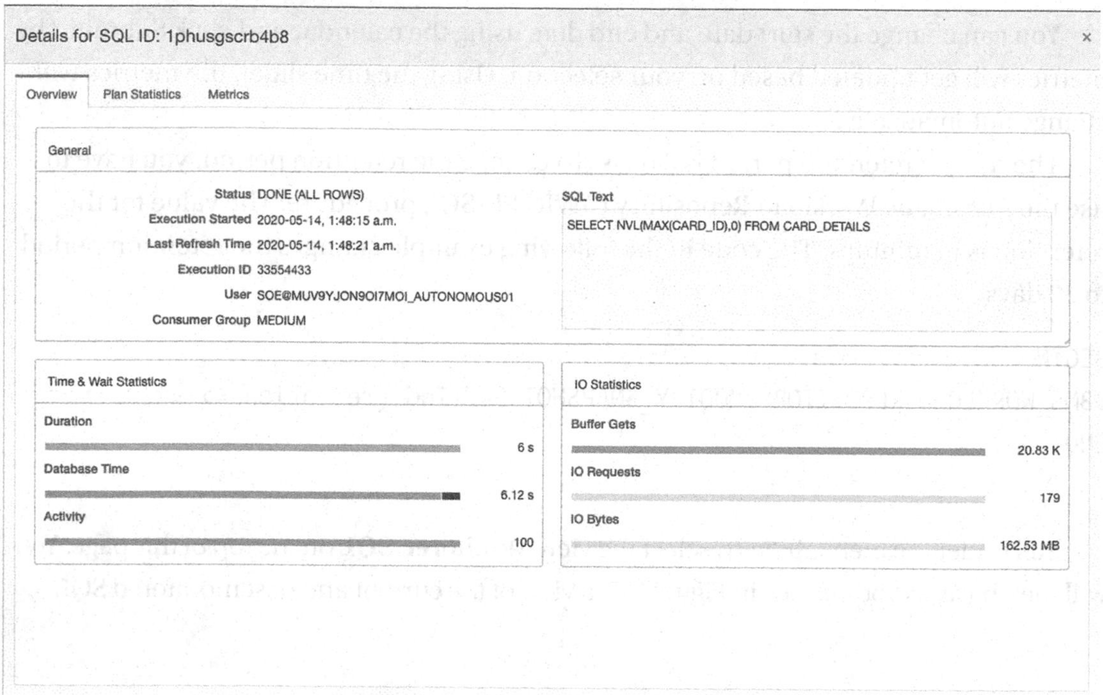

Details for SQL ID: 1phusgscrb4b8   ×

Overview   Plan Statistics   Metrics

General

Status	DONE (ALL ROWS)
Execution Started	2020-05-14, 1:48:15 a.m.
Last Refresh Time	2020-05-14, 1:48:21 a.m.
Execution ID	33554433
User	SOE@MUV9YJON9OI7MOI_AUTONOMOUS01
Consumer Group	MEDIUM

SQL Text

SELECT NVL(MAX(CARD_ID),0) FROM CARD_DETAILS

Time & Wait Statistics

Duration — 6 s
Database Time — 6.12 s
Activity — 100

IO Statistics

Buffer Gets — 20.83 K
IO Requests — 179
IO Bytes — 162.53 MB

Figure 7-10. Monitored SQL Overview tab

The tab *Overview* is providing general information on the selected SQL statement. You will see the status, the user that executed that request, the consumer group, SQL Text, and so on. You can see some metrics related to the execution of the request, Duration, IO Statistics, and so on. If you move over your mouse on the metrics, you will get more details. The tab *Plan Statistics* will provide you the entire execution plan. You can see the sequence of operations Oracle performs to run this request. The tab *Metrics*, as you can see in Figure 7-11, will give you information about CPU used, memory usage, I/O throughput, and I/O requests of the execution of this specific SQL. If you bring you mouse over some metrics, you will have more detailed information.

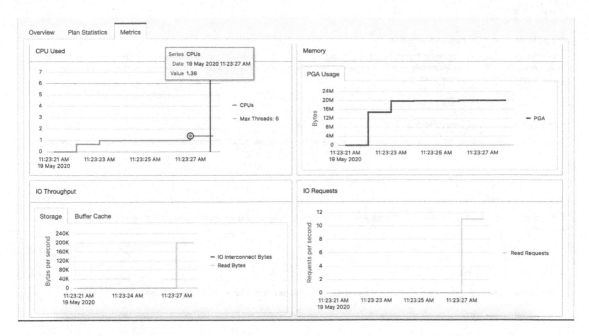

Figure 7-11. *Metrics tab*

The HTML report can also be downloaded and share with your colleagues.

The Administration Menu

The Administration menu allows you to perform some administration tasks. Figure 7-12 shows the different tasks that are available.

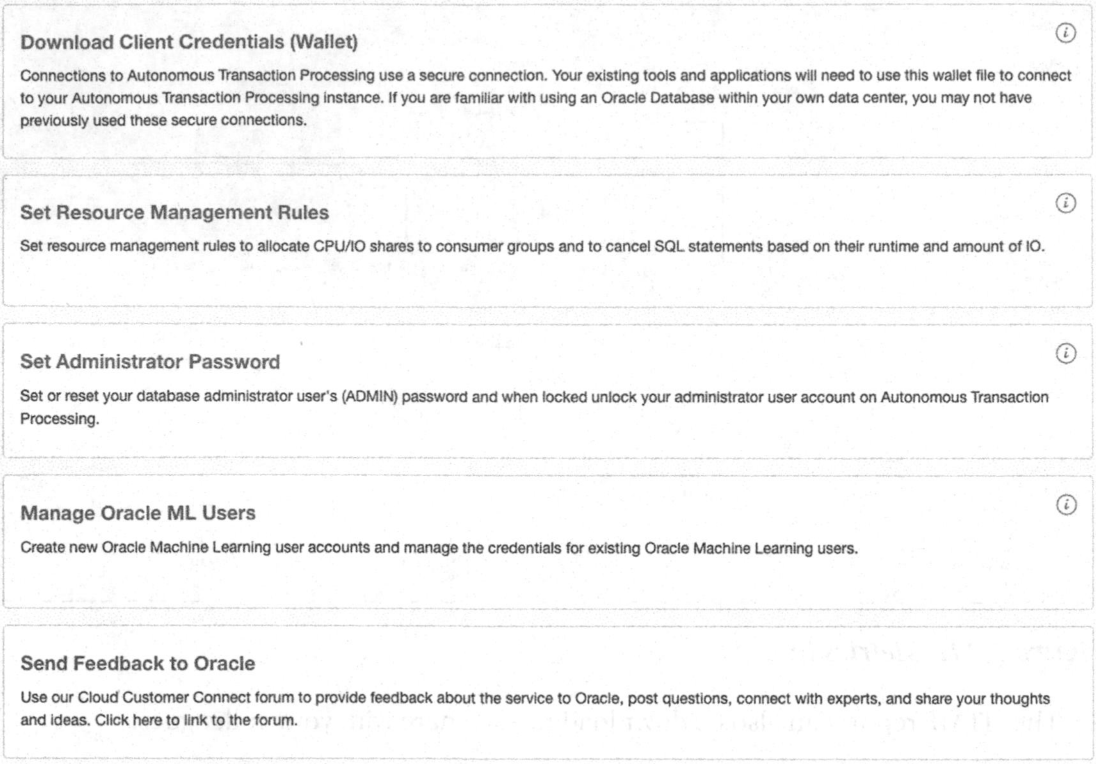

Download Client Credentials (Wallet)   ⓘ

Connections to Autonomous Transaction Processing use a secure connection. Your existing tools and applications will need to use this wallet file to connect to your Autonomous Transaction Processing instance. If you are familiar with using an Oracle Database within your own data center, you may not have previously used these secure connections.

Set Resource Management Rules   ⓘ

Set resource management rules to allocate CPU/IO shares to consumer groups and to cancel SQL statements based on their runtime and amount of IO.

Set Administrator Password   ⓘ

Set or reset your database administrator user's (ADMIN) password and when locked unlock your administrator user account on Autonomous Transaction Processing.

Manage Oracle ML Users   ⓘ

Create new Oracle Machine Learning user accounts and manage the credentials for existing Oracle Machine Learning users.

Send Feedback to Oracle

Use our Cloud Customer Connect forum to provide feedback about the service to Oracle, post questions, connect with experts, and share your thoughts and ideas. Click here to link to the forum.

Figure 7-12. *Administration page*

Download Client Credentials (Wallet): The first link in this page is to download the client wallet. We have already seen a way to download the wallet from the *DB Connection* button.

Set Resource Management Rules: This link is used to perform two tasks. We can set *Run-away criteria*, per consumer group. If a request is reaching defined thresholds, this request will be cancelled. Thresholds are *Query run time* and *Amount of IO*. For example, if I set the *Query run time* to 180 seconds and *Amount of IO* to 2000 MB for the consumer group *HIGH*, as we can see in Figure 7-13, every running SQL statement that reaches these limits will be terminated.

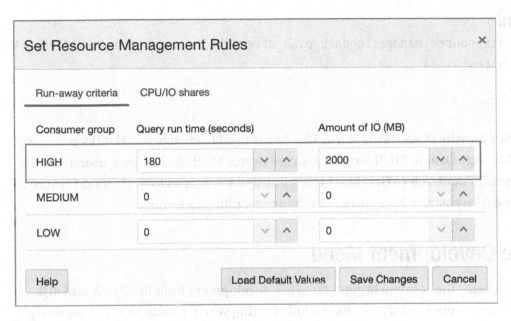

Figure 7-13. *Resource Management Rules*

We can also change the *CPU/IO shares* per consumer group. The shares determine how much CPU/IO a consumer group can use with respect to the other consumer group. Table 7-1 shows the default shares for an ATP.

Table 7-1. *Default shares*

Consumer Group	CPU/IO Shares
TPURGENT	12
TP	8
HIGH	4
MEDIUM	2
LOW	1

For example, the consumer group *TPURGENT* can use 12 times more CPU/IO resources compare to *LOW*. You can then change the shares from this page, or you can use the PL/SQL package. Here is an example for changing the shares for *TPURGENT* to 14:

```
BEGIN
    cs_resource_manager.update_plan_directive(consumer_group => 'TPURGENT',
    shares => 14);
END;
/
```

Set Administrator Password: This link is used to change the ADMIN password.

Manage Oracle ML Users: To manage Oracle Machine Learning user accounts.

Send Feedback to Oracle: This is a link that brings you to the "Cloud Customer Connect" website, where you can exchange on different forums.

The Development Menu

The Development menu brings you to the development tools like APEX and SQL Developer Web. You will also have a link to bring you to *Oracle Machine Learning Notebooks*. You will have more information in Chapter 14 about machine learning.

This *Service Console* has a lot of information, especially in regard to real-time and historical performance metrics. This is an interesting page to quickly get an idea of the ADB performance.

Performance Hub

Now let's see what we have in the *Performance Hub* page by clicking the *Performance Hub* button. The first thing you will see is a drop-down menu where you can select a specific time period:

- Last hour

- Last 8 hours

- Last 24 hours

- Last week

- Custom

After you have selected the time period, you can slide the window over the period you would like to analyze the activities. Figure 7-14 gives an example of period.

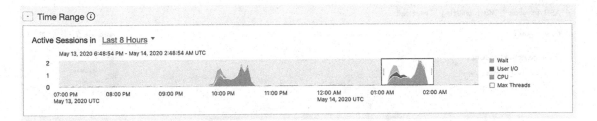

Figure 7-14. *Selected time period*

Once you have selected the period you would like to focus on (usually this is a period with abnormal peak of activities), we will be able to drill down into this period and have a deeper look at these activities. The objective will be to understand and analyze the SQL statement that were running during this period and identified any improvement that could be done in order to reduce the consumption of resources and increase the general health of the system.

Below the time slider, you will then get the first deeper view of the activities within the select period. You can select from three options: ASH Analytics, SQL Monitoring, and Workload.

ASH Analytics

ASH graphs show the Active Session History data. You can explore the data using different dimensions like Consumer Group, Wait Class, User Session, Module, and so on. When users are complaining about performance issues, I personally like to have a view on the Wait Class dimension. To select the desired dimension, click the drop-down list next to *ASH Dimensions*. Figure 7-15 shows an example of data.

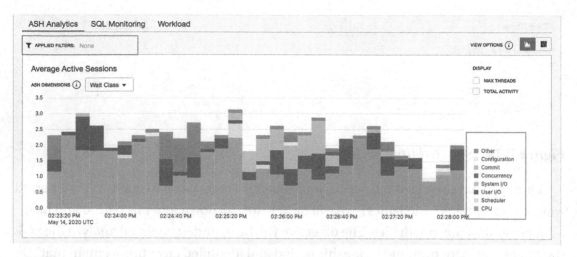

Figure 7-15. *Example of ASH data using dimension Wait Class*

The first element to notice, under the menu *ASH Analytics*, is the ability of using filters. I will come back to the concept later. On the right side of the image, we can see the *Wait Class* categories. We can quickly say that CPU (green) is the most important *Wait Class*.

Let's go down the page. In the next figure (Figure 7-16), we get a deeper look into the dimension *Wait Class* selected earlier. We can now drill down into this dimension and use two extra dimensions. In this example, I'm using the dimensions *SQL ID* and *Consumer Group*.

SQL ID ▾	by Wait Class		Columns ▾		Consumer Group ▾	by Wait Class	
SQL ID	**Activity (Average Active Sessions)**		**SQL Type**		**Consumer Group**	**Activity (Average Active Sessions)**	
aruq406dxd66n	CPU: 0.3 (15.9%) 0.43		SELECT		LOW	2.13	
2axzhrx4tmyby	0.27		SELECT		Internal	0.05	

Figure 7-16. *Extra dimensions*

In terms of CPU wait class, we can identify the SQL ID "aruq406dxd66n" as the one using the most CPU during that period – the same as for the consumer group *LOW*.

I encourage you to explore the different dimensions and the combinations of these together; you will find a lot of useful information when it comes to explaining a performance issue. The ability to use filters is very useful when you want to drill down into a problematic situation. Let say, your user *SOE* contacted you saying his process is slower than usual. As you can see in Figure 7-17, I did use the dimension *User Name* in order to have the list of username connected on ADB.

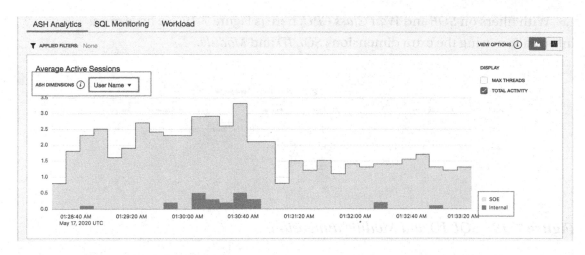

Figure 7-17. *User Name dimension*

On the right side of the graph, click *SOE,* and you will see the user added in the filter list. You will notice the main dimension is back to *Wait Class.* Figure 7-18 is now showing, using the filter on the username *SOE,* the *Wait Class* dimension during that period, associated with this user.

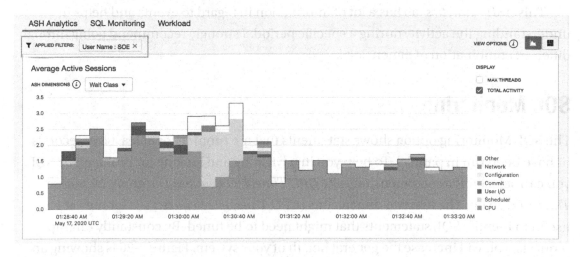

Figure 7-18. *Wait Class associated with SOE*

You can also add more filter. As you can see here, the Wait Class CPU is the most important one. You can decide to add this Wait Class into the filter, and you will be able to deeply drill down and have more information in regard to the Wait Class CPU, associated with the user *SOE,* during this selected period.

With filters on *SOE* and *Wait Class CPU*, here is Figure 7-19; we have more information using the extra dimensions *SQL ID* and *Module*.

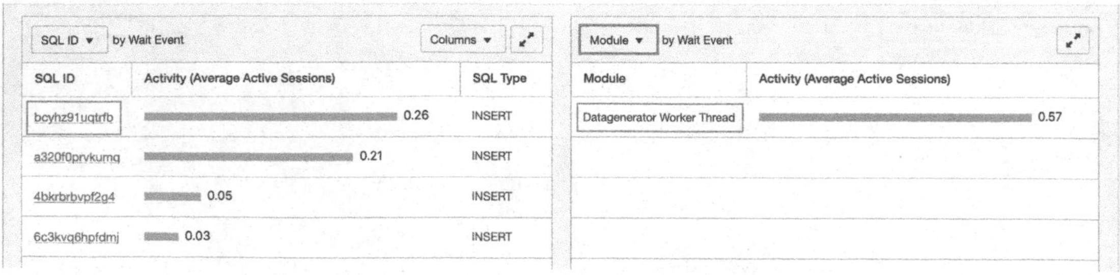

Figure 7-19. *SQL ID and Module dimensions*

I can already note the module or program involved during this period, which is "Datagenerator Worker Thread". This process is executing a lot of requests, and the one that consumes the most CPU is the SQL ID "bcyhz91uqtrfb". We are already able to provide explanation on why the system is running slower during that period. We were able to isolate what was running, and now, by clicking the *SQL ID*, we will have a deeper look at this specific SQL statement.

This *ASH Analytics* tab has a lot of information in regard to events and helps in understanding the activity during a specific period. I strongly recommend going through different combination of dimensions.

SQL Monitoring

The SQL Monitoring option shows statements that are running for at least five seconds or have been run in parallel. To help you in navigating and looking for problematic SQL, you can select different dimensions like *CPU Time, I/O Request, Duration, Database Time*, and so on. The first two dimensions (*CPU Time, I/O Request*) are for me very useful to identify SQL statements that might need to be tuned. By constantly tuning requests, you will increase the general health of your system. Figure 7-20 is showing an example of this tab using the dimension *Database Time*.

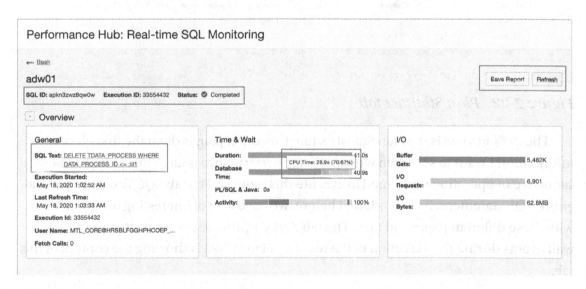

Figure 7-20. *SQL Monitoring*

First of all, you can see the status as either running, completed, failed, or queued and other pieces of information, like *SQL ID*, *User Name*, and *I/O Requests*. Another column that we can't see in the figure is the *SQL Text*. Once you have identified a SQL statement you would like to get more details on, you can click the *SQL ID* of this request. This will bring you the *Real-time SQL Monitoring*, as you can see in Figure 7-21.

Figure 7-21. *Real-Time SQL Monitoring*

This page contains a lot of information. First of all, by clicking the *Save Report* button, you can generate an HTML page and share it with other people. Under the name of the ADB, you have the summary of the request, *SQL ID*, *Execution ID,* and the status of this request. Just below, you have a section called *Overview*. In this section, you have three panels, *General, Time & Wait,* and *I/O. In* the *General panel,* you will find the *SQL Text,* last execution time, as well as the username of the user that executed this request. In the *Time & Wait* and *I/O* panels, you will find information in regard to waits during the execution of the request. If you move over your mouse, more information will be displayed. In this example, we can see the most important wait was the *CPU Time* with 28.9 seconds, out of the 41 seconds of the total duration time.

Below the Overview section, you will have the Details section. You will see four tabs in this section, *Plan Statistics*, *SQL Text*, *Activity*, and *Metrics*. Figure 7-22 gives an example.

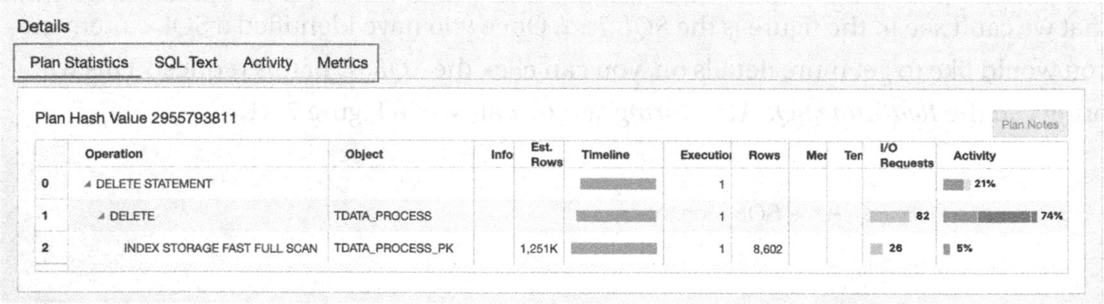

Details

| Plan Statistics | SQL Text | Activity | Metrics |

Plan Hash Value 2955793811

	Operation	Object	Info	Est. Rows	Timeline	Execution	Rows	Mer	Ten	I/O Requests	Activity
0	⊿ DELETE STATEMENT					1					21%
1	⊿ DELETE	TDATA_PROCESS				1				82	74%
2	INDEX STORAGE FAST FULL SCAN	TDATA_PROCESS_PK	1,251K			1	8,602			26	5%

Figure 7-22. *Plan Statistics tab*

The default view is the Plan Statistics tab. Execution plan is often the first piece of information I want to see when we experience performance issue. This gives you the sequence of operation performed to execute this request. The tab *SQL Text* gives you the entire SQL statement. As I mentioned before, we have a lot of interesting information with these different pages and tabs. The tab *Activity* provides, second after second, the wait events during the execution of the request. Figure 7-23 is showing the content of this tab.

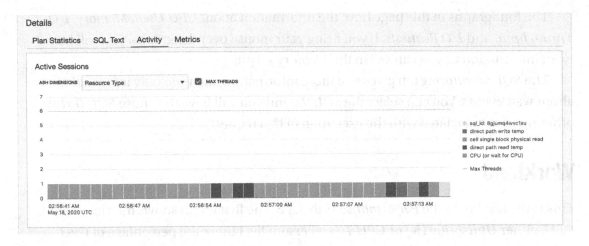

Figure 7-23. *Activity tab*

As mentioned, we can see what was happening every second, from the start time of the execution to the end of the execution. In this example, dark blue is the *direct path read temp* event, pink is the *cell single block physical read* event, and green is the CPU event. It is amazing how we can exactly see the progression of the execution of this request.

The last tab in the Details section is *Metrics*. Again, the four graphs present very interesting information. Figure 7-24 provides an example.

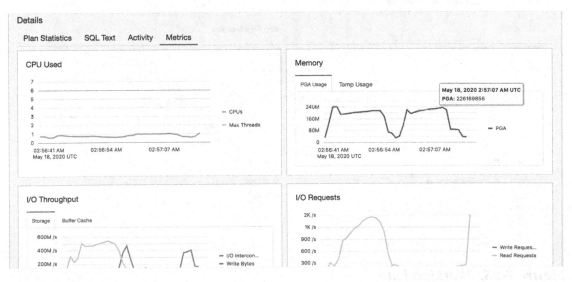

Figure 7-24. *Metrics tab*

The four graphs in this page have the information about *CPU Used*, *Memory*, *I/O Throughput,* and *I/O Requests*. If you bring your mouse over the graphs, you will have extra information as you can see in the *Memory* graph.

The *SQL Monitoring* tab gives you more information and then only information about wait events. You can select the *SQL ID,* and you will have the entire *SQL Text* and other metrics associated with the execution of this request.

Workload

This is the last tab in the *Performance Hub* page. The first graph shows metrics about *CPU*, either *Utilization* (%) or *CPU Time*. Personally, I think the percentage of *CPU Utilization* is easier to understand. The second graph shows the wait time statistics during this period. In this example, the user I/O seems to be the most important *Wait Class*.

The third graph shows metrics in regard to *User Calls, Transactions, Running Statements*, and so on, per consumer group. This could give you an idea of the workload in terms of queries during that period. The last graph shows metrics on *number of sessions* or *current logons*, during the select period. Figure 7-25 is an example of the tab *Workload*. The gray section represents the selected period.

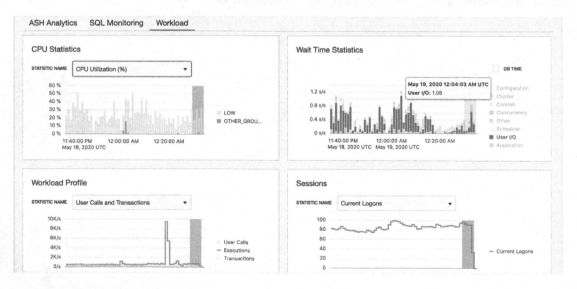

Figure 7-25. *Workload tab*

The tab *Workload* provides an overview of the workload on the ADB during the desired period. Before going deeper in troubleshooting nonperformant request, this view could reassure you on the general health of the system.

Automatic Backups

During the creation and configuration of the ADB, Oracle schedules automatic backups with a retention period of 60 days. For non-Always Free ADB, you are able to restore the ADB at any point in time in this retention period, which is unfortunately not possible with Always Free. From the ADB main page, click the menu *Backups* under *Resources*. Figure 7-26 is showing an example of backups information.

Backups

Backups are automatically created daily.

Create Manual Backup

Display Name	State	Type	Started	Ended	
May 16, 2020 18:45:51 UTC	● Active	Incremental, initiated by Auto Backup	Sat, May 16, 2020, 18:44:52 UTC	Sat, May 16, 2020, 18:45:51 UTC	⋮
May 15, 2020 18:57:05 UTO	● Active	Incremental, initiated by Auto Backup	Fri, May 15, 2020, 18:46:25 UTC	Fri, May 15, 2020, 18:57:05 UTC	⋮
May 15, 2020 00:34:22 UTC	● Active	Incremental, initiated by Auto Backup	Fri, May 15, 2020, 00:09:08 UTC	Fri, May 15, 2020, 00:34:22 UTC	⋮

Figure 7-26. List of ADB Backups

Form this page, you can see the information on the existing backups. You can see a button called *Create Manual Backup*, but unfortunately, Always Free Autonomous Database doesn't allow you to create manual backup.

Cloning

As mentioned, Always Free doesn't allow you to restore an ADB, but you are allowed to use the clone feature. You can use this feature to create an exact copy of the ADB at any point in time. This could be very useful to start a development project, to test new functionalities, and so on. You have the option of creating a clone from an active Autonomous Database or from a backup. You also have the option of creating a full clone that includes the metadata and the data, or a clone that contains the metadata only.

For the creation of the clone from the active ADB, click the *More Actions* button and select *Create Clone*. You will be redirected to the *Create Autonomous Database Cloud*, as you can see in Figure 7-27. This example is a metadata clone of the active ADB.

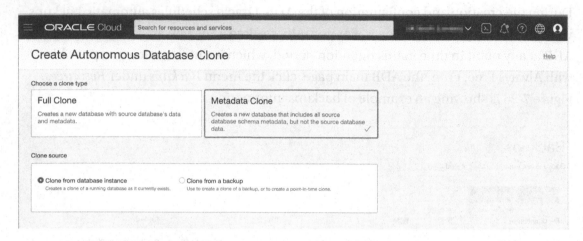

Figure 7-27. Metadata Clone

You will have to provide the following information:

- Compartment.

- Display Name of the new ADB.

- Database Name of the new ADB.

- Database Version: You can use the clone feature to upgrade your ADB.

For the other items, you have to provide the same information when you provision a new ADB. Please refer to the section "ADB Provisioning." Click *Create Autonomous Database Clone* to launch the clone process.

Note   Don't forget you have a limit of two Always Free ADB.

Once the clone process is completed, you will see your new ADB in *Autonomous Database* list page.

Limitations

Oracle's Always Free offering is quite generous. Even so, there are limitations that you should be aware of ahead of time so that you can plan your development around them and know when it's time to upgrade to a paid offering.

Storage

A non-Always Free Autonomous Database is provisioned with 1 TB of storage. You can use the *Scale Up/Down* button to increase the amount of storage. Unfortunately, with Always Free, you are allowed to use 20 GB of storage only. This limitation of storage is related to the entire system. In terms of database storage, we are estimating at around 12 GB of database storage.

Scaling

One of the biggest advantages of using Autonomous Database is the ability of scaling up/down the CPU and scaling up the storage. Using the console, you can dynamically increase or decrease the number of CPU and add storage to your ADB. You can also enable the auto-scaling which will automatically increase up to three times the CPU. Once the demand on CPU is over, auto-scaling will decrease the number of CPU. This way, the right number of CPU is always in use, and you are controlling the cost of the system.

Unfortunately, Always Free Autonomous Database doesn't allow us to use the scaling feature. You are then limited to 1 OCPU and 20 GB of the entire storage.

Automatic Shutdown and Destruction

Oracle is controlling the amount of resources assigned to Always Free Autonomous Database. In order to do that, Oracle will automatically stop your Always Free ADB after 7 days of inactivity. Your data will be preserved, and you can, from the console, start your ADB as usual. Connections using SQL*Net or HTTP reset the measurement to zero.

Oracle will automatically terminate your Always Free ADB after an inactivity or in a stopped state for 90 days. Starting the ADB will reset the measurement to zero.

Before either stopping or terminating your Autonomous Database after 7 days or 90 days of inactivity, you should have a banner alert informing you of these future actions.

Summary

The *Oracle Cloud Free Tier* offering from Oracle has the objective to allow anyone to use, learn, build, and get experience on Oracle Cloud *Always Free* resources for unlimited time. This offer includes the new Autonomous Database with *self-driving*, *self-securing*, and *self-repairing* capabilities.

Depending of your needs, you will decide to choose either the *Autonomous Transaction Processing* or the *Autonomous Data Warehouse*. The management of either type is exactly the same, and it is totally centralized in the OCI console. You are able to create, configure, manage, monitor, start, stop, restart, and clone your system using different menus and tabs like *Service Console, Performance Hub, Metrics,* and so on.

We have seen that provisioning and managing the ADB are pretty simple as it's a fully managed cloud service. On the other end, monitoring the ADB requires more time and efforts (as it always did), but the console is providing a lot of pages and features like ASH to help you identify problematic SQL statements or processes that would require some tuning. This new database service has a lot of advantages and deserves that you take some time exploring them all.

CHAPTER 8

Load Balancers

Load balancers are an important component for defining scalable and high-availability web application infrastructures. They are responsible for directing incoming network traffic to backend servers using predefined policies and algorithms.

While several networking equipment manufacturers offer dedicated, hardware-based load balancers, there are also many solutions using only software to provide these services. Generally, most cloud vendors offer load balancers as a software-defined network component, including the *Oracle Cloud*.

Every *Oracle Cloud Free Tier* account comes with one *Always Free* eligible Load Balancer. We will explore in this chapter how we can take advantage of this offering.

Our Goal

In Part 3 of this book, we will build a front-end application for the fictional *Always Cloud Conference* (ACC) website. With the popularity of Oracle Cloud on the rise, we anticipate that this will be a high-traffic website. To ensure that we can maintain high availability and website performance, we should host these applications on multiple servers and then have a load balancer marshal incoming web traffic to an appropriate *backend server*.

Always Free Limitations

The list of Always Free cloud services includes a single instance of a load balancer. This is a powerful feature that is provided at no cost, but it comes with some limitations.

Load balancers can be provisioned in four different bandwidth limits. These limits are based on an aggregate of both ingress and egress traffic. The various options and their bandwidth are listed in Table 8-1.

© Adrian Png and Luc Demanche 2020
A. Png and L. Demanche, *Getting Started with Oracle Cloud Free Tier*,
https://doi.org/10.1007/978-1-4842-6011-1_8

Table 8-1. *Maximum total bandwidth for the*
available Load Balancer options

Name	Maximum Total Bandwidth (Mbps)
Micro	10
Small	100
Medium	400
Large	8000

If you have not upgraded to a paid account, then you may only select *Micro*. That is the only option available as Always Free.

While Oracle recommends that backend servers performing the same functions be placed in different *Availability Domains*, there are some considerations as to whether this is possible. Some data regions only have one availability domain. For redundancy, we sometimes use other regions as a fallback. However, if you are strictly using Always Free *compute* instances, these approaches are not possible. Always Free resources may only be created in the account's Home Region. However, this is moot, since Always Free Compute shapes are typically bound to one Availability Domain.

Last but not least, when designing public web resources, backend servers should preferably be placed on private subnets, while load balancers are attached to a different public subnet. However, this may not be feasible given the limited number of compute instances that we can create. Placing these resources in a private subnet, or removing their public IP addresses, will require direct access to the *Virtual Cloud Networks* (VCN). We can do that by setting up *VPN Connect*, which establishes an IPSec connection between your network and the VCN securely. While this is a free-to-use feature, it is only available to paid accounts. You will also need to have network equipment that is compatible and able to set up these connections. You may set up a VPN server on a Compute Instance, in place of a VPN Connect, but that means consuming an additional Always Free resource.

Despite having these drawbacks, it is still possible to take advantage of the OCI load balancing service. Even if you are merely using it as a web proxy service, it does alleviate your backend servers from performing this role.

Load Balancer Overview

With these considerations in mind, let us begin by understanding what the load balancing service entails, starting with a list of components. To successfully create and run a load balancer, here are some concepts that we need to familiarize ourselves with:

- Backend sets

- Backend servers

- Health check policies

- Traffic distribution policies

- Security list changes for backend servers and listeners

- Listeners

- SSL certificates

- Path route sets

- Rule sets

- Hostnames

- Reserved public IP addresses

A backend set is a logical grouping of backend servers that deliver the service required. It has a health check policy that describes how to determine the availability of each backend server in the set. Together with a traffic distribution policy, the health of the servers helps load balancers decide which server to direct traffic to. It is important to ensure the security lists attached to the servers' subnet must be updated to allow the necessary traffic for health status determination and service delivery.

A load balancer will have one or more listeners to be useful. A listener may support one of the following protocols: HTTP, HTTPS, or TCP. To support HTTPS, a certificate will need to be created prior to creating the listener. Listeners can be customized by changing ports and tuning the idle timeout, but more importantly, you can introduce rule sets that allow you to specify the following:

- **Access Control Rules**: These rules help listeners determine, based on IP addresses, what traffic to allow access.

- **Access Method Rules**: Select one or more HTTP methods, for example, GET, PATCH, OPTIONS, and so on, to allow access.

139

- **URL Redirect Rules**: Use these to redirect browsers or a different
  URL. A common use case would be to convert all nonsecure HTTP
  requests to HTTPS.

- **Request Header Rules**: Using these rules, you may modify the HTTP
  request header.

- **Response Header Rules**: Likewise, a HTTP response header can be
  modified by the listener.

Note   Listener idle timeouts are set to 60 seconds by default. This might be too little especially for websites expecting to receive large file uploads or other similar web transactions.

Listeners must be assigned to a backend set, but you may specify a path route set to choose a different backend set based on the request's path. An interesting use case for path route sets is renewing Let's Encrypt (*https://letsencrypt.org*) SSL certificates. The Let's Encrypt certificate enrollment and renewals are performed by applications like Certbot (*https://certbot.eff.org/*). If you use Certbot's stand-alone authenticator, it runs a web server on port 80 and writes to the path /.well-known during the challenge-response phase.

This poses a problem the HTTP port 80 might already be used. Typically, administrators need to write pre-hook and post-hook scripts. These scripts are called before and after the verification step is completed and are often used to stop and start the web server. This may be unacceptable if maximum uptime of the service is required. With path route sets, you can easily create a rule to redirect any Certbot traffic to a backend set to servers or *Docker* (*www.docker.com*) containers that perform the challenge-response.

When a load balancer is created, a reserved IPv4 address is automatically created. For public load balancers, this will be a public IP address that you may then use to map a domain name to. Unfortunately, at this time, OCI does not allow us to precreate a reserved IP address and then assign it to the new load balancer created.

A more recent addition to the load balancer features is support for virtual hostnames. HTTP and HTTPS listeners can be assigned zero or more hostnames. This is very similar to virtual hosting solutions provided by popular web servers like *Apache HTTP Server* and *Nginx*.

Load Balancer Walkthrough

The best way to digest and understand what we have learned about load balancers is by doing. In this next section, we will set up the load balancer to prepare the environment for the ACC website development.

Create the Backend Servers

Using what you have learned in Chapters 3–6, create and set up a VCN that will host two compute instances. You may create these instances using the Oracle Autonomous Linux image. Provide the necessary information and attach the instance to a public subnet. Before clicking *Create*, we will provide a *cloud-init* script (Figure 8-1).

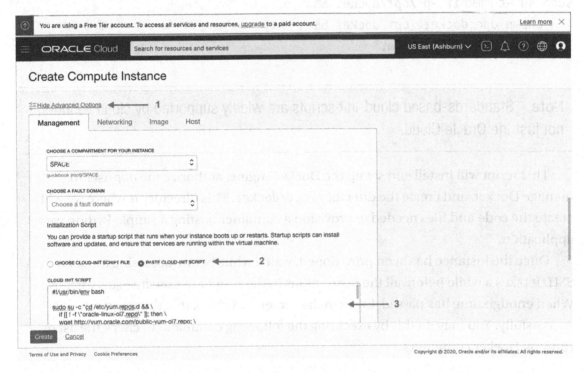

Figure 8-1. *Standing up servers with cloud-init scripts*

These options are hidden by default, so click *Show Advanced Options* (step 1) to expose the required fields. Next, select *Paste Cloud-init Script* (step 2) that will enable the text field for entering the script contents. Enter the following code in the text field (step 3):

```
#!/usr/bin/env bash

sudo su -c "cd /etc/yum.repos.d && \
    if [[ ! -f \"oracle-linux-ol7.repo\" ]]; then \
    wget http://yum.oracle.com/public-yum-ol7.repo; \
    fi;"

sudo yum-config-manager --enable ol7_addons ol7_latest

sudo yum install -y docker-engine

sudo usermod -aG docker opc

sudo su -c "systemctl enable docker && systemctl start docker"

sudo su -c "mkdir -p /opt/docker && \
    chown opc:docker /opt/docker && \
    chmod 2770 /opt/docker"
```

Note   Standards-based cloud-init scripts are widely supported by cloud vendors, not just the Oracle Cloud.

This script will install and set up the Docker engine, authorize the *opc* user to manage Docker, and create the directory /opt/docker. This directory is where we will create the code and files needed to provision a container hosting a simple Python web application.

Once the instance has been provisioned, wait a while before accessing the server *via* SSH. It takes a while before all the instructions in the script are executed successfully. When enough time has passed, log in to the server and check that the script ran successfully. You may do this by executing the following command to check the list of running Docker containers:

```
docker ps
```

Create the following directory structure:

```
/opt/docker/lbdemo-web
    |- templates/
       |-base.html
    |- Dockerfile
    |- main.py
    |- requirements.txt
    |- run.sh
```

The contents of each file are listed as follows, beginning with base.html:

```
<!DOCTYPE html>
<html lang="en">
<head>
  <meta charset="UTF-8">
  <meta name="viewport" content="width=device-width, initial-scale=1.0">
  <title>{{ title }}</title>
</head>
<body>
  <h1>{{ title }}</h1>
  <p>
    {{ body_text }}
  </p>
  <footer>
    Hostname: {{ hostname }}
  </footer>
</body>
</html>
```

The Dockerfile for building the Docker image that we will use:

```
FROM python:3

ENV FLASK_APP=main.py \
    FLASK_PORT=5000

WORKDIR /app
```

143

```
COPY requirements.txt /tmp/requirements.txt

RUN pip install --no-cache-dir -r /tmp/requirements.txt && \
  rm -f /tmp/requirements.txt

CMD [ "sh", "-c", "flask run --host 0.0.0.0 --port ${FLASK_PORT:-5000}" ]
```

The main Python application code main.py:

```python
from flask import Flask, render_template
import os

app = Flask(__name__)

@app.route("/")
def root():
    return render_template(
        "base.html",
        title = "Load Balancer Demo",
        body_text = """
        Demonstrating the use of Load Balancers to support highly scalable
        web applications.
        """,
        hostname = os.environ.get('DOCKER_HOST')
    )
```

A requirements.txt file for defining the Python application's dependencies:

```
Flask
```

Finally, a *Bash* script (run.sh) for building and then running a container using the Docker image:

```bash
#!/usr/bin/env bash

APP_NAME=lbdemo-web

docker build -t ${APP_NAME} .

docker rm -vf ${APP_NAME}

docker run -d --name=${APP_NAME} \
```

```
-e DOCKER_HOST=$(hostname) \
-p 8000:5000 \
-v ${PWD}:/app \
${APP_NAME}
```

Once the files have been staged, run the following command to run the Python web application:

```
cd /opt/docker/lbdemo-web && ./run.sh && \
    docker logs -f lbdemo-web
```

If successful, the Docker container's logs should display the following messages:

```
* Serving Flask app "main.py"
 * Running on http://0.0.0.0:5000/ (Press CTRL+C to quit)
 * Environment: production
   WARNING: This is a development server. Do not use it in a production
   deployment.
   Use a production WSGI server instead.
 * Debug mode: off
```

Press *Ctrl+C* to exit the logs. You may then test the website functionality using the *curl* command:

```
curl http://localhost:8000
```

A valid HTML output would indicate that the container was launched and is running successfully.

Perform these steps for both instances and then we will be ready to proceed to the next steps of creating the load balancer.

Important   As warned in the Docker container's logs, the method used to host a Python web application is for development purposes only. There are better alternatives to hosting the applications, but this approach will be sufficient for our use.

Create the Load Balancer

From the OCI console's home page, click the navigation menu (α) at the top right of the page. Place the mouse cursor over the menu item *Networking* and then click *Load Balancers*. On the Load Balancers page, ensure that you are creating the components in the correct compartment. If so, click the button *Create Load Balancer* to begin creating the network component. This launches the guided process of creating the load balancer (Figure 8-2).

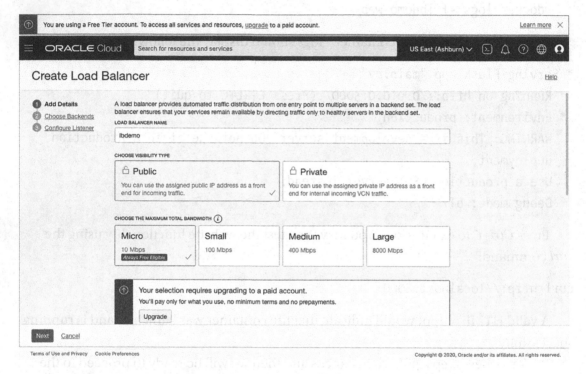

Figure 8-2. *Guided creation of load balancers*

You will need to provide the following information or selections:

- A name for the load balancer.

- Select the *Public* visibility type.

- Only the *Micro* option is available as an Always Free resource, so please select this.

- Select the appropriate VCN and public subnet that the load balancer will be assigned to.

Click the button *Next* to proceed to the second of three steps. There are three traffic distribution (load balancing) policies that may be selected (Figure 8-3).

Figure 8-3. *Choose an appropriate traffic distribution policy*

The options are as follows:

- Weighted Round Robin

- IP Hash

- Least Connections

Select the most suitable depending on the backend service behaviors. Generally, a round-robin approach will work, where the load balancer simply rotates the backend server to use. You will also be able to assign weights to backend servers, and this will influence how many times it will redirect to the same server until the limits are reached. A weight of "5" vs. a second with a weight of "1" means that the former will be used at least five times before the load balancer directs traffic to the second backend server.

The *IP Hash* policy provides some degree of connection "stickiness" based on the IP address of the client. However, this may not be efficient when an IP address is shared among multiple network clients. This is common in organizational networks where clients are assigned internal network addresses, but access the Internet using a NAT Gateway.

The third policy, *Least Connections*, simply routes traffic based on the connection counts to each backend server.

Next, add the backends to the set. Click the button *Add Backends* (Figure 8-4).

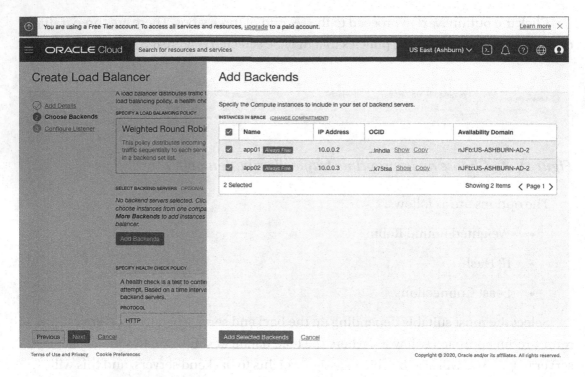

Figure 8-4. *Add backend servers to the backend set*

Then select the backends to add. In our demo, select all and then click *Add Selected Backends*. The backend servers added will be assigned the communication port and health check ports to 80 (Figure 8-5).

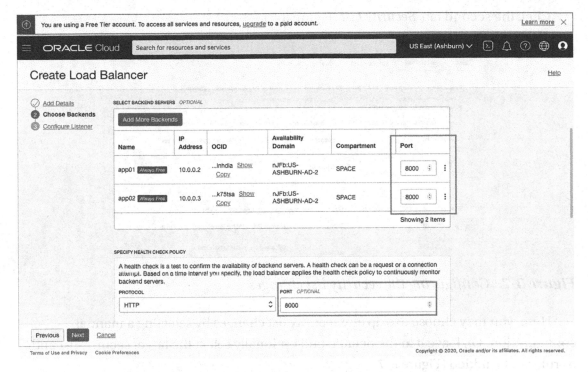

Figure 8-5. *Update the backend server and health check ports*

This is incorrect for our Python web server. In the Docker run command, we had specified that the web server port 5000 is to be mapped to the host's port 8000. Update the fields accordingly.

Before moving to the third and final step, click the *Show Advanced Options* to expose additional settings. The first is to specify a backend set name. Change this as preferred (Figure 8-6).

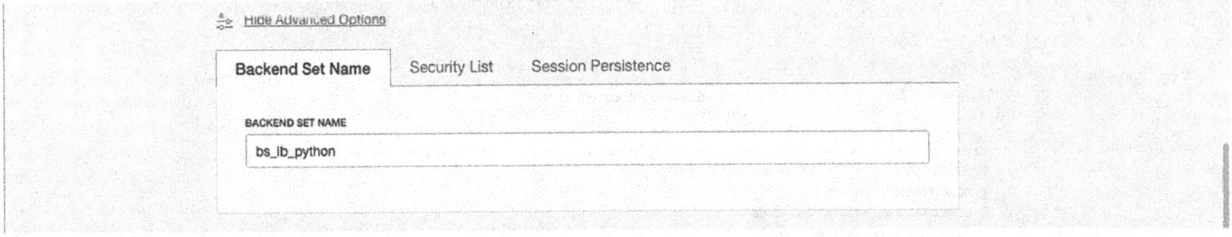

Figure 8-6. *Specify a preferred backend set name*

Click the second tab, *Security List* (Figure 8-7).

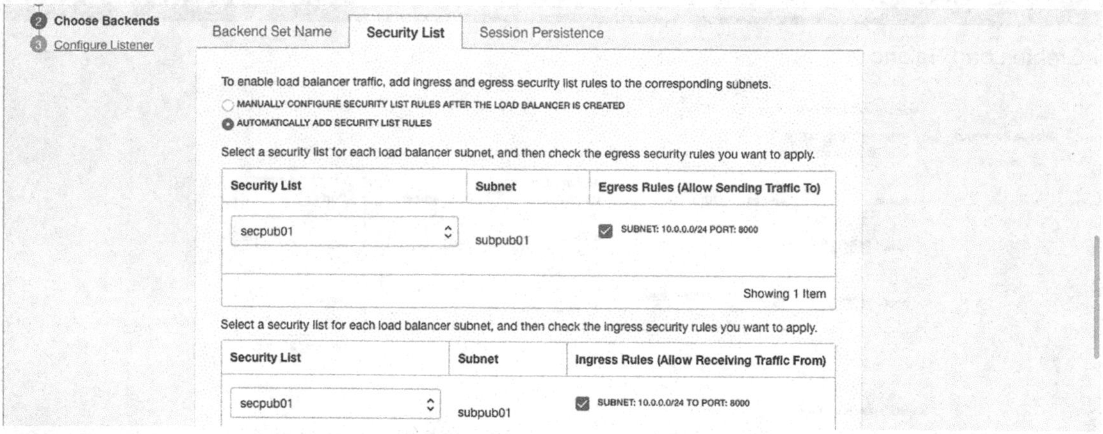

Figure 8-7. *Configuring the security list changes*

Here, you may choose to skip any security list changes by selecting a manual configuration. Or, leave it to the default, and optionally select the target security list and/or rules to be added (Figure 8-7).

Important   At the time of writing, there appears to be a bug in the OCI console. Although the backend server and health check ports are updated to 8000, they are reset to 80 when the load balancer is finally created. Likewise, though the console indicates that the corresponding security list rules will open the requested ports, it also sets them incorrectly to 80.

The last tab to review is *Session Persistence* (Figure 8-8).

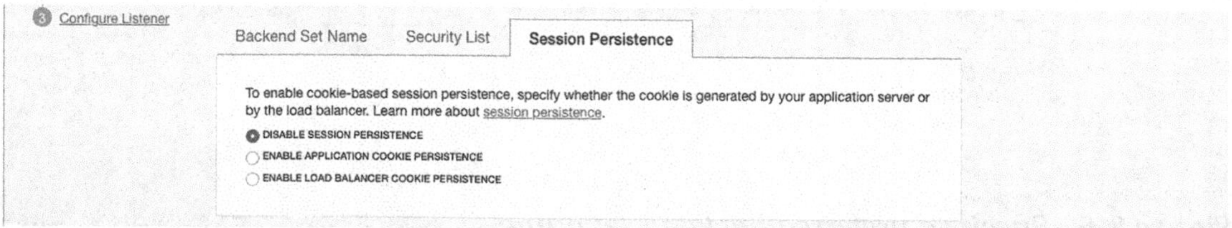

Figure 8-8. *Select the required session persistence*

Here, you may select the session persistence required. Earlier, we had discussed the IP Hash load balancing policy and suggested that it offers, to some extent, session stickiness. The settings here, however, will provide more specific backend server adhesion to clients.

Click the button *Next* and move on to the third and final step for creating the load balancer (Figure 8-9).

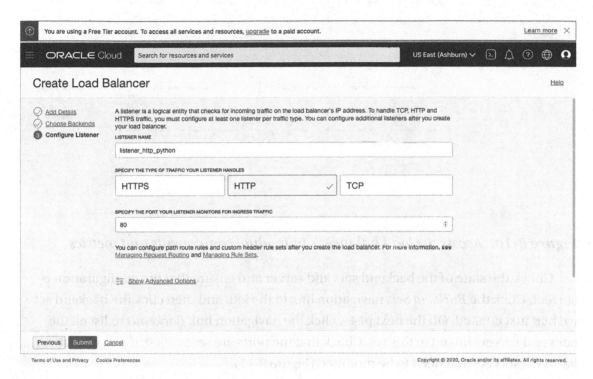

Figure 8-9. *Final set of questions before proceeding to create the load balancer*

In this last step, you will have the opportunity to define an appropriate listener name and select the listener traffic type and specific port to listen to. For now, let's specify a HTTP listener that listens on port 80 for web traffic. Click the button *Submit* to initiate the creation of the new load balancer.

After the load balancer has been created successfully, you will have access to manage its individual components and, also, the metrics to monitor activity and performance (Figure 8-10).

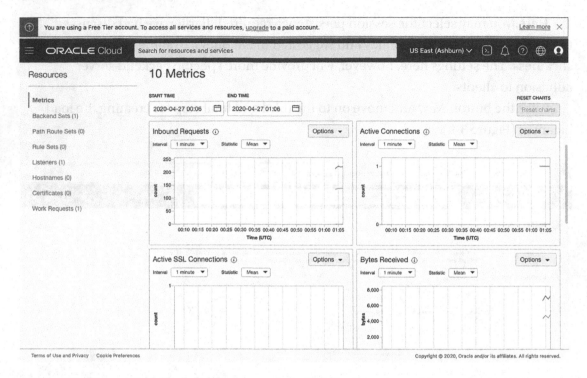

Figure 8-10. *Access the load balancer's individual components and metrics*

Check the state of the backend sets and server and ensure that the configuration is correct. Click the *Backend Sets* navigation link to the left, and then click the backend set we had just created. On the next page, click the navigation link *Backends* to list all the backend servers linked to this set. Check that the ports are set to 8000; if not, click the backend servers that need to be modified (Figure 8-11).

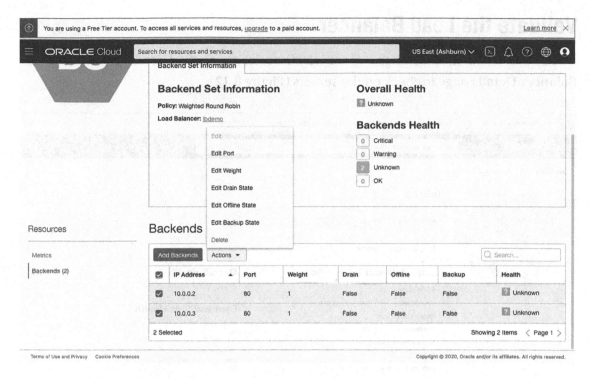

Figure 8-11. *Update the backend servers if necessary*

Click the *Actions* drop-down menu and then click *Edit Port*. This opens a modal dialog. Correct the port number and then click *Save Changes*. A work request will be submitted, and the changes will be processed in the background. When the modal closes, scroll to the top of the page and click the button *Update Health Check*. The monitored port should also be 8000. Correct this value if necessary.

You may check the status on all work requests by returning to the Load Balancer Details page and then click the navigation link *Work Requests*.

Security Lists

Rules are required for the load balancer to access the backend servers' ports and for external clients to access the web servers using the listener's HTTP ports. The former may be automatically created along with the load balancer, but always check that they were created correctly, or the backend servers will be inaccessible. The rules for accessing the listener must be manually created and assigned.

Validate the Load Balancer

Once the load balancer settings and security list rules are verified, return to the Load Balancer Details page to check on the servers (Figure 8-12).

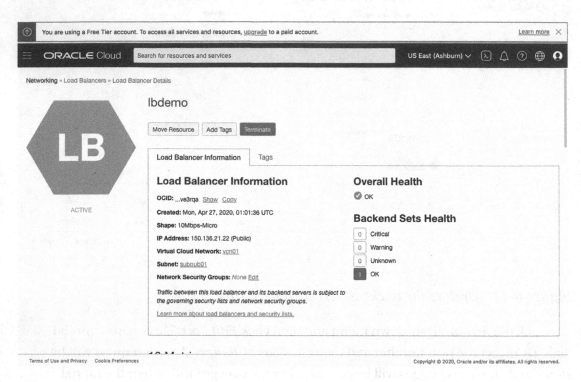

Figure 8-12. *Load balancer status*

The overall health and backend sets health status should all be green. Test your access to the Python web server by entering the load balancer's public IP address in the web browsers location. You should see a simple web page displayed (Figure 8-13).

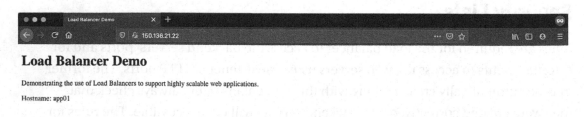

Figure 8-13. *Simple web page demonstrating that the load balancer is working as expected*

With equal weights set on both backend servers, refreshing the page each time displays a different hostname.

Summary

Load balancers play an important role in scalable and resilient web architectures. Web applications can be hosted on multiple servers, built on top of separate underlying hardware infrastructure, and then rely on load balancers to redirect web traffic as defined by their policies. The Oracle Cloud Infrastructure provides this service out of the box with only minimal setup necessary.

An Oracle Cloud Free Tier account offers one micro-sized load balancer for use in the account. While there are limitations that prevent us from maximizing its potential, it will nevertheless alleviate the need to dedicate a Compute Instance to perform its functions. The managed, software-defined service assures us that it is secure and well configured.

CHAPTER 9

Notifications and Monitoring

The purpose of this chapter is to provide information on two Oracle Cloud Infrastructure Services tightly related, *Notifications* and *Monitoring* services. We have seen, so far, great Oracle Cloud Infrastructure Services, going from *Compute*, *Autonomous Database* (ADB), *Block Volume*, *Object Storage*, and so on. Now we will see the *monitoring* and *notification* mechanisms Oracle Cloud Infrastructure uses to manage your system. This helps you to react as quickly as possible when a particular situation happens. We will see how the *Monitoring* service monitors cloud resources and has the ability to publish messages using the *Notification* service.

Notifications

In order to use the Notification service, we have to understand three concepts:

- **Topic**: The channel used to publish messages.

- **Subscription**: Messages will be sent to endpoints subscribed to the topic.

- **Message**: The content to be published.

When a situation needs to notify an individual or a process, a published message will be transmitted to the subscribers through the notification topic. On a paid account, notifications can be sent in three ways: when event rules are triggered, alarms are breached, or messages are manually published. Unfortunately, *Oracle Cloud Free Tier* supports only notifications from alarms and manually published messages.

157

© Adrian Png and Luc Demanche 2020
A. Png and L. Demanche, *Getting Started with Oracle Cloud Free Tier*,
https://doi.org/10.1007/978-1-4842-6011-1_9

Note   *Oracle Cloud Free Tier* does not support the *Events* service.

There are five types of subscriptions:

- **Email**: The service will send an email.

- **Function**: The service will send a message to run a function.

- **HTTPS**: The service will send a message to an endpoint (URL using HTTPS protocol).

- **PagerDuty**: Create a PagerDuty incident by sending to an endpoint (URL).

- **Slack**: The service will send a message to a Slack channel.

Note   Oracle Functions is not supported on *Oracle Cloud Free Tier*.

First task we have to do is the creation of the *Notification Topic*. Let's imagine we would like to use a topic for the monitoring of your *Compute* and your *Autonomous Database*. Typically, DBA will subscribe to the topic.

Creating Topics

Click the *navigation* icon and select *Application Integration* and *Notifications*. For the creation of the topic, make sure you are in the right compartment and click the *Create Topic* button. You will have to provide the topic name and a description. For the example let's use *FreeTier_Monitoring* as the name and *Topic been used for Free Tier Monitoring* for the description. Then click *Create*.

Once created, you will be back to the Topics main page. You will see the list of Topics for this compartment as we can see in Figure 9-1.

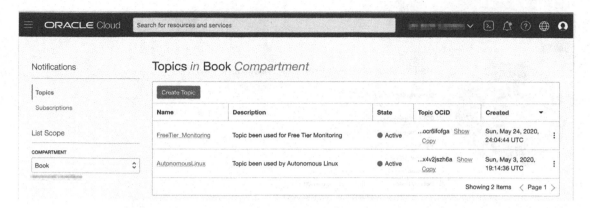

Figure 9-1. *List of Topics*

Subscribing to a Topic

To receive the message published using a topic, the individual, utility, or process should be subscribed to this topic. We will demonstrate the subscription process for two types of endpoints, *email* and *Slack*.

Email

Select the topic you would like to subscribe an email address to. Click *Create Subscription*. Provide the following information and click *Create*:

- **Protocol**: Email
- Email address

The subscriber will receive an email to confirm the subscription to this topic. Once confirmed, you will see the active subscription, as what we have in Figure 9-2.

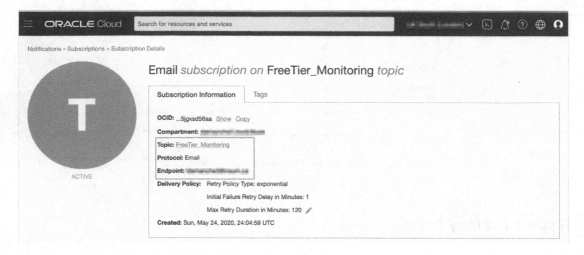

Figure 9-2. *Active subscription*

You can see here the topic, the protocol, and the endpoint associated with this subscription.

Slack

Let see now how we can subscribe a Slack channel to a topic. Let's imagine a DBA group using a Slack channel to communicate with each other and to centralize the notifications. Notification service is using *webhook* to communicate with the Slack channel. Before subscribing the channel to the topic, we have to activate the *incoming webhooks* for the Slack channel. Please follow the instructions from Slack Help Center. Take note of the *Webhook URL* generated by the activation.

Tip   See the help article at `https://slack.com/help/` `articles/115005265063-Incoming-Webhooks-for-Slack` for details on setting up incoming webhooks.

Select the topic you would like to subscribe to on the Slack channel. Click *Create Subscription*. Provide the following information and click *Create*:

- **Protocol**: Slack

- Webhook URL provided by Slack

A message will be sent in the Slack channel to confirm the subscription request. Once confirmed, you will see the active subscription that corresponds to the Slack subscription.

Both subscriptions are in place, and in order to validate them, we will manually send a message. Click the navigation menu, select *Notifications* under *Application Integration*, and then select the right topic. From this page, click Publish Message as you can see in Figure 9-3.

Figure 9-3. *Publish Message*

You will get a window where you can add a message and a title, and you can click *Publish*.

Monitoring

This service is using two concepts: *Metrics*, emitted from Cloud resources, and *alarms* to notify users. By default, Cloud resources are sending metrics to the *Monitoring* service and these metrics are evaluated. If the metrics reach defined thresholds, the alarm will be triggered.

Metrics

Monitoring service includes metrics related to health, capacity, and performance of the system. By querying the data in this service, you can gain a better understanding of the state of your system or application.

With *Oracle Cloud Free Tier*, metrics are available for Cloud resources like *Compute*, *Autonomous Database, Load Balancer, Block Volume, Object Storage,* and *Vault.* In this chapter we will give an example of metrics and alarms for *Compute* and *Autonomous Database.*

Here is a table listing the metrics associated with Compute.

Table 9-1. *Metrics associated with Compute*

Metric Display Name	Description
CPU Utilization	Percentage of used CPU
Disk Read Bytes	Read throughput, in bytes read
Disk Write Bytes	Write throughput, in bytes read
Disk Read I/O	I/O reads activity
Disk Write I/O	I/O writes activity
Memory Utilization	Memory currently in used
Network Receive Bytes	Network receipt throughput, in bytes
Network Transmit Bytes	Network transmission throughput, in bytes

This table lists the metrics associated with the Autonomous Database on Shared Infrastructure.

Note   ADB on Dedicated Infrastructure is not allowed on *Oracle Cloud Free Tier.*

Table 9-2. *Metrics associated with the Autonomous Database service*

Metric Display Name	Description
Connection Latency	Latency, in milliseconds, between a compute and the ADB in the same region
CPU Utilization	Percentage of CPU used across all consumer groups
Current Logons	Number of successful logons
Execute Count	Number of executed SQL statements
Failed Connections	Number of failed database connections
Failed Logons	Number of failed logons because of invalid username or password
Parse Count	Number of hard and soft parses
Query Latency	Time to display the results of a single query
Queued Statements	Number of queued statements across consumer groups
Running Statements	Number of running statements across consumer groups
Sessions	Number of sessions in the database
Storage Utilization	Percentage of provisioned storage capacity currently in use
Transaction Count	Combined number of user commits and rollbacks
User Calls	Combined number of logons, parses, and executed calls

Service Metrics

Service Metrics is the first link we have under the Monitoring menu. First thing to do is to make sure you are using the proper compartment and select the desired *Metric Namespace*. As an example, select the Metric Namespace *oci_computeagent*. You can use filters by using the concept of *Dimension*. As you can see in Figure 9-4, use the *resourceDisplayName* dimension and select a Compute Instance you would like to see metrics on.

Service Metrics

COMPARTMENT

Book

Idemanche3 (root)/Book

METRIC NAMESPACE (i)

oci_computeagent

Dimensions ✎ Edit

☑ **resourceDisplayName:** AppServerBook02

☐ AGGREGATE METRIC STREAMS

START TIME

May 24, 2020 12:14:08 / 📅

END TIME

May 24, 2020 1:14:08 AI 📅

QUICK SELECTS

Last hour

Not seeing all of your resources? (i)

↻ Reset charts

CPU UTILIZATION (i)

Options ▼

Interval | 1 minute ▼   Statistic | Mean ▼

```
100
 80
 60
Percent
 40
 20
  0
   00:15 00:20 00:25 00:30 00:35 00:40 00:45 00:50 00:55 01:00 01:05 01:10
```

MEMORY UTILIZATION (i)

Options ▼

Interval | 1 minute ▼   Statistic | Mean ▼

```
100
 80
 60
Percent
 40
 20
  0
   00:15 00:20 00:25 00:30 00:35 00:40 00:45 00:50 00:55 01:00 01:05 01:10
```

Figure 9-4. *Metrics for a Compute*

I have highlighted the important information in this page. In order to see metrics emitted from Compute, we have to use the metric namespace *oci_computeagent*. To filter on a specific Compute Instance, we have used the dimension *resourceDisplayName* and we have identified a specific period of time. The figure shows the first two metrics, *CPU Utilization* and *Memory Utilization*. You can scroll down the page to see the other six metrics associated with this Compute Instance. Now, let's see how we can explore the metrics and the different options we have. For every graph, you can see the button *Options*. Figure 9-5 is showing the options.

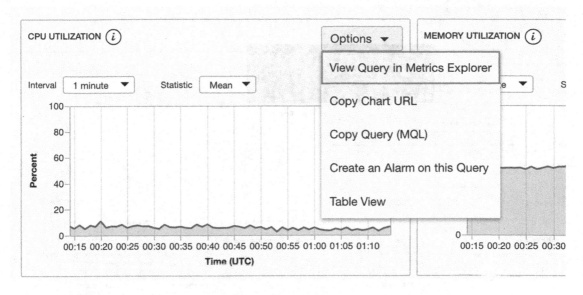

Figure 9-5. *Options for exploring Metrics*

Here are the options:

- **View Query in Metrics Explorer**: This brings you to the *Metrics Explorer* page, where you can edit the query.

- **Copy Chart URL**: Copy the URL to share the chart.

- **Copy Query (MQL)**: This copy the Monitoring Query Language (MQL) query.

- **Create an Alarm on this Query**: This brings you to the *Alarm Definitions* page where you can create an alarm using this query.

- **Table View**: This switch from Graph view to a Table view.

Metrics Explorer

This second link under the *Monitoring* menu, *Metrics Explorer*, helps you to explore all the possibilities with metrics, graphs, and how to build queries. Figure 9-6 shows you an example of queries and graphs for the *compute* instances in this compartment.

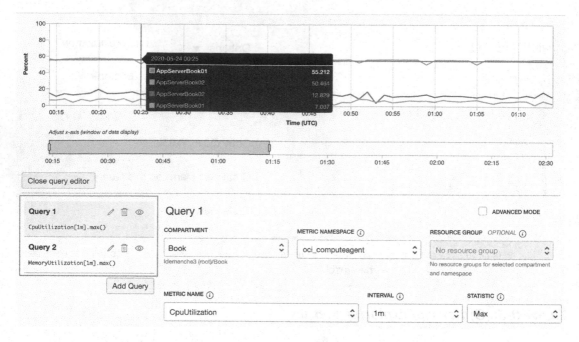

Figure 9-6. *Metrics Explorer for Computes*

I have highlighted the two queries I have built. You can see the results in the graph. The first query is

```
CpuUtilization[1m].max()
```

This MQL provides the maximum CPU Utilization for the interval of one minute for every *Compute* Instance in this compartment. The two lines in the graph, below 20%, are the CPU Utilization for my compute instances AppServerBook1 and AppServerBook2.

The second query is

```
MemoryUtilization[1m].max()
```

This MQL provides the maximum Memory Utilization for the interval of 1 minute for the same two compute instances. The lines around 60% represent their memory utilization.

Note   The different intervals are *1 minute*, *5 minutes*, *1 hour*, and *1 day*.

As you can see, if you bring your mouse over the graph, you will get more details on the metrics. In this example I'm using the *max* statistic. Here is a table with the possible statistics.

Table 9-3. *MQL statistics*

Statistic Name	MQL Expression	Description
Mean	mean()	Returns the value of Sum divided by Count
Rate	rate()	Returns the average rate of change
Sum	sum()	Returns all values added together
Min	min()	Returns the lowest value
Max	max()	Returns the highest value
Count	count()	Returns the number of the observations received
P50	percentile(0.5)	Returns the estimated value of the specified percentile
P90	percentile(0.9)	Valid values are between 0.0 and less than 1.0
P95	percentile(0.95)	
P99	percentile(0.99)	
P99.5	percentile(0.995)	

Now, let's have a look at an example that we can see in Figure 9-7, of queries and graphs for *Autonomous Database* in terms of *CPU* and *Running Statements*.

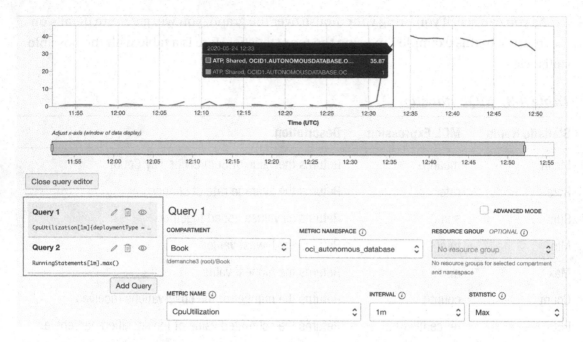

Figure 9-7. *Metrics Explorer for Autonomous Database*

I have highlighted the queries using the metrics of the Autonomous Database. The first query is about *CPU Utilization,* where I use MQL to query the metric and create a graph. The second query is about *Running Statements*.

Here are the two queries:

```
CpuUtilization[1m]{deploymentType = "Shared", resourceName =
"AUTONOMOUS01"}.max()
```

The first query is using dimensions to filter on a specific resource using *deploymentType* and *resourceName*. It gives the maximum *CPU Utilization* during the interval.

```
RunningStatements[1m].max()
```

The second query gives the maximum number of running statements during the interval. You can see the metric values when you bring your mouse over the graph.

Alarms

Alarms are triggered when a metric has reached a defined threshold. The alarms can use the Notification service to be published to the subscribers.

Note   Alarms are based on metrics. You have to make sure the resource you want to monitor can emit metrics.

There are at least three methods to create an alarm. The first one is by using the *Alarm Definitions* page. Click the navigation menu, *Monitoring, Alarm Definitions*, and *Create Alarm*. Let's create an alarm based on the CPU Utilization usage reaching 80%. A notification will be sent by email, and a message is created on the DBA Slack Channel. We have six sections on the *Create Alarm* page:

- **Define Alarm**: Provide information like

  - **Alarm Name**: Name of the alarm

  - **Alarm Severity**: Critical, Error, Warning, or Info

  - **Alarm Body**: Description of the alarm

- **Tags**: Optionally, you can assign tags.

- **Metrics Description**: Refer to the latest section to get the required information to complete the creation of the alarm.

- **Metrics Dimensions**: You can filter by using dimension like *resourceDisplayName*.

- **Trigger Rule**: Condition to trigger an alarm. For this example, use *greater than* with a *value* of 80.

- **Trigger Delay Minutes**: Number of numbers the condition must be maintained before triggering the alarm.

- **Notifications**: Select the desired Notification Topic.

- **Repeat Notification**: Resend notifications even if alarm is in firing state.

- **Suppress Notifications**: To disable the notification for the specific period.

Make sure *Enable This Alarm* is checked and click *Save alarm*. Perform the same steps to create the alarm for *Autonomous Database CPU Utilization* that reach 20% and use the same Notification Topic.

Once completed, go back to the *Alarm Definition* page and you will see these two alarms shown in Figure 9-8.

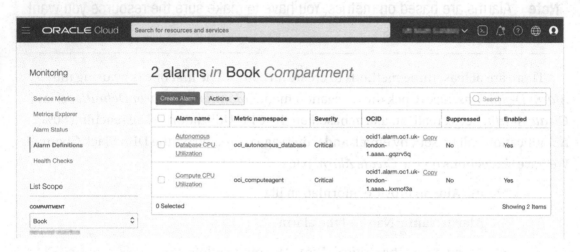

Figure 9-8. *Alarms created*

Now that we have the two alarms in place, let's create a CPU load on the application server and on the Autonomous Database. By creating this load, we can validate that the resources are sending metrics to the *Monitoring service*, trigger alarms, and publish messages to the *Notification service*.

To generate a load on the Linux application server, I'm using a utility called *Stress*. This utility will generate a load, and we will see the load average going up, from the operating system point of view and from the *Monitoring* Service.

Log in to the Compute Instance. Then switch (using sudo) to the root account. Once connected, run this command:

```
[root@appserverbook02 ~]# stress --cpu 8 --timeout 300s
```

Open another terminal and you will immediately see the load average going up using the *TOP* command:

```
top - 23:12:40 up 23:20,  3 users,  load average: 6.10, 3.82, 2.34
Tasks: 141 total,   9 running,  79 sleeping,   0 stopped,   0 zombie
%Cpu(s): 24.8 us,  0.2 sy,  0.0 ni,  0.0 id,  0.0 wa,  0.0 hi,  0.0 si, 75.0 st
```

For the ADB, I will use a utility called *Swingbench* to generate a load on the database.

Note   You can download Swingbench and find the documentation on this utility from this URL: *www.dominicgiles.com/swingbench.html*.

Once both load generated tools are running, you can validate the alarms are triggered by going to *Monitoring ➤ Alarm Status* menu. Figure 9-9 shows both alarms with firing status. If you remember, the alarm definitions mentioned the interval of one minute before triggering the alarm, so you will have to wait one minute before seeing the alarms with firing status.

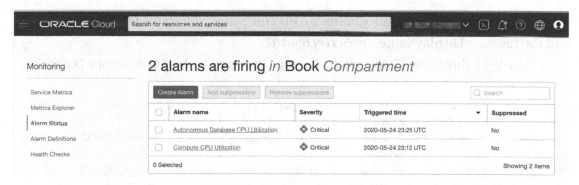

Figure 9-9. Triggered alarms

Last validation we would like to perform is if the *Notification* service sent the message to the subscribers. Earlier we created two subscribers for this Notification Topic: *Email* and a *Slack channel*.

Figure 9-10 shows the JSON format message received in Slack in regard to the *Compute CPU Utilization*.

{"dedupeKey":"d7b515b0-36d7-4a51-b87b-9c372005/8b4","title":"Compute CPU Utilization","body":"CPU High Usage for Compute","type":"OK_TO_FIRING","severity":"CRITICAL","timestampEpochMillis":1590361920000,"alarmMeta Data":[{"id":"ocid1.alarm.oc1.uk-london-1.aaaaaaaa2doi4n4t5oaziq6lyrnubyqrunahbpnfndb7adotqzqj3kxmof3a","status":"FIRING","severity":"CRITICAL","query":"CpuUtilization[1m].max() > 80","totalMetricsFiring":1,"dimensions":[{"instancePoolId":"Default","resourceDisplayName":"AppServerBook02","faultDomain":"FAULT-DOMAIN-2","resourceId":"ocid1.instance.oc1.uk-london-1.anwgiljtv4fcskyciwxhkngj63okygpgupvznwmajygt6z6chw57mi34jlfa","availabilityDomain":"vcAf:UK-LONDON-1-AD-1","imageId":"ocid1.image.oc1.uk-london-1.aaaaaaaaz57okycdlykwzwegouf6p4fl6leo3mf7zs2setxxbls26hctpkgq","region":"uk-london-1","shape":"VM.Standard.E2.1.Micro"}]}],"version":1.0}

Figure 9-10. *Compute CPU Utilization*

We can see the Alarm name *Compute CPU Utilization*, the status *OK_TO_FIRING*, and the resourceDisplayName *AppServerBook02*.

Figure 9-11 shows the JSON format message in regard to the Autonomous Database.

{"dedupeKey":"780182df-ff64-424d-a628-ed67eb73cc57","title":"Autonomous Database CPU Utilization","body":"High CPU Utilization for Autonomous Database","type":"OK_TO_FIRING","severity":"CRITICAL","timestampEpochMillis":1590362700000,"alarmMeta Data":[{"id":"ocid1.alarm.oc1.uk-london-1.aaaaaaaarpivljkowvl37xzkmbaabjjgxldmtimapa6xth4is6svjloqpiza","status":"FIRING","severity":"CRITICAL","query":"CpuUtilization[1m].max() > 15","totalMetricsFiring":1,"dimensions":[{"AutonomousDBType":"ATP","deploymentType":"Shared","resourceId":"OCID1.AUTONOMOUSDATABASE.OC1.UK-LONDON-1.ABWGILJSNAGIUHXVM4J5GCPXR3FQOYPX3TJXWUG3V6HSVZBSH3OWHXAG7JXA","resourceName":"AUTONOMOUS01","region":"uk-london-1","displayName":"CpuUtilization"}]}],"version":1.0}

Figure 9-11. *Autonomous Database CPU Utilization*

We can see the Alarm name *Autonomous Database CPU Utilization*, the status *OK_ TO_FIRING*, and the resourceDisplayName *AUTONOMOUS01*.

These examples showed how we can use *Monitoring* service, using Cloud resources metrics, and create alarms using thresholds and how these messages are published using *Notification* service.

Summary

In this chapter we have covered two Oracle Cloud Infrastructure Services, the *Notification* service and the *Monitoring* service. Using the *Notification* service, we can create topics and have one or more subscribers. The message is then published through a topic and the subscribers receive it. In this chapter we have used only two types of subscriptions: *Email* and *Slack Channel*. The other types of subscriptions are Functions, HTTPS, and PagerDuty.

Monitoring service uses the metrics emitted by Cloud resources. We did focus on only two cloud resources (Compute and Autonomous Database), but a lot of cloud resources emit metrics. The metrics are categorized into different categories like general heath, capacity, and performance. A way to consume these metrics is to build alarm using Monitoring Query Language. When an alarm is triggered, a message can be sent with the *Notification* service.

PART 3

Applications

CHAPTER 10

SQL Developer Web

Now that we have a deep understanding of the various Oracle Cloud Infrastructure (OCI) Always Free resources and created some, let us now explore how we can create web applications to make the best use of them. For Part 4 of this book, please create the following OCI resources:

1. Autonomous Database for Transaction Processing (ATP)

2. Compute Instance running Oracle Autonomous Linux 7.x

3. Virtual Cloud Network (VCN) to support the Compute Instance

All Autonomous Databases (ADBs) come with several tools preinstalled. These include SQL Developer Web (SQLDEV Web), Oracle Application Express (APEX), and Oracle Machine Learning (OML) Notebooks.

Most Oracle Database developers are accustomed to using *Oracle SQL Developer* (SQLDEV), a desktop application that you can download from Oracle's website (*www.oracle.com/tools/downloads/sqldev-downloads.html*) and use for free! This application was built with Java and will run on all major operating systems: Microsoft Windows, macOS, and Linux.

SQLDEV is a comprehensive toolkit. The application (Figure 10-1) allows database administrators, analysts, and developers to work with the Oracle Database including ADBs. Depending on their user roles, these activities may include, but are not limited to

- View and manage database objects

- Execute SQL queries

- Check database parameters, storage, and memory consumption

- Import and export data

- Design and execute Machine Learning models

© Adrian Png and Luc Demanche 2020
A. Png and L. Demanche, *Getting Started with Oracle Cloud Free Tier*,
https://doi.org/10.1007/978-1-4842-6011-1_10

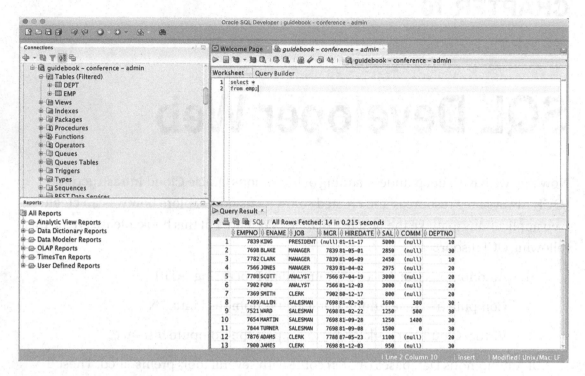

Figure 10-1. *Screenshot showing the SQLDEV user interface*

It also includes SQL Data Modeler (SDDM) that allows database analysts to design and document data models and then generate the necessary Data Definition Language (DDL) files for creating the objects in the database. With so many features packaged into this platform-independent application, it is not surprising that it has a large storage footprint and can consume large amounts of memory.

SQLDEV Web was first revealed along with launch of the Autonomous Database service. It contains a subset of key features from its desktop counterpart, but importantly, could be accessed on any network-connected computer using only a web browser. The software was eventually made available for on-premise deployment with the release of Oracle REST Data Services (ORDS) version 19.4.

This valuable tool will be the focus of this chapter, but first, an overview of the multitiered application we will create in subsequent chapters. Most IT professionals would have attended a technical conference at least once throughout the span of his or her career. The goal of the project we are about to embark on is to create a suite of web applications to support the fictional *Always Cloud Conference* (ACC).

There are typically a few activities before, during, and after the event that are best managed using a web-based database application. These include abstract submission, scheduling of sessions, and downloading of presentation materials. Our goal is to build this application with a variety of software development platforms:

1. **Abstract Submission and Selection:** To help select the best content for conferences, organizers often launch a *Call for Proposals* (CfP) weeks ahead of the event. Technical experts who wish to present at the conference will submit one or more abstracts that describe what they will be speaking on. Organizers use this information to select would-be speakers. We will develop this component using APEX in Chapter 11.

2. **Session Schedule:** After selecting the best sessions, organizers will the use the same APEX application to create a schedule. Speakers will also be able to upload their presentation slides that will be stored using the Oracle Cloud Object Storage Service (OSS). In Chapter 13, we will explore different web application frameworks for rendering the conference schedule and deploy them on an Always Free Compute Instance.

Python, Node.js, and ASP.NET Core will be used to create different examples of the conference schedule display application. The Python web application will access the database using *cx_Oracle* (*https://oracle.github.io/python-cx_Oracle/*) to connect to the ADB. For Node.js and ASP.NET Core applications, we will rely on RESTful services instead.

ORDS is the cornerstone of many of the tools that come with the ADB. It is required for running both SQLDEV Web and APEX. In Chapter 12 though, we will use ORDS to develop the RESTful services needed to support the front-end applications.

Accessing SQLDEV Web

Start by signing in to the OCI console, click the navigation menu at the top right of the landing page (≡), and then click Autonomous Transaction Processing. Look for the ATP created for your web applications (Figure 10-2) and then click to access the instance's details.

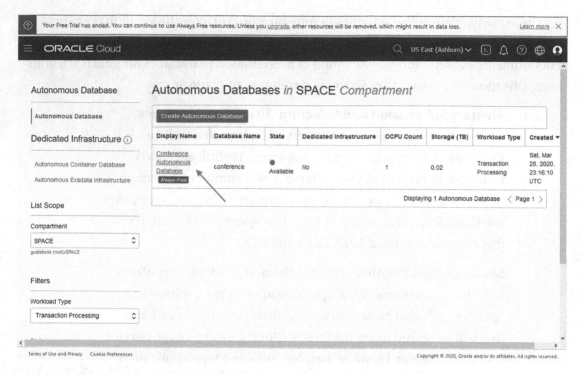

Figure 10-2. *Access the ATP created for the ACC web applications*

Next, on the *Autonomous Database Details* page, click the *Tools* tab for quick access to buttons linking to various utilities available with each ADB instance (Figure 10-3).

Note   The OCI console and the numerous features it provides are ever evolving. When the Autonomous Database service was first launched, administrators needed to first access the Service Console, before reaching a page with links to the individual tools. Adding the Tools tab was a definite improvement to the administrator's workflow.

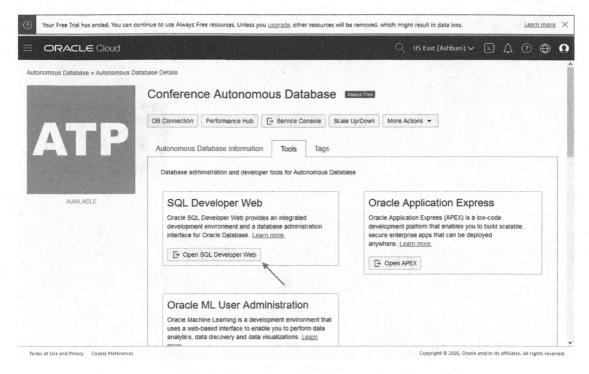

Figure 10-3. *Quick access to tools preinstalled with each ADB instance*

With every Autonomous Database instantiated, an administrative user, aptly named *admin*, is created. During the provisioning process, you would have been asked to secure this account with a password that meets the OCI's complexity requirements. By default, the admin account would have been provided the necessary access to SQLDEV Web. We will use this account to perform some user management tasks.

Note   While the admin user is the most powerful account available to the ADB owner, it does not have *SYSDBA* privileges. Hence, there are limitations on some database operations that are either not allowed or have restrictions. For example, changing certain database initialization parameters, running SQL commands like altering profiles, creating tablespaces, and executing some PL/SQL packages.

Upon successful login, a new *Worksheet* will be created. If this is your first time accessing SQLDEV Web, a sequence of wizard dialog boxes will pop up to walk you through various features of the worksheet. Step through the introductions to quickly familiarize yourself with the user interface (UI) (Figure 10-4). We will examine them more thoroughly later in the chapter.

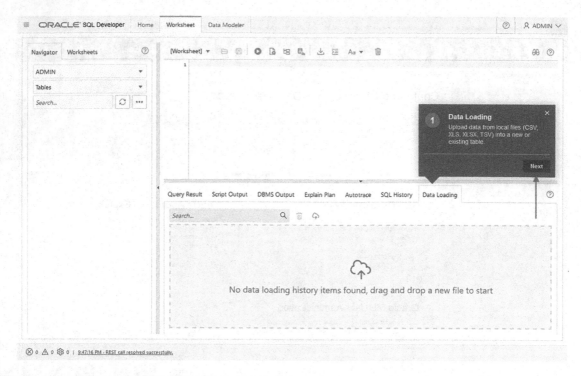

Figure 10-4. *The SQLDEV Web Worksheet guided tour*

Managing Access

Never use the *admin* account for your day-to-day development work. As with all privileged accounts, they should only be used for performing administrative tasks on a database, for example, creating users, granting privileges, and dropping objects belonging to other schemas.

To build your applications, create a separate schema and assign it the minimal privileges needed to perform database operations required by the application. You may perform these tasks using SQLDEV Web.

Let's begin by creating the application schema, or as we sometimes refer to in APEX, the *parsing schema*. Execute the following command:

```
create user ocftconf identified by "my-secret-Password-is-123.";
```

This creates the *ocftconf* schema that we will use to store information about speakers, session proposals, and conference timeslots.

When APEX is installed in the Oracle Database, a database role called *APEX_ GRANTS_FOR_NEW_USERS_ROLE* is created. It captures all the database privileges needed for an APEX parsing schema, and since we intend to build an application using APEX, we can use it as a template of grants for our new schema. Execute the following:

```
declare
  c_schema_name constant varchar2(8) := 'ocftconf';
begin
  for r in (
    select privilege
    from dba_sys_privs
    where grantee = 'APEX_GRANTS_FOR_NEW_USERS_ROLE'
  ) loop
    execute immediate 'grant ' || r.privilege || ' to '
      || c_schema_name;
  end loop;
end;
/
```

To store data successfully, we need to define a storage quota for the parsing schema. You may opt to specify a specific amount of space the user can use by executing the procedure DBMS_CLOUD_ADMIN.GRANT_TABLESPACE_QUOTA. The next script grants the user up to two gigabytes of storage space on its default tablespace:

```
declare
  c_schema_name constant varchar2(8) := 'ocftconf';
begin
  dbms_cloud_admin.grant_tablespace_quota(
    username => c_schema_name
    , tablespace_quota => '2G'
  );
end;
/
```

Or, simply allow the user to use an unlimited amount of space by granting the UNLIMITED TABLESPACE privilege:

```
grant unlimited tablespace to ocftconf;
```

183

Finally, we would like to also give this user access to SQLDEV Web. To do so, we will need to

1. "REST-enable" the schema

2. Generate a personalized URL by specifying a unique *schema alias*

Run the next script to perform this function.

```
declare
  c_schema_name constant varchar2(8) := 'ocftconf';
  c_schema_alias constant varchar2(8) := 'user0001';
begin
  ords_admin.enable_schema(
    p_enabled => true
    , p_schema => c_schema_name
    , p_url_mapping_type => 'BASE_PATH'
    , p_url_mapping_pattern => c_schema_alias
    , p_auto_rest_auth => true
  );
  commit;
end;
/
```

The personalized URL for the user to log in to SQLDEV Web is defined in the template shown in Figure 10-5. The placeholder values can be obtained from the initial URL when the application was launched through the OCI console.

https://<UNIQUE_STRING>-<DATABASE_NAME>.adb.<DATA_REGION>.oraclecloudapps.com/ords/<SCHEMA_ALIAS>/_sdw/?nav=worksheet

Figure 10-5. *SQLDEV Web URL template*

For my ATP instance, I can determine the following:

- **UNIQUE_STRING:** A random string of alphanumeric characters, for example, *zqbtnc5yxpr941f.*

- **DATABASE_NAME:** This is the database name specified when creating the instance. My database name is called *conference.*

- **DATA_REGION:** This will be the *region identifier* of your Oracle Cloud account's Home Region. You can find a full list of data regions and their identifiers here (*https://bit.ly/oci-docs-regions*). The Home Region for my account is US East (Ashburn) and the region identifier is *us-ashburn-1*.

- **SCHEMA_ALIAS:** This value is determined by the parameter p_url_mapping_pattern when the schema was REST-enabled, for example, *user0001*.

With the required values in hand, the SQLDEV Web URL for the user *ocftconf* is derived as shown in Figure 10-6.

https://zqbtnc5yxpr941f-conference.adb.us-ashburn-1.oraclecloudapps.com/ords/user0001/_sdw/?nav=worksheet

Figure 10-6. *Example SQLDEV Web URL for the user ocftconf*

User Interface Explained

After the parsing schema has been created successfully and granted the necessary privileges, log out of SQLDEV Web immediately, and then log in as the user using the personalized URL generated. We will step through the various UI components of SQLDEV Web using this account.

Worksheet

The landing page upon login is the Worksheet module. For most database developers, this is the main area that most work is done. Conceptually, there are little differences between the web and desktop versions of SQL Developer, but the available features in the web version are limited as it relies heavily on REST APIs provided by ORDS.

Tip   If you prefer the landing page to be the *Home* page instead, change the query parameter *nav* value (see Figure 10-5) from *worksheet* to *home*.

The UI is broken up into three key sections (Figure 10-7). On the left, labeled "A", are two tabs for finding and listing database objects and saved worksheets.

Figure 10-7. The Worksheet module is divided into three main sections

The *Navigator* tab is selected by default and is further subdivided into two regions. The top region contains fields and controls for search and filtering database objects that are then rendered below.

When you select and right-click over a database object, you will have access to additional action items that you can choose to perform on the selected object (Figure 10-8). This is similar to the desktop version but with a lot less functionality.

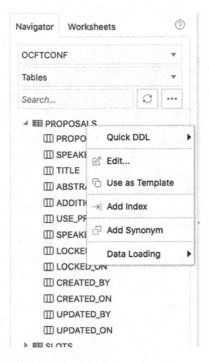

Figure 10-8. *Accessing database object-specific*

For some object types like tables, clicking "Edit..." opens up a modal window (Figure 10-9) that allows you to view and edit many object attributes, for example, changing attribute types, adding indexes, and removing constraints.

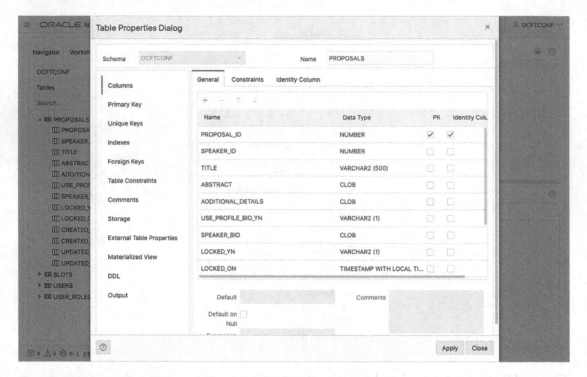

Figure 10-9. *Edit table attributes with SQLDEV Web*

Again, remember that software features and functionalities are constantly evolving. At this time, do not be surprised to find that some object changes cannot be performed using the available features. For such cases, revert to using either the desktop version, your favorite command-line database client, or simply executing SQL commands in the Worksheet (region labeled "B" in Figure 10-7).

Like its desktop counterpart, you may enter one or more SQL statements to execute. You may also execute PL/SQL block statements. The group of buttons, labeled "E" in Figure 10-10, are very similar to what you can find in SQL Developer.

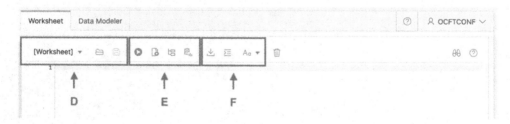

Figure 10-10. *The Worksheet toolbar*

The two buttons on the left let you run (from left to right) either a single statement or the entire script. The keyboard shortcuts are also the same. To perform these actions using on a keyboard, press *Ctrl+Enter* and function key *F5,* respectively. The remaining two buttons in Group "E" allow you to generate an *Explain Plan* and set *Autotrace,* or simply use the keyboard shortcuts *F10* and *F6,* respectively.

Note   In Figure 10-10, the toolbar functions in "D" allow users to manage saved worksheets. Use these to store worksheets with specific tasks for reuse. There are buttons in "F" that also allow users to download these worksheets and format code.

The outputs from executing SQL queries, PL/SQL statements, generating explain plans, and so on can be found in the third region (labeled "C" in Figure 10-7). They are organized in several tabs (Figure 10-11).

Figure 10-11. *Tabbed regions displaying outputs from various actions in SQLDEV Web*

Starting from the left, *Query Results* is where SQL query results are formatted neatly in a table and can be downloaded in CSV, JSON, XML, and tab-delimited text files. The outputs from any other SQL statements are displayed in the *Script Output,* along with the results from executing PL/SQL statements. Outputs from the PL/SQL package DBMS_ OUTPUT are exclusively channeled to the tab *DBMS Output.* There are also dedicated tabs for explain plans and Autotrace reports.

SQL History, as its name implies, lists all the SQL and PL/SQL statements that have been executed and is maintained even after you log out. It displays when the statements were last executed, and how many times it has been called. There is also an improvement over one feature in the desktop version, and that is how it responds to a double-click event on a statement. Instead of clearing the worksheet, the selected statement is appended to the currently opened worksheet for easy re-execution.

Note   Saved worksheets and SQL history are stored locally in your browser using IndexedDB (*https://w3c.github.io/IndexedDB/*), a browser-based storage system and API. For that reason, it is highly recommended that you should always store important scripts on file storage systems, preferably with source control management.

Last but not least, let's explore a very useful functionality in SQLDEV Web: Data Loading. If you have data tucked away in comma- or tab-delimited files and wish to put them in a database where they belong, then you are in luck. These can be either imported by creating a new table, or into existing tables.

If you are introducing data in destined for a new table, then click the Data Loading tab (see Figure 10-11). Either click the darker grayed area indicated by a red arrow (Figure 10-12) or drop the source file inside. Alternatively, click the button marked by a red circle.

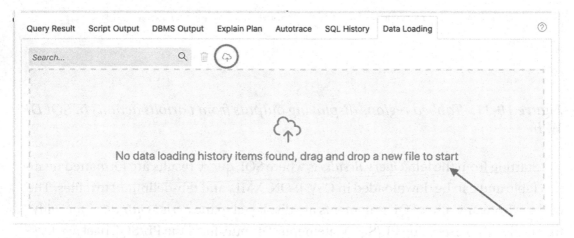

Figure 10-12. *Drag and drop a CSV file to begin the data import process*

This will trigger a new modal window with a wizard to guide you through the data import process. The first step involves customizing any import parameters and previewing the parsed data. By default, column names are expected in the first row, and each column value is enclosed in double quotes. Tweak these if necessary. These options are not displayed initially, so click the button next to the filename (Figure 10-13).

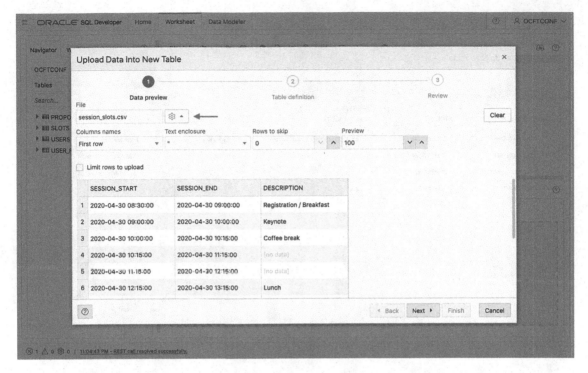

Figure 10-13. *Click the button next to the filename to customize the file import parameters*

In step 2, select the target schema and provide a unique table name to create. Select the columns that you wish to import and customize their attributes. For example, you may change the column names created, specify the data types, and indicate if a value is required.

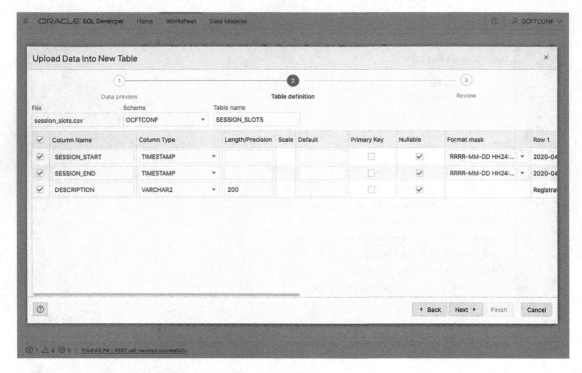

Figure 10-14. *Customize the new table*

Finally, in step 3, do a check on the DDL generated and column mappings. If everything looks correct, start the import process by clicking the button *Finish* (Figure 10-15).

Figure 10-15. *Final checks before starting the data import process*

The process will take a while depending on how large the file is. When it is completed, the Data Loading history will report on the outcome of the process, showing the number of rows read and how many failed. In the Navigator, you will also find the target table created and another that is autogenerated by SQLDEV Web (Figure 10-16). The latter logs any errors and includes the error message and submitted data for easy troubleshooting. You will find this valuable information in the table prefixed with *"SDWERR_"*.

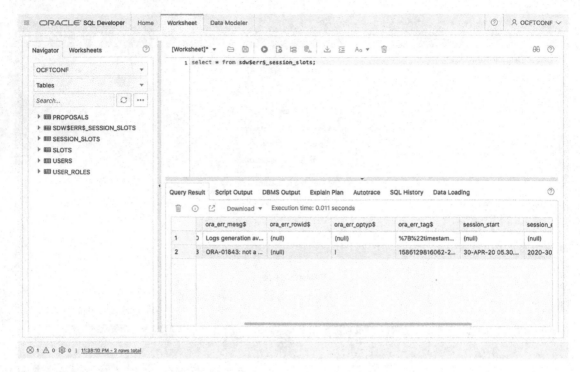

***Figure 10-16.** Autogenerated logs produced during data loading*

Note   For importing into existing tables, trigger the wizard from the target table's context menu (see Figure 10-8). Place your mouse over Data Loading and then click "Upload Data…".

Data Modeler

Besides worksheets, SQLDEV Web also provides Data Modeler to assist in better database design. Like the Worksheet, the user interface includes a left pane, labeled "A", that allows you to navigate database objects, plus any saved diagrams from this tool (Figure 10-17).

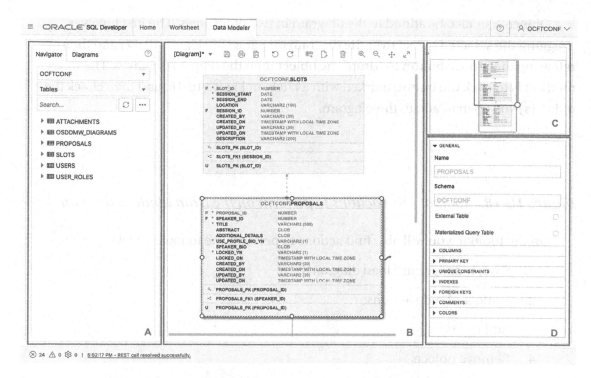

Figure 10-17. *The Data Modeler user interface is divided into four panes*

To access the context menu available on each object, table, or view, right-click the target object. For tables, in addition to the actions available in Worksheet, you may add the object to the currently opened *Diagram*, with or without dependencies, or as a *Star Schema*. While the latter is similar to adding the selected object to the diagram with dependencies, it also does the following:

- Automatically detects implied foreign keys and adds them to the diagram, along with any defined foreign keys

- Automatically positions the object and its dependencies in a Star layout

---

Note   Star Schemas are often used in data warehouses where foreign keys are not explicitly defined in the database, though such relationships could be derived between the fact table (the select object) and dimension tables.

Objects can also be added to the diagram in two other ways. The first involves dragging the selected object over the diagram on pane "B" (Figure 10-17) and then releasing the mouse button to "drop" the object onto the diagram's canvas. The other method is to click the button marked with a circle in Figure 10-18, and then check the object(s) you wish to add to the diagram.

Figure 10-18. *Toolbar with actions to perform on the Data Modeler diagram*

On the toolbar, you will also find actions to perform the following tasks:

1. Save, manage, and load diagrams

2. Undo and redo actions

3. Add notes

4. Remove objects

5. Control the diagram's viewing properties

6. Auto layout items

7. Generate DDL statements, reports, and graphics for reporting purposes

8. Find objects

Note   Unlike worksheets, saved diagrams are stored in a database table as opposed to using the browser-based IndexedDB. When the first diagram is saved in your schema, a table named *OSDDMW_DIAGRAMS* is created. This allows users to access diagrams in any SQLDEV Web session, and they won't mysteriously disappear should you accidentally clear your browser cache.

Last but not least, on the rightmost pane (Figure 10-17), pane "C" provides an overview map of your diagram and is especially useful in large and complex schemas. The area bounded in the red rectangle corresponds to the current view port in pane "B". The fourth and final pane "D" lists the attributes of the selected object in the diagram for easy analysis.

Data modeling is an important step in determining the correct data structure of applications, ensuring that they are maintainable and to generate key deliverables like reports for communicating to customers and other developers (Figure 10-19). While there are many concepts and functionality not available in SQLDEV Web, compared to its desktop counterpart, the current feature set should be sufficient for creating quality applications.

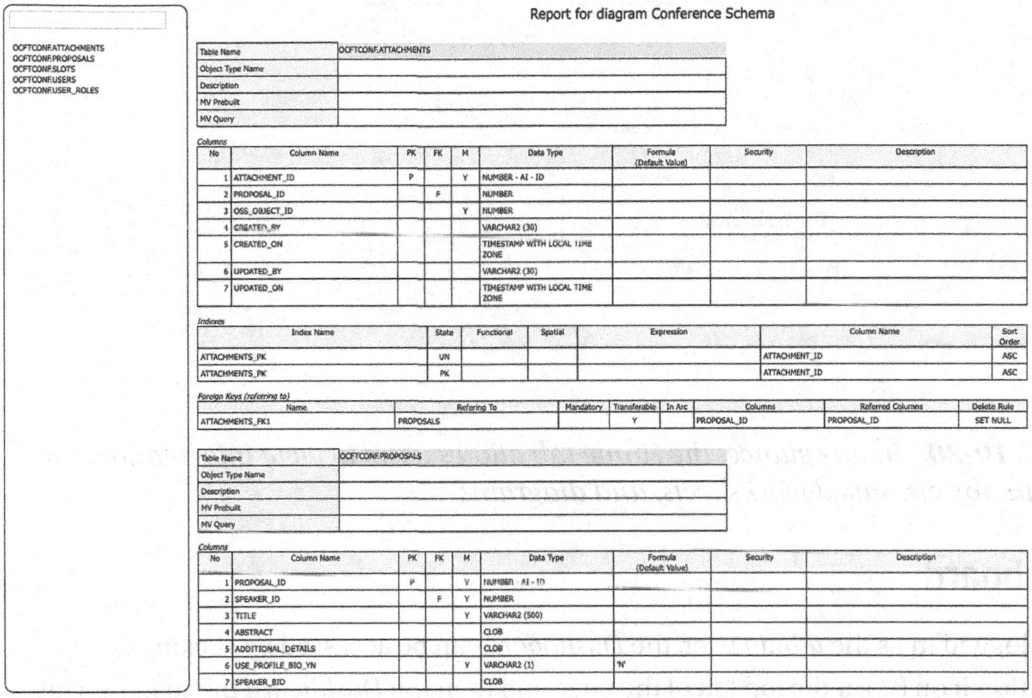

Figure 10-19. *A sample report generated for the Conference database schema*

Other Features

Home Tab

The Home tab in SQLDEV Web provides a quick overview of your assets in the current schema (Figure 10-20). This includes a list of saved worksheets and diagrams. It also provides information about invalid objects, simple table metrics, and a timeline of activities.

Figure 10-20. *In one glance, the Home tab allows users to view information about schema objects, saved worksheets, and diagrams*

Dashboard

When logged in as the *admin* user, the *Dashboard* can be accessed by clicking the navigation icon (≡) at the top left of the page and then the *Dashboard* menu item. This page provides administrators with a quick overview about the Autonomous Database's current status (Figure 10-21).

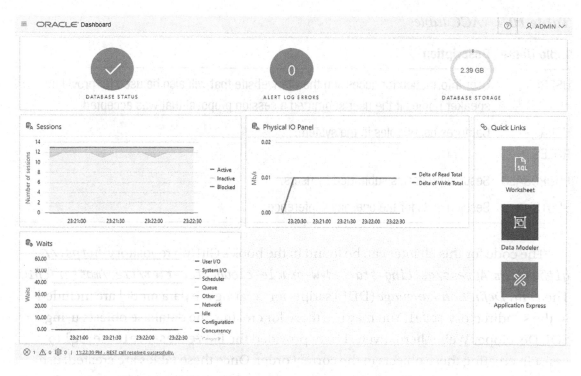

Figure 10-21. *The SQLDEV Web Dashboard provides an overview of the ADB's current status*

The Dashboard provides details like storage usage and number of alert logs generated. Three charts also provide administrators with details about the number of database sessions open, physical input and output disk operation rates, and amount of database waits. While these charts give a general overview of database performance, the best tool to monitor these parameters is the Autonomous Database's *Performance Hub*.

Modeling the ACC Website

The data model for the ACC website will consist of a few entities that will help us capture speaker information, session proposals, and schedules. We will create the following tables.

Table 10-1. *ACC tables*

Table Name	Description
USERS	User information for accessing the CfP website that will also be used for providing speaker names if the user submitted a session proposal that was accepted.
USER_ ROLES	Captures users' roles in the system.
PROPOSALS	Session proposals submitted by users.
SLOTS	Session slots for the one-day conference.

The code for this chapter can be found in the book's GitHub repository: *https:// github.com/Apress/getting-started-w-oracle-cloud-free-tier/tree/master/ch10*. The *Data Definition Language* (DDL) scripts for creating the data model are included in the subdirectory model. You may use these for creating the database objects using SQL Developer Web. Alternatively, I have provided the file release/release.sql to assist in creating these objects in the correct order. Once these tables are created, use data loading features of SQL Developer Web to populate the SLOTS table with the data contained in the file data/sessions_template.csv. When completed, you will be ready to proceed to the next chapter where you will create the ACC CfP website using APEX.

Summary

In the absence of a direct database connection, developers who are accustomed to *SQL Workshop* in APEX as an alternative for managing database objects would deeply appreciate the SQLDEV Web user interface. SQL Workshop is a web-based tool for developers to browse and manage database objects and has been a core component in the APEX ecosystem for quite a while. While useful, I have experienced some challenges in using it productively. The ability to browse database objects with the flexibility to execute SQL commands without navigating away is a huge boost to productivity.

However, it is not without its limits. The Data Modeler features are far fewer than what one could expect from running the software from the desktop. And while SQLDEV Web offers developers the ability to save scripts and data model diagrams, the lack of version control support means that developers need to be diligent in saving them on to a physical drive, and then check into a code repository. Until then, it is hard to imagine a development workflow that does not include our usual tool suite consisting of SQL Developer, SQLcl, and SQL*Plus.

Last but not least, in this chapter, we had a brief look at the simple database schema enabling the web applications that we will build using various software development platforms in the coming chapters.

CHAPTER 11

Oracle Application Express

The *World Wide Web* (WWW) was invented by renowned British computer scientist Sir Tim Berners-Lee in 1989. He had proposed three fundamental concepts that have today become ubiquitous to many. It provides us timely information, a way to access services, and more. These principles include the *HyperText Markup Language* (HTML), the *Uniform Resource Identifier* (URI) (also commonly known as URL), and the *Hypertext Transfer Protocol* (HTTP). URIs are human-friendly addresses on the Internet that allow us to identify and locate web resources, which are then transmitted over the network, to web browsers, using HTTP. The most common web resources are web pages formatted using HTML.

The most basic web page is static and can be hosted on any server application that could present the content over HTTP. However, many web pages these days are data-driven and dynamic. Data is stored in a database and then presented as web pages using an intermediary that typically uses a programming language that helps render HTML.

Oracle Application Express (APEX) plays that crucial role in transforming data in the *Oracle Database* into standards-compliant web pages. On the backend, APEX is driven by the robust and proven programming language PL/SQL that runs efficiently on the database. While on the browser, content is driven by *Cascading Style Sheets* (CSS), HTML, and *JavaScript*. In an *Autonomous Database* (ADB), there are no additional servers or applications to install. This full-stack web application environment comes preinstalled and ready to use.

These are not the only essential ingredients needed to build secure web applications. We have to think about security issues like user authentication, data encryption, and access control (authorization). Application and data must also have a backup and recovery strategy. The APEX rapid application development platform offloads these

203

© Adrian Png and Luc Demanche 2020
A. Png and L. Demanche, *Getting Started with Oracle Cloud Free Tier*,
https://doi.org/10.1007/978-1-4842-6011-1_11

concerns to the network and database administrators and leaves software developers to focus on understanding the business, design the data schema, and implement the business logic.

This chapter provides a quick overview of the technology; however, there is so much to discover and learn about the power of APEX and *Low Code* development. I will attempt to provide you sufficient information to help get a sense of what APEX can do for you. As a follow-up, I strongly encourage that you read the APEX official documentation, access the large collection of videos on *YouTube* (`https://bit.ly/orclapex-youtube`), and/or check out the vast number of books, including many published by Apress. The APEX development team maintains a web page (`https://apex.oracle.com/shortcuts/`) with links to many of these resources, so check them out when you are done with this book.

Note   Low Code development generally refers to the process of building functional applications using graphical user interfaces, involving very little amount of traditional programming code.

APEX Workspace

The *Oracle Cloud Free Tier* offering provides users with two *Always Free Autonomous Databases*. Every Autonomous Database (ADB), regardless of workload type, comes with *Oracle Application Express* (APEX) preinstalled. To create APEX applications, you will first need to provision a *workspace* and *schema*.

You may access APEX for your ADB through its *Service Console*, or *Oracle Cloud Infrastructure* (OCI) console. The latter is similar to the steps outlined in Chapter 10, for accessing *SQL Developer Web*. Click *Open APEX* to launch a new browser window or tab (Figure 11-1).

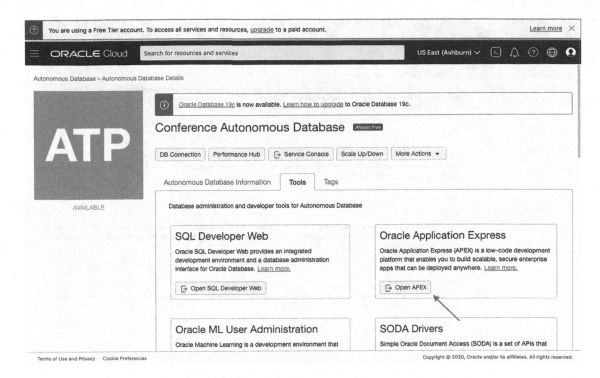

Figure 11-1. *Launch APEX from the OCI console*

You can find the link to your APEX instance through the Service Console under the tab *Development* (Figure 11-2).

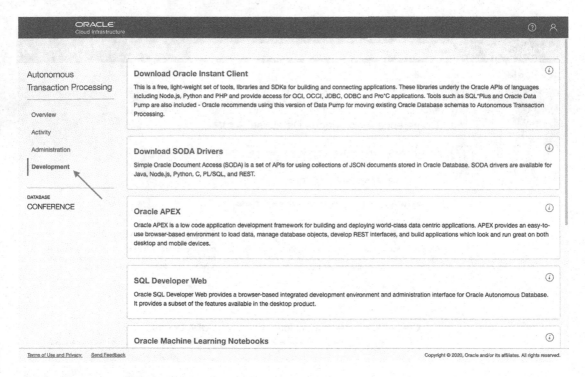

Figure 11-2. *Launch APEX from the ADB Service Console*

Like SQL Developer Web, you may also access APEX using a personalized URL for your instance (Figure 11-3).

https://<UNIQUE_STRING>-<DATABASE_NAME>.adb.<DATA_REGION>.oraclecloudapps.com/ords/apex

Figure 11-3. *APEX URL template*

For my ATP instance, I can determine the following:

- **UNIQUE_STRING**: A random string of alphanumeric characters, for example, *zqbtnc5yxpr941f*.

- **DATABASE_NAME**: This is the database name specified when creating the instance. My database name is called *conference*.

- **DATA_REGION**: This will be the *region identifier* of your Oracle Cloud account's Home Region. You can find a full list of data regions and their identifiers here (`https://bit.ly/oci-docs-regions`). The Home Region for my account is US East (Ashburn) and the region identifier is *us-ashburn-1*.

Freshly provisioned, there will not be any usable workspace to develop an application. As such, you will be redirected to the *Administration Services* (Figure 11-4) where you will log in as the *admin* user.

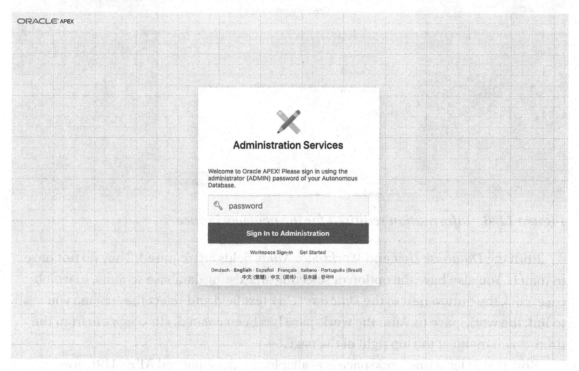

Figure 11-4. *Administration Services login page*

You will immediately be prompted to create a workspace. Click Create Workspace (Figure 11-5).

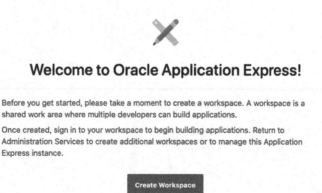

Figure 11-5. *Invitation to create a workspace*

Provide the information request for the new workspace (Figure 11-6).

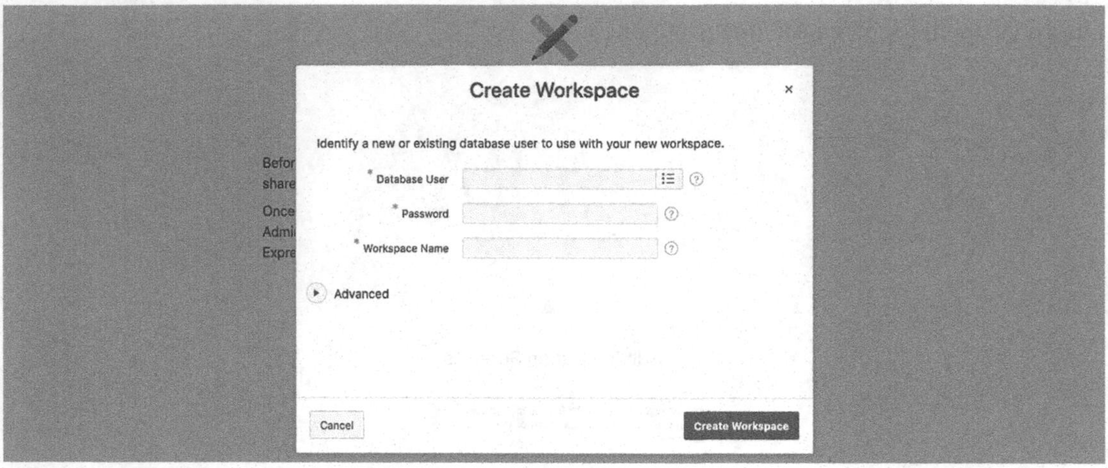

Figure 11-6. *Information required for the new workspace*

Both the *Database User* and *Workspace Name* fields are required. They **do not** have to match. You also have the option of selecting an existing database schema, in which case, click the button next to the *Database User* text field and select the schema you wish to link the workspace to. After the workspace has been created, click *Sign out* from the drop-down menu at the top right of the page.

Now that at least one workspace is available, the personalized APEX URL now redirects you to the *Workspace Sign-In* page instead (Figure 11-7).

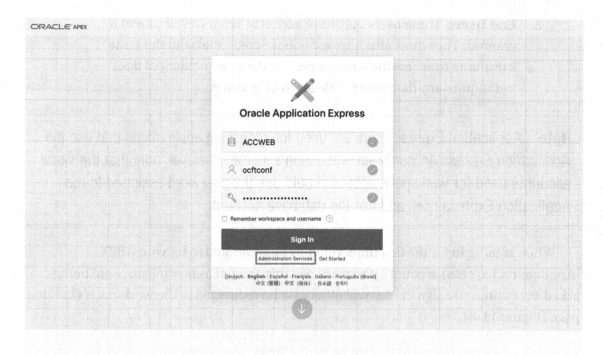

Figure 11-7. *The APEX Workspace Sign-In page*

If you wish to return to the Administration Services, click the link below the *Sign In* button (highlighted with the red box). Otherwise, enter the required information to log in to the workspace.

The APEX *Development Environment* in ADBs uses an *Authentication Scheme* called *Database Accounts*, which relies on database credentials for access. However, for managing workspace privileges, APEX requires a matching *Application Express* user account that you must create for every developer and then assign a role. There are three roles that you may assign a user to:

1. **Workspace Administrators**: Members of this group may manage applications, database objects, user accounts, groups, workspace preferences, and access workspace utilities, for example, *Team Development*.

2. **Developers**: Members of this group may manage applications, database objects, and access workspace utilities if granted.

3. **End Users**: These users only have access to Team Development if granted. They must also have a database credential with the same username to access the workspace. The database credential does not require any database privileges to be granted.

Note   Application Express users are used for accessing applications that use the *Application Express Accounts* authentication scheme. However, note that the same accounts used for workspace access should use the password assigned to the Application Express user, and **not** the database account.

When signing in for the first time, you may be prompted to set your APEX (Application Express) account's password. Set this as soon as possible to avoid being asked every time you sign in. You will otherwise be redirected to the workspace's landing page (Figure 11-8).

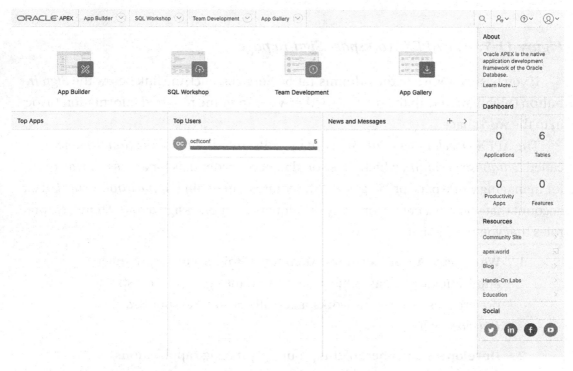

Figure 11-8. *APEX workspace landing page*

From here, workspace administrators will have access to the following:

- App Builder
- SQL Workshop
- Team Development
- App Gallery

Let's examine what each of these provides.

App Builder

The *App Builder* is central to the APEX development environment. Here, workspace administrators and developers perform a variety of actions involved in building modern web applications (Figure 11-9).

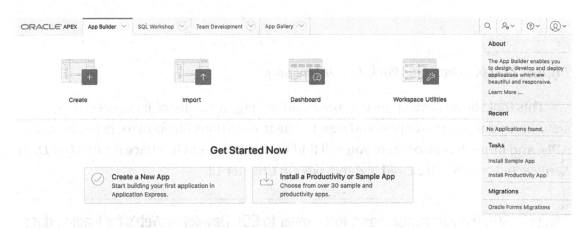

Figure 11-9. The App Builder home page

These include the creation of new applications, importing existing ones from other APEX instances, and defining external REST-based data sources.

SQL Workshop

In Chapter 10, we had examined in depth the features of SQL Developer Web. *SQL Workshop* has been available in APEX workspaces for quite a while (Figure 11-10).

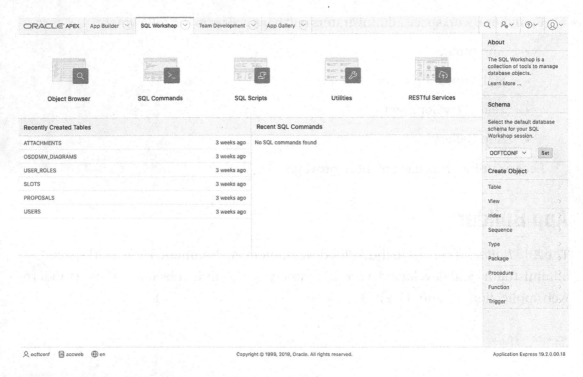

Figure 11-10. *The SQL Workshop home page*

This tool allows developers to browse and manage database objects, execute SQL statements and scripts, import and export data from various file formats, generate table APIs, and more. It is also where you will find the management interface for *RESTful Data Services* that will be discussed in depth later in Chapter 12.

Note   SQL Workshop also has a tool similar to SQL Developer Web's for loading data onto the database, and it is called *Data Workshop*. This tool actually predates SQL Developer Web and is an alternate starting point for creating an APEX application.

Team Development

Like SQL Workshop, the *Team Development* tool has been a feature in APEX for a long while. It has, however, recently undergone a major update with APEX release 19.2. If you plan to use Team Development as part of your development workflow, then you will need to first prepare the environment for use (Figure 11-11).

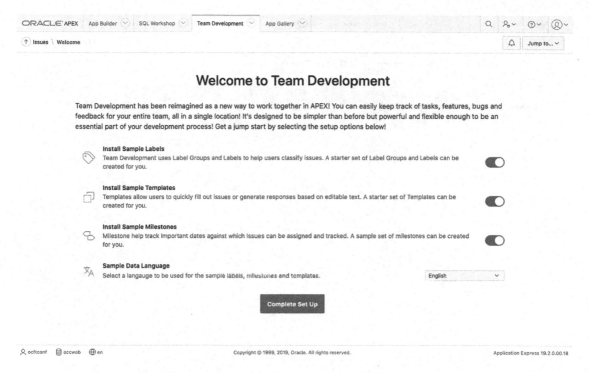

Figure 11-11. *Set up Team Development for initial use*

If you are new to Team Development, it might be a great idea to install the sample data to visualize and learn the various features of the tool.

Once the setup is completed, you will have access to the tool's home page where you can proceed to manage your settings (Figure 11-12).

Figure 11-12. *Manage Team Development settings*

Similar to applications like *Jira* and *GitHub*, Team Development has features that allow you to create issues, manage their statuses and assignments, and monitor progress using milestones. What it lacks, however, is tight integration with a source code version control system at this time, commonly found in other issue management systems.

Team Development can also be used to help monitor user feedback. APEX has built-in support for users to submit feedback from within applications. Each entry contains crucial session information that is logged when submitted. This allows developers to be more efficient in troubleshooting and fix problems in the application. Feedbacks can be accessed either from the top navigation bar, under the Team Development drop-down menu, or by clicking the links in the *Feedback* dashboard found on the bottom right of the home page (Figure 11-12).

Caution   The Feedback functionality is linked to the legacy Team Development in APEX release 19.2. Creating linked "issues" from a feedback entry will be deposited in the older utility. Both features will be better integrated when the version of APEX in ADB is upgraded to 20.1.

App Gallery

All installations of APEX come with a suite of ready-made applications designed to support common business needs, for example, managing customer relations and creating surveys and polls (Figure 11-13).

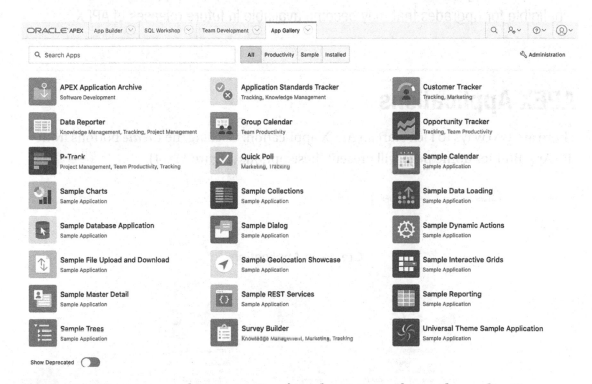

Figure 11-13. *A comprehensive suite of productivity and sample applications*

These are called *Productivity Apps* or *Packaged Apps*. Also included are sample applications that, together, help demonstrate various capabilities of this Low Code platform. There is no coding involved in deploying any of these applications. With only a few options to set, these applications come with SQL scripts that automatically create dependent database objects. However, should you wish to extend their functionalities, then unlock the application. You will have full access in the App Builder to customize and develop a version to call your own.

> **Caution**   Productivity Apps are fully supported by Oracle, subject to your database support contract. If you do not upgrade to a paid account, you will not enjoy this entitlement. Support will only be available through public forums. Also, Oracle will not support applications that have been unlocked. Unlocked applications are also ineligible for upgrades that may become available in future releases of APEX.

APEX Applications

There are two ways to kick-start an APEX application. Clicking the *Create* buttons from the App Builder home page will present these options (Figure 11-14).

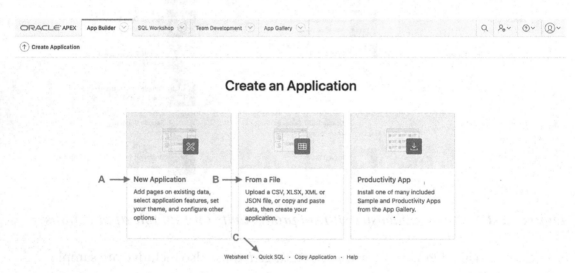

Figure 11-14. *Create an APEX application*

The most common approach is to start by clicking New Application (labeled "A"). The other is to start with a file containing your data in an appropriate format, for example, CSV, JSON, TXT, XLSX, or XML. You also have the option to perform a copy and paste operation, or simply select from a list of sample data provided by Oracle (labeled "B"). The other interesting link on this page is *Quick SQL* (labeled "C"). This tool allows you to generate SQL statements from a text format that defines the target schema (Figure 11-15).

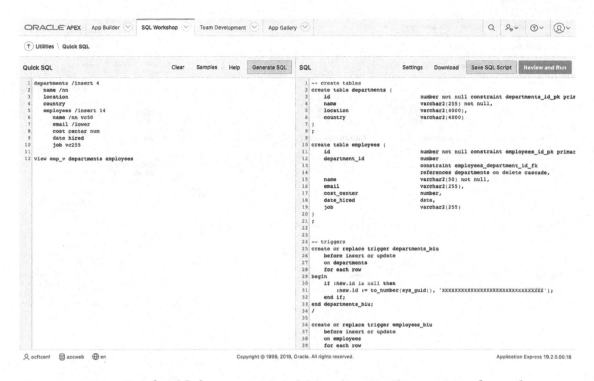

Figure 11-15. *Quick SQL for generating SQL statements to create a desired database schema expressed using a simplified text format*

In the example, I had loaded a sample structure and generated the corresponding SQL statements that can then be executed in the database, either using the APEX utilities or an external application like SQL Developer Web or SQL*Plus.

When applications are created, APEX automatically generates an *Application ID* (APP_ID) that you can change. However, this identifier must be unique within the APEX instance.

APEX workspaces can be associated with one or more database schemas. If there is more than one schema, you may select a different *parsing schema* for the application. Your parsing schema may or may not own all the database objects required for the application. However, if they are located in other schemas, then provide the necessary database grants. Often, database administrators or architects may opt to isolate critical tables and allow access and manipulation of data through database *Views* and or *Table APIs* implemented as PL/SQL packages. In this application, neither were changed.

Once the application has been created, you will have access to the application's home page (Figure 11-16).

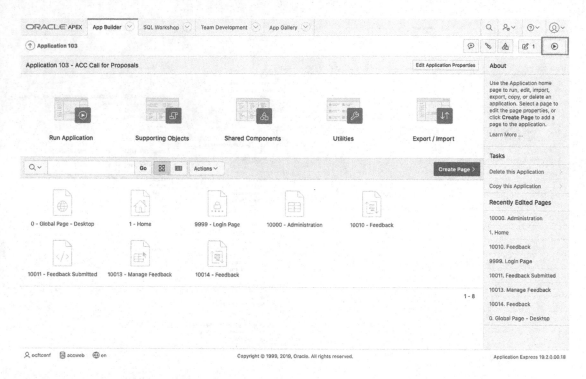

Figure 11-16. *APEX application home page*

From here, workspace administrators and developers may manage all elements of the APEX application, starting with creating, editing, and deleting pages. APEX pages are the backbone of the application and will be discussed later in the chapter.

Using the *Supporting Objects* features, you may also manage installation and deinstallation scripts, as well as any prompts required during application deployments. These prompts help determine what application features are enabled and set APEX *Substitution String* values. The latter act as placeholders for "constant" values that might be used throughout the application.

Other elements of the APEX application are managed under *Shared Components*. These components and settings directly impact the application's visual display and behavior. There are many, and unfortunately, we will not be able to address all of them in a single book chapter. We will, however, examine some of the key components that should excite you.

Finally, to view the application, simply click *Run Application*. You may also run the application with the highlighted button at the top right of Figure 11-16. This button appears also on each page that you are editing, allowing you to run the current page.

The running application renders on a different browser tab or window. This allows you to conveniently edit the page, save the changes, and then view the result in a different area of your screen, without unnecessarily switching back and forth.

Application Security – Authentication Schemes

APEX applications are designed to be secure, ground up. When creating applications, the wizard automatically selects a default authentication scheme. All pages are set to require *Page Authentication*, and a login page will be automatically added to the application that then relies on the current (active) authentication scheme to identify users.

As of release 20.1, there are nine types of authentication schemes that you can define and use with your APEX application. Let's examine each of these to understand their capabilities, limitations, and suitability for your projects.

Application Express Accounts

This is most commonly the default authentication scheme selected when an application is created. These accounts are also used for accessing the workspace and come with many built-in functionalities for managing user accounts. When using this scheme, administrators may manage user accounts using the workspace utilities. Application developers do not need to worry about issues like encrypting passwords, routinely expiring passwords, and so on. PL/SQL APIs are also available that you can use in applications to facilitate user registrations and password and personal profile changes. However, note that some of these requires certain application attributes to be changed to nondefault values (Figure 11-17).

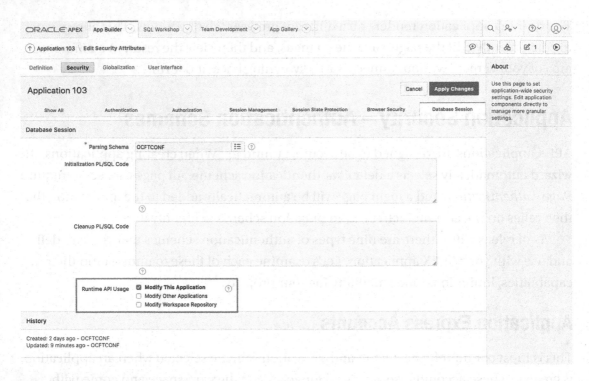

Figure 11-17. *Change the application's runtime API usage to perform limited user management functions*

Custom Authentication

This is another popular authentication scheme. It is often used when developers implement security using schema objects. For example, user information is stored in tables and then managed using PL/SQL APIs that also ensure passwords are stored encrypted in the database. This is the authentication that we will use in the APEX application that we will create later in this chapter.

Database Accounts

For seasoned APEX developers, you would be accustomed to developing applications using Application Express Accounts to log in. On ADBs, the equivalent would be to use Database Accounts. This is convenient; however, bear in mind that application users will require database access should they need to change their passwords.

Note   Database users in ADB are created with the *DEFAULT* profile with a password lifetime of 360 days. Any attempts to change a user's profile, for example, by executing the ALTER USER command, will be ignored. You will also have no rights to create a new profile or change any profile's limits.

HTTP Header Variable

This authentication scheme relies on an external server that acts as a gateway to APEX (Figure 11-18).

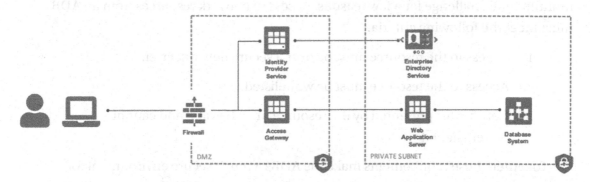

Figure 11-18. *A typical topology to support authentication using HTTP header variables*

The gateway is responsible for authenticating the user and then injecting a specially named *HTTP Header Variable*, containing a value that would then be used for the application's username (*APP_USER*). Finding this variable in the headers was sufficient to gain access to the application.

This creates a dangerous scenario since anyone with knowledge of this variable and the right tools would be able to assume the identity of anyone in the system. Hence, when using this authentication scheme, it is extremely important that no person or system, other than the gateway, has access to the instance. You may use the *Access Control List* to lock down access to the ADB instance.

However, with the current methods used by ADBs to support APEX, there is no effective way to create a topology that would allow us to construct such a topology, so at the moment, this is pretty much just a theoretical approach.

LDAP Directory

The *Lightweight Directory Access Protocol* (LDAP) is an industry-standard protocol for systems to access directory information over the Internet. It enjoys support by many vendors including *Microsoft Active Directory, NetIQ eDirectory, OpenLDAP,* and many more. However, unlike the HTTP traffic, LDAP typically runs over TCP ports 389 or 636. Most enterprise directories will not be accessible outside of a protected network, either on-premise or on an Oracle Cloud Virtual Cloud Network. For Always Free ADBs, you cannot provision it with a private endpoint, and that is needed for the database to communicate with the LDAP server hosted on-premise.

Setting up APEX hosted on ADBs to access these servers would also be a monumental challenge for a few reasons. Access to network resources from an ADB must meet the following criteria:

1. Access to the resource must be over a secure network layer.

2. Access to the resource must be whitelisted.

3. Certificates presented by the resource must be valid and cannot be self-signed.

Together, these requirements make the ADBs a much secure environment for everyone to operate in. However, given these limitations and challenges, using LDAP Directory for APEX authentication may not be a viable solution for an Always Free ADB.

No Authentication

Of the nine available schemes, this one sounds somewhat like a misnomer, but it can be useful when switching applications from "public" to "private" just by changing the active authentication scheme.

Open Door Credentials

This authentication scheme does not attempt to authenticate a user. Using the application's login page, APEX would simply set your logged in username to the value provided in the login page. This authentication scheme is only useful during development, where this ability allows you to test, for example, an application's authorization schemes and rules.

Oracle Application Server Single Sign-On

This is one of the oldest *Single Sign-On* (SSO) approaches provided by Oracle. Unfortunately, this product only works with an Oracle Application Server. This authentication scheme type is not relevant to you unless your organization has access to this product.

Social Sign-In

Introduced with release 18.1, support for *OAuth2* (`https://oauth.net/2/`) and *OpenID Connect* (`https://openid.net/connect/`) was a game changer. OAuth2 is yet another industry-standard protocol for an application, a *service provider* (SP), to request a user's permission and authorization to use his/her identity and information, through an *identity provider* (IdP). Out of the box, APEX allows developers to create applications that work with IdPs like *Google* and *Facebook*. Any other OAuth2-compliant providers, for example, *Microsoft Azure Active Directory*, *LinkedIn*, *Okta*, and so on, can also be configured for use as your application's authentication scheme. Multiple IdPs may also be configured for a single application, allowing users to choose between their favorite networks.

For ADBs, this is perhaps the best approach for offering the benefits of SSO for users. It is also worthwhile mentioning that the relationship with the IdPs can be further extended to access REST-based resources that the user can authorize. You may then, using the same authorization, access a user's *Microsoft OneDrive* content, or create an appointment on a *Google Calendar*.

Making Choices

Choosing the appropriate authentication often relies on several factors. Here are some considerations, in no particular order of importance:

1. User requirements

2. Integration with corporate IT systems

3. Implementation costs

4. The application's target audience

5. Security compliance based on industry, type of data managed, and jurisdiction

Application Security – Authorization Schemes

Authentication is the process of identifying users based on what they know (username and passwords) and, for greater security, what they have (personal mobile device or biometrics). For the application, it answers the question: "Who are you?" Authorization, on the other hand, is the process of establishing what you are allowed to do on the system. In APEX, authorization rules can also be defined declaratively, and you have the option of choosing from 11 scheme types.

Some of the most common approaches involve using *Bind Variables* :APP_USER, the username as returned by the APEX authentication process, and a SQL query or PL/SQL function to return records and/or a TRUE/FALSE value, respectively. You may even use any of these with the Social Sign-In authentication scheme to build compelling authorization rules based on information obtained from the IdPs.

Application Structure and Components

APEX applications are primarily composed of pages, regions, page items, and buttons. Pages are literally rendered as an HTML page. Regions are rendered based on their assigned template, but most rely on the HTML <div> tag. Page items are commonly rendered using an HTML *input* element, but not always. For buttons, either the *button* or *anchor* HTML elements are commonly used, but they can be changed through their assigned *Template*. The relationship between these elements is illustrated in Figure 11-19.

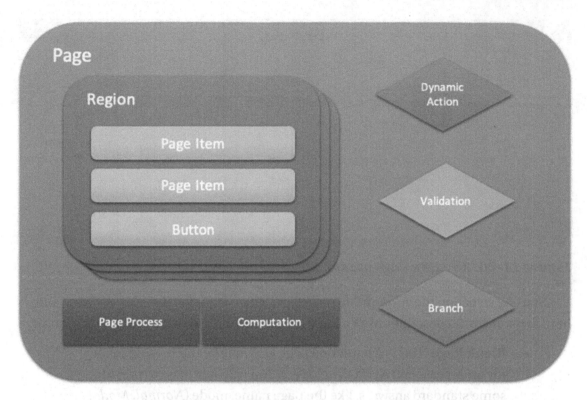

Figure 11-19. *Structure of an APEX page*

Pages

From the application's home page, creating a page is easy. Start by clicking the button *Create Page*. This triggers a wizard that will assist you in creating the page or pages, depending on the page type you select (Figure 11-20).

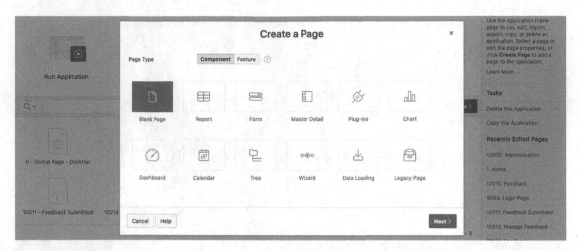

Figure 11-20. *Create a Page wizard*

Start by selecting the appropriate page type. There are several to choose from, and here are some brief descriptions of what they are and the use cases they intent to solve:

- **Blank Page**: This is a barebone page and may be the starting point for most seasoned APEX developers. You will only need to provide some standard answers, like the page name, mode (*Normal, Modal Dialog*, or *Non-Modal Dialog*) and whether to associate the page with a navigation menu entry. Page numbers are autogenerated and can be changed. However, they must be unique within an application. If you associate a navigation menu entry, it is added to an appropriate *List* linked to the application's active *Navigation Menu.*

- **Report**: The wizard walks through several steps to create a report page, one of which requires the developer to specify either a table, SQL query, *REST Enabled SQL Service*, or Web Source Module as a data source. There are several report types and formats to choose from. These reports are regularly associated with "form" pages to allow application users to manage records.

- **Form**: These work alongside report pages, but they are not required to. In some cases, users may want to edit data like in a spreadsheet application. In that case, developers can choose to create an *Editable Interactive Grid*. Together with report pages, they are perhaps the most common type of pages that you will create in an application.

- **Master Detail**: These pages are intended to manage records in tables with parent-child relationships. Most normalized database schemas will have these types of tables, and the master detail pages will greatly ease data entry and management for the application user.

- **Plug-ins**: Plug-ins will be discussed in a later segment, but to be clear, there are no page plug-ins. Selecting this page type will allow developers to select region type plug-in to be included in the page created.

- **Chart**: This option requires developers to specify the chart type that will be added as a region, the data source, and choose the appropriate columns to be used for the chart's data. These are great for situations where only one chart is required. However, most visualization use cases would include more than just a single chart.

- **Dashboard**: More than likely, if you wish to create data visualization pages, then you will want to include multiple charts. Dashboard page type only requests that you specify the preferred layout. It will create the chart regions and layout requested. Each chart will need to be configured by specifying the data source and mapping.

- **Calendar**: Selecting this creates a page with a calendar region. You will need to specify the data source and columns that will be mapped to render as content. The data source must include at least one column with date or timestamp data type.

- **Tree**: Trees are useful for both visualizing and navigating hierarchical data. However, they are better used alongside other components. This is a great starting point but expect to include more regions after the page is created. Like the chart and calendar page types, you will need to specify the data source and map the columns required to generate the tree.

- **Wizard**: Selecting this page type will walk you through a few simple steps to create a series of interlinked pages. Once the pages are created, you will need to customize the content and implement any additional validations, processes, and so on. Wizard pages are great examples for implementing multistep data collection workflows.

- **Data Loading**: This page type creates a series of wizard pages, modeled after APEX's own data loading features. The underlying data loading workflow is defined in the associated *Data Load Definition*. You might use this approach to assist application users to upload structured data, such as a spreadsheet. It is also worthwhile to note that in APEX release 19.1 and later, a new PL/SQL package APEX_DATA_PARSER allows you to create a single one-step data loading functionality on just about any page.

- **Legacy Page**: APEX evolved and improved over its long history. Older page types are deprecated but remain in the platform to maintain compatibility with older applications and give developers ample time to transition and update these older pages.

Note   APEX provides the option to create pages as a *Feature*. Selecting a feature would create the required pages and any other components required to support the functionality.

In APEX applications, there is a special *Global Page*, also commonly known as Page Zero, and there can only be one. If you accidentally delete it, you can create a new one when you click to create a page. The Global Page plays a unique role in the application. Inside, developers may create regions, page items, buttons, and dynamic actions, but you may not create any processes, validations, or branches. Any component you add to this page will appear on all pages, subject to applied rules, such as authorization schemes, build option, and server-side conditional logic. Global pages are a great place to share common components throughout the entire application.

Page Designer

Clicking any of the pages from the application home page will take you to the *Page Designer* (Figure 11-21).

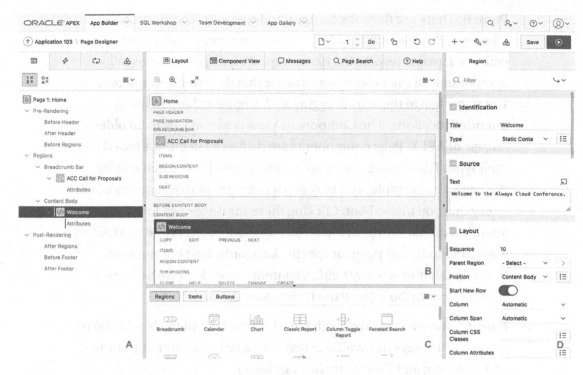

Figure 11-21. *The Page Designer layout*

At the top of the Page Designer, you will find buttons and items that you can use to navigate between pages, undo/redo actions, access page utilities, and more. Importantly, you will find buttons to save changes to the application and run the page.

By default, the Page Designer is broken into four panes. They are separated by adjustable splitters and may even be hidden by clicking the tiny chevrons found in the center of each splitter.

- **Pane A:** There are four tabs on this pane. The contents in these tab regions are displayed as a tree with collapsible branches. Right-clicking branches and nodes will further reveal more actions that you may perform, like creating additional components or managing existing ones. Under the tab *Rendering*, you may manage page components like regions, page items, buttons, processes, and more. You may switch between logically grouping them by processing order (default) or component type. The second tab lets you manage dynamic actions, and the third, other components involved in page validation, processing, and branching. The final tab lets you manage any shared components used, for example, *List of Values, Authorizations, Templates,* and so on.

- **Pane B**: There are five tabs on this pane – *Layout, Component View, Messages, Page Search*, and *Help*. Most developers work primarily with the Layout view. As the name implies, it displays the visual components in the positions and order that they will be rendered. You may change these by dragging and dropping them in the intended locations. The Component View is a legacy from an older release of APEX. Page components are displayed in groups based on their type. The Message tab displays errors and hints when editing the page. For example, you may add a component that requires a SQL query that you missed out. Clicking these messages will focus your attention on the source of the error. Page Search tab is one of a few ways to search your page for specific keywords. Last but not least, the Help tab displays any helpful content on working with the page component attribute (on Pane D) is selected.

- **Pane C**: This pane is only available when the Layout tab is selected in pane B. It displays the available regions, page items, and buttons that you may drag and drop onto the page layout.

- **Pane D**: When a component in either the Region tab on Pane A, Layout or Component View on Pane B is selected, its attributes are displayed in Pane D. For example, selecting a *Text Field* page item will allow you to change the field's label, its position and span on the region it is displayed in, or the template for rendering the item. There are typically many attributes, so make use of the grouping or filter function found on the top of the pane.

Developer Toolbar

When you run the application or page, it opens a new browser window or tab depending on the preference you set in the workspace. By default, the application runs with a *Developer Toolbar* that floats at the bottom of the page. You may change the position of the toolbar, make it auto hide or not display it at all by changing the application's build status.

Inside this toolbar, you will find easy access to return to the application's home page, or the Page Designer to edit the current page. There are also buttons to view the data stored for the current session. Clicking the *Debug* button reloads the page in the debug mode – a useful mode for tracking down potential issues during page execution. You can find useful trace messages by clicking the *View Debug* button. Last but not least, there are tools to make quick edits to the user interface and instantly preview the changes. The *Theme Roller* will be discussed in greater detail later in the chapter.

Regions

If an APEX page were a page on your local newspaper, then regions are blocks of text, photo inserts, and informational charts. There are a great variety of built-in regions that can be added to pages (Figure 11-22).

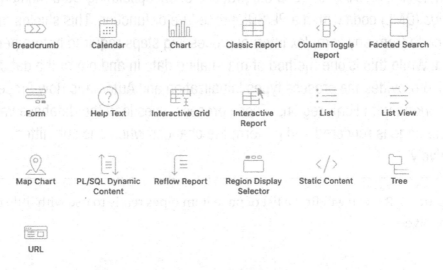

Figure 11-22. A grid displaying the available regions in APEX

While most regions have specialized functions to display content, they also act as canvases for placing page items. Regions also have attributes and you may access them on the expanded right pane. The attribute types vary, but generally, regions will allow developers to manipulate the region's appearance and layout on a page. Several of them, like *Interactive Grids*, *Chart*, and *Form*, are dependent on an association with a data source. This is an attribute that a developer would then need to either define declaratively and providing a SQL query, define a PL/SQL function that returns a SQL query, or specify a predefined *Web Source Module* (WSM). When specifying a data source declaratively, you may either select a local database object or a remote endpoint supporting *REST Enabled SQL*, a feature provided by *Oracle REST Data Services* (ORDS).

Page Items

Page items in APEX are the smallest units for interacting with data. They are linked to *session state*, which you may choose to persist over a single request, or in the database for as long as the session remains valid. You may refer to them in various points in the execution workflow or within dynamic actions, in order to execute the relevant business logic. For example, during page processing, you may create a process that uses a *Table API* to create or update a record.

Tip Table API, or *TAPI*, refers to the practice of encapsulating *Data Manipulation Language* (DML) code within a PL/SQL procedure or function. This shields the calling code from any complex internal processing steps required before persisting the data. While this is one method of marshaling data in and out of the database, APEX also provides the process types Initialization and Automatic Row Processing when working with Form regions. These process types load the database values when the page is rendered and perform the changes when it is submitted, respectively.

In Figure 11-23, you will find a list of page item types ready to use with little or no coding involved.

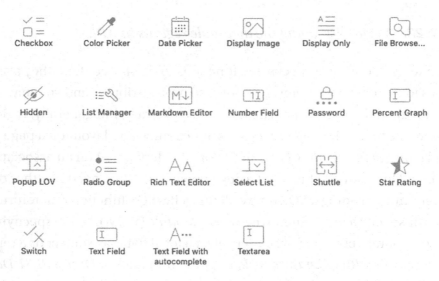

Figure 11-23. *A grid displaying available page item types in APEX*

Dynamic Actions

Dynamic actions (DAs) in APEX provide a declarative approach for defining the application's client-side behavior and response to user actions, such as changing value of a text field or toggling a radio button. Internally, the APEX engine generates the necessary JavaScript code to provide the interactivity on the browser.

Developers do have the option of writing their own JavaScript code to create more advanced behaviors. And to facilitate that, the framework also exposes a comprehensive JavaScript API. On top of that, you will have access to some rather powerful JavaScript libraries, such as *jQuery*, *D3.js*, and *Knockout.js*, which was introduced as part of the platform's support for *Oracle JET* (`https://oraclejet.com`).

Validations

Validations are conditional logic executed when the page is submitted with a request to execute validations. This will ensure data submitted through the page is valid. There are several methods for validating the data, and you may implement it using either SQL, PL/SQL, or declaratively. Depending on the validation approach adopted, the validation may return either a Boolean value or an error message, where a *NULL* return indicates valid input.

Page Processes

Page Processes may run at different points of the page execution workflow. They often embody business logic that might involve processing user inputs, moving data in and out of the database or changing the application's session variables. Some examples of how page processes can be used include the following:

- Executing a page process, before a page is rendered, that uses submitted parameters from a previous page and uses it to filter and retrieve values from a table.

- When the page is submitted, execute a PL/SQL function to calculate a value based on the user's input, and then save that value in the database.

- Triggered by a dynamic action, call an *AJAX* process to update a database record and then refresh an Interactive report, without needing to submit the page.

Computations

Computations are like page processes, but are used primarily for initializing page item values, usually before the page is rendered, but could be after. When creating computations, the two main tasks are as follows:

1. Specify the target page item.

2. Select the computation type and provide the appropriate value.

Branches

Last but not least, pages may contain *Branches*. These encapsulate the page flow logic and may be triggered before or after a page is submitted. Like page processes though, they are typically used after the page is submitted and page processes are completed.

Theming

The "look and feel" of APEX applications is defined by *Themes*. In older versions, APEX had several included in all installations; however, the product development team had since focused on maintaining a single *Universal Theme* (`https://apex.oracle.com/ut`).

This theme is responsive and compliant with accessibility standards. It is also easy to customize to meet corporate branding requirements using the *Theme Roller* (Figure 11-24).

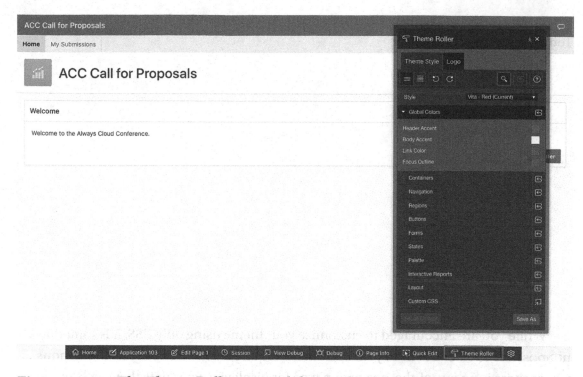

Figure 11-24. *The Theme Roller is a tool that makes it easy to customize the "look and feel" of the application*

There are many aspects of the UI that can be changed to modify the aesthetics of the application. These are primarily colors and sizes of the various UI components like the box that skirts the APEX regions, buttons, and many more. For anything else, there is the *Custom CSS*, where you might override existing CSS classes or create new ones. And note that as you work on all these changes, the page previews the changes "live," giving you immediate feedback without needing to go back and forth with saving and refreshing the site to validate your work. When you are done tweaking the UI, save the style and set it as the current (active) style.

Note   There is great emphasis on accessibility compliance. When choosing colors, the tool provides a contrast score and validates if it meets the *Web Content Accessibility Guidelines* (WCAG). Any color selection that does not meet these standards is immediately flagged with a warning.

Besides styles, a theme is also made up of templates for the different UI components. Templates can be created for

- Pages

- Regions

- Reports

- Labels

- Lists

- Buttons

- Breadcrumbs

- Legacy Calendars

- Pop-ups

While you are encouraged to customize your theme using only CSS, it is sometimes not possible to cater the UI to your customer's requirements. There are also situations where there is no out-of-the-box region type for displaying your data that can be easily rendered using a *Class Report* with a custom template. If there is a need to customize templates for your application, avoid unsubscribing the theme and overriding any built-in templates. Rather, you should create new ones so that you can patch your theme with updates and fixes when a new APEX release becomes available. Templates can be found under the application's shared components.

Earlier in this chapter, we had also talked about the many attributes of an APEX region. These are also found when working with other elements like page items and buttons. Attributes relating to themes can be found under the group *Appearance*, where you can select the desired template to use and change any *Template Options*. The latter can also be tweaked using the *Quick Edit* feature found on the developer toolbar (Figure 11-25).

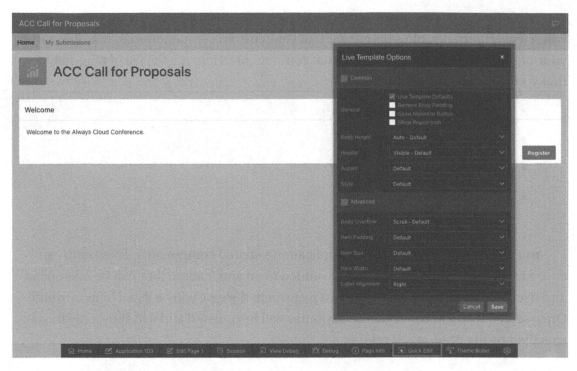

Figure 11-25. *The Quick Edit feature in the developer toolbar lets developers tweak template options and preview the changes instantly*

When working with themes, documentation is your friend. On the Universal Theme website shared earlier, you will find extensive write-up on all built-in UI components, samples, and tools that will help you with your application's visual makeover.

Plug-ins

APEX is more than a low-code development platform, and that's what makes it appealing. While the built-in regions and page items cover the majority of use cases, sometimes, they are not enough. Fortunately, APEX has an extensible framework that lets developers create custom modules that can be "plugged in" very easily. Backed by a strong global community, many such plug-ins are available to download and use, often without needing to pay a fee. You can find a comprehensive listing on the *apex.world* website (*https://apex.world*).

While you are encouraged to share any plug-ins you build, you do not have to. Even when used internally, plug-ins ensure that your custom components are reusable within your organization. And it isn't just visual components. Here is a full list of plug-in types that you can create and use:

- Authentication Scheme

- Authorization Scheme

- Item

- Process

- Region

You will find plug-ins under an application's shared components. There, you can either create or import a plug-in. Once added to an application, they can be referenced and used, for example, when you add a page item, the type will be listed in its attribute. Once selected, the item's available attributes will be updated and will show only those specified by the plug-in's developer.

Web Source Modules

When extensibility is discussed, we often think of application components and processes. One other issue that needs to be discussed is integration with external systems. These days, interoperability between various applications and platforms is through the use of web services, or more specifically, RESTful web services.

APEX has provided developers an easy way to work with RESTful web services for quite a while, mainly through the use of its `APEX_WEB_SERVICE` PL/SQL API. It supports both *Simple Object Access Protocol* (SOAP) and *Representational State Transfer* (REST) protocols, and the API includes support for service authentication using a limited number of OAuth grant types. You also have the option of creating *Web Service References* that will allow you to easily link components like reports to a REST endpoint.

WSM is a new feature release with APEX version 18.1 and supersedes the Web Service References. It introduces a seamless integration of the REST service and APEX components. This allows you to both render data and update records like you would with a local data source. Another benefit of using WSM is the support for OAuth2 authentication and, in release 19.2, generating *Request Signatures* required to call *Oracle Cloud Infrastructure* (OCI) REST APIs. The latter allows you to easily work with OCI objects, for example, storing files in the *Object Store*.

> **Note**   As part of the security enhancement strategy undertaken by Autonomous Databases, all outgoing network requests must be protected by a secure transport layer. For web service calls must be made using HTTPS. In an Oracle Database, a successful SSL/TLS connection requires certificate verification that is performed with the use of *Oracle Wallets*. In the ADB, a majority of all known root certificates have been added to the shared wallet, and so, most web resources using certificates signed by a recognized *Certificate Authority* will connect successfully. Self-signed certificates will **not** work!

Email Support

The APEX_MAIL API allows APEX applications to send emails. To do so, the instance must be configured with the correct *Simple Mail Transfer Protocol* (SMTP) information. Unlike in a traditional Oracle Database, the instance settings that administrators have access to are limited in an ADB. The SMTP settings can be modified but are not available through the APEX *Administration Services*. They must be set using the APEX_INSTANCE_ADMIN API, specifically the APEX_INSTANCE_ADMIN.SET_PARAMETER procedure, for example:

```
begin
  apex_instance_admin.set_parameter(
    p_parameter => 'SMTP_HOST_ADDRESS'
    , p_value => 'smtp.us-ashburn-1.oraclecloud.com'
  );
  commit;
end;
```

The parameter names associated with SMTP server settings are list in Table 11-1.

Table 11-1. *List of SMTP-related parameters*

Parameter Name	Description
SMTP_HOST_ADDRESS	SMTP server address
SMTP_HOST_PORT	SMTP server port number
SMTP_TLS_MODE	The connection's encryption mode
SMTP_USERNAME	SMTP server username for connecting to the server
SMTP_PASSWORD	Password for the username specified

However, while the platform supports sending emails, there are limitations with an Autonomous Database to consider. To secure the platform, you may only use the OCI *Email Delivery Service* SMTP servers to send emails. Unfortunately, you will need to upgrade to a paid account to use these services. It isn't expensive, but Oracle will need a credit card to bill for emails sent through its servers.

Deployment Strategy

As we come to the end of this quick APEX overview, there is one last critical issue I would like to address. A question I often ask when learning a new programming language or framework is: "How do we deploy the application in production?" It is extremely important that we are able to take our product and reproduce it across multiple stages of deployment, from development, to test and then onto production. And it is good practice, in my opinion, to have separation of roles in a software development team. As developers, we need to be able to describe and document clearly what the deployment process is, so that another person on the team is able to deploy the application and any changes in the destination environment.

For APEX, this process depends on your organization's approach to development. In its simplest form, an APEX application can embody all the code and static file resources. Deployment would then simply involve exporting the application into a single SQL file and then importing it to the target server. However, as our APEX development skills mature, we should consider the following:

- Capture business logic in PL/SQL packages that can be stored in a file and eventually checked into a version control system such as *Git* or *SVN*. Keep the amount of PL/SQL code to a minimum, usually only for marshaling data between the session state and database.

- While it is tempting to use a tool like SQL Developer to manage the database objects, it is recommended that any *Data Definition Language* (DDL) statements be written in files.

- As with PL/SQL code, we should attempt to keep complex JavaScript code out of APEX and organize them in files. These files can then be deployed either in the *Static Application Files* or on a web server for performance.

Exporting and Importing

There are a few ways to export and import APEX applications:

- App Builder

- SQL Developer

- SQLcl

Of the three, the most straightforward method to deploy the application is to use the App Builder. However, using a tool like SQLcl can be a great way to automate deployments for consistency and productivity. Deploying applications could simply be executing a single, well-written SQL script that calls dependent scripts that create or modify database objects, compile PL/SQL packages, and even install the APEX application.

Supporting Objects

Running SQL scripts using a command-line interface isn't everyone's cup of tea. For that reason, APEX development team has been delivering productivity applications that can be installed with a click of a button. This is made possible by Supporting Objects. If you have dutifully created DDL and other scripts to create the dependent database objects, then the next steps are simple. You can add these as installation, upgrade, and deinstallation scripts to the supporting objects before exporting them for your clients. On their end, all they need to do is import the applications and then install the supporting objects to have a fully functional application.

The Call for Proposals Application

Armed with knowledge about APEX, let us now examine what's involved in creating a simple web application in record time!

In Chapter 10, we discussed the data model and generated the database entities needed for the *Always Cloud Conference Call for Proposals* (CfP) website. The code for this chapter can be found in the book's GitHub code repository at *https://github.com/ Apress/getting-started-w-oracle-cloud-free-tier/tree/master/ch11*. Before we begin though, log in to the database as the *admin* user, and execute the following:

```
grant execute on dbms_crypto to ocftconf;
```

This provides the grant necessary to compile the packages.

Next, compile all package specifications and bodies found in the directory `packages`. As its name implies, the package `user_security` provides functions and procedures for security-related code. This includes a method for securely hashing passwords, authenticating users, and performing any post-authentication actions, while the `user_admin` package is responsible for creating users and assigning the *ADMIN* role to a specified user. The compilation of these packages may also be performed by simply executing the script `release/release.sql`.

Last but not least, there are two additional scripts in the subdirectory `scripts` that will assist you in staging sample records for users and proposals. Just remember to commit any changes.

With the dependent database objects created, let us now proceed to create the application beginning from the App Builder home page; click the *Create* button and then *New Application* on the next page. As you might recall, this launches the *Create Application Wizard*, from where you can quickly customize your new application (Figure 11-26).

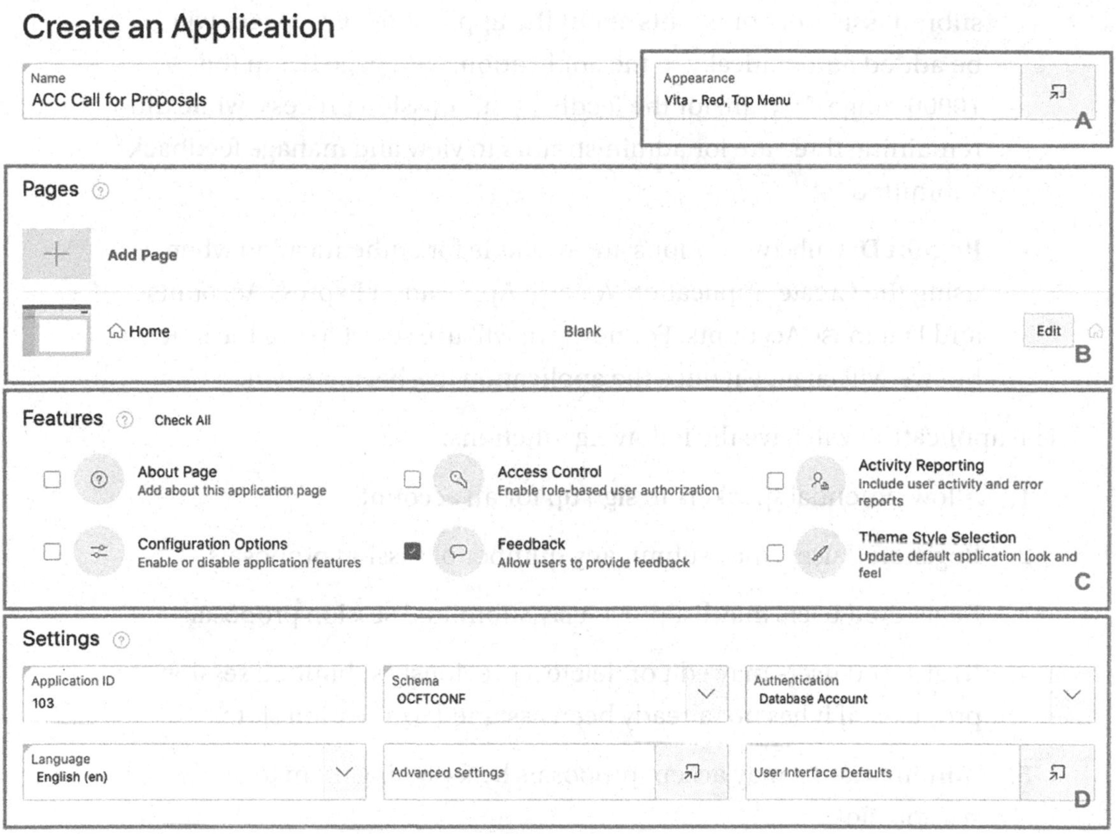

Create an Application

Name
ACC Call for Proposals

Appearance
Vita - Red, Top Menu

A

Pages ⍰

＋ Add Page

⌂ Home   Blank   Edit ⌂

B

Features ⍰   Check All

☐ ⍰ **About Page**
Add about this application page

☐ 🔍 **Access Control**
Enable role-based user authorization

☐ 👥 **Activity Reporting**
Include user activity and error reports

☐ ⚌ **Configuration Options**
Enable or disable application features

☑ 💬 **Feedback**
Allow users to provide feedback

☐ ✎ **Theme Style Selection**
Update default application look and feel

C

Settings ⍰

Application ID
103

Schema
OCFTCONF ⌄

Authentication
Database Account ⌄

Language
English (en) ⌄

Advanced Settings ⤢

User Interface Defaults ⤢

D

Figure 11-26. *Create Application Wizard*

Here are some changes that we can make for the CfP website:

- **Region A**: For this application, we have opted for the *Vita – Red* theme style with the navigation menu located at the top of all pages.

- **Region B**: By default, APEX will add a Home page with no content regions. Here, you may add pages with a choice of page types and a corresponding wizard to help set them up. We left this unchanged in the example.

- **Region C**: Oracle provides several common features that are found in web applications. Everyone has different approaches for implementing these types of features that are completely optional to add. In the example application, we chose to adopt one of these and added the *Feedback* functionality. Feedback, as previously mentioned in this chapter, provides built-in support for users to submit issues or comments about the application. Five pages will be added automatically to the application, with page IDs in the 10000 range. Two are for the feedback submission process, while the remaining three are for administrators to view and manage feedback submitted.

- **Region D**: Only two options are available for authentication when using the Create Application Wizard: Application Express Accounts and Database Accounts. For now, we will use select to use the latter, but we will change it once the application has been created.

The application will have the following functions:

1. Allow potential speakers to sign up for an account.

2. Registered users may submit any number of session proposals.

3. Registered users may list previously submitted session proposals.

4. Registered users may edit or delete a previously submitted session proposal, if it has not already been assigned to a session slot.

5. Administrators may accept proposals by assigning them to a session slot.

Public Pages

By default, any page created by APEX will require authentication. However, at times, we might want some pages to be accessible by anyone on the Internet. For example, on the ACC CfP home page, we might want to publish some information about the event, submission criteria and deadlines, and so on. We want our reach to be as wide as possible.

To make a page public, please do the following:

1. Go to the application's home page. That should list all available pages using an Interactive report. You may choose to view the pages as a grid or table, change the sort order, or choose the number of rows to view at once. When you find the page you wish to edit, click the page name.

2. On the Page Designer, the page will be initially selected, exposing its attributes on the right pane. Filter on the keyword "authentication". There should only be one attribute named *Authentication*, and it has two options: *Page Requires Authentication* or *Page is Public*. Select the latter and then click the *Save* button.

In this application, there are four other pages that will require this attribute:

- **Page 2**: User Registration (to be created)

- **Page 9999**: Login Page

- **Page 10010**: Feedback

- **Page 10011**: Feedback Submitted

The Login Page was created by APEX when the application was provisioned and should already be set as a public page. We want anyone to be able to submit feedback, so do the same for the two pages that were autogenerated when we enabled the feedback feature. As for the User Registration page, we can set this when the page is created next.

User Registration

All proposals must be linked to the user. Hence, users must log in before they are allowed to submit one. The User Registration page will be used to collect basic information about the potential speaker and then create the account. Let's create the page.

1. From the application's home page, click the *Create Page* button.

2. Click the Form type, which will bring you to the next step automatically. Click *Form* again.

3. In the next step, the page number should be "2". Enter the page name *User Registration* and then select *Modal Dialog* for the page mode. Click *Next* to proceed.

4. We will launch this modal page from a button on the website's home page, so select *Do not associate the page with a navigation menu entry*, and then click *Next*.

5. You will be asked to select a *Data Source* next. Select *Local Database* and the source type *Table*. Ensure the correct owner is selected and then use the pop-up search dialog to pick the USERS table. Click *Next* to proceed.

6. Not all the details in the USERS table require the user's input. Use the directional buttons to move columns and leave the ones required on the right. The following are the required fields:

   a. USERNAME

   b. USER_PASSWORD

   c. FIRST_NAME

   d. LAST_NAME

   e. EMAIL_ADDRESS

   f. AGREE_TO_TERMS_YN

7. Finally, choose *Select Primary Key Column(s)* for the primary key type, select USER_ID for the primary key column, and then click *Create*.

The User Registration needs to be public. When the page is created, you will be redirected to the Page Designer. Set the page's authentication attribute to public and save the changes.

We will need the user to confirm the submitted password. Under the Rendering tab on the left pane, right click the generated page item *P2_USER_PASSWORD* and click *Duplicate* (Figure 11-27).

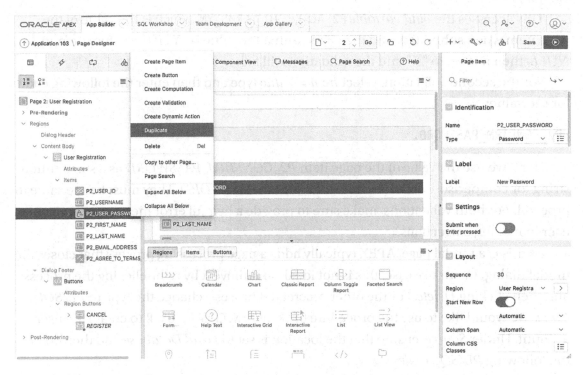

Figure 11-27. *Duplicate a page item*

The new page item should appear just underneath. Rename it to *P2_CONFIRM_ PASSWORD*. Also, delete the *UPDATE* and *DELETE* buttons, and then rename the *CREATE* button to *REGISTER*. The label on the button would be updated automatically.

For the page item P2_AGREE_TO_TERMS_YN, we would like the users to indicate their acceptance of the website's policies before the account can be created. First, change the page item type to *Switch*. By default, the switch will be configured to use its *Component Settings*, and it sets the value to either "Y" or "N", which is what we require.

Next, we will need to add two validations. The first is a check that the user has accepted the terms, so *P2_AGREE_TO_TERMS_YN* must return a value of "Y", and the second checks that the passwords entered by the user match. To add a validation, go to the Processing tab on the left pane, right-click validations, and then click *Create Validation*.

For the first validation, set the type to *PL/SQL Expression* and add the following code:

```
coalesce(:P2_AGREE_TO_TERMS_YN, 'N') = 'Y'
```

This accesses the *bind variable* P2_AGREE_TO_TERMS_YN, which is the value of the page item when submitted, and then checks that the value is "Y". If the value is empty or *NULL*, then it is set to "N" and the validation will fail.

For the second validation, select *Item = Value* type and then enter the following code for the value:

```
&P2_CONFIRM_PASSWORD.
```

Here, we use the value of the page item *P2_CONFIRM_PASSWORD* as a substitution string for comparison with the value in *P2_USER_PASSWORD*. They must be the same to proceed. For both validations, make sure to provide a helpful error message to assist the user in making corrections.

As this is a modal page, APEX typically adds a page processing process that closes the modal dialog. In our use case, this is not ideal, so remove it by right-clicking the process and then clicking *Delete*. For the other precreated process, change the type to *PL/SQL Code*. We would like to use the procedure USER_ADMIN.CREATE_USER to create the user account. Under *Source*, ensure that the location is set to *Local Database* and then enter the following *PL/SQL Code*:

```
user_admin.create_user(
    p_username => :P2_USERNAME
    , p_password => :P2_USER_PASSWORD
    , p_password_repeat => :P2_CONFIRM_PASSWORD
    , p_first_name => :P2_FIRST_NAME
    , p_last_name => :P2_LAST_NAME
    , p_email_address => :P2_EMAIL_ADDRESS
    , p_agree_to_terms => :P2_AGREE_TO_TERMS_YN
    , p_user_id => :P2_USER_ID
);
```

This procedure ensures that the user's password is hashed based on the algorithm specified in USER_SECURITY.HASH_PASSWORD before it is stored in the database.

Finally, add a *Success Message* and *Error Message* to the process, and then create an *After Processing* branch that redirects the browser to the home page. For both the process and branch, we want to ensure that they only happen when the *REGISTER* button is clicked. Under *Server-side Condition*, select REGISTER for the attribute *When Button Pressed*.

Authentication Scheme

We will be using the credentials stored in the USERS table and the function USER_SECURITY.AUTHENTICATE_USER to authenticate users to the application. Go to the application's shared components and click *Authentication Schemes*, and then do the following:

1. Click the *Create* button.

2. Select *Based on a pre-configured scheme from the gallery* and then click *Next*.

3. Enter a name, for example, *ACC Accounts*, and then select the scheme type *Custom*. This will reveal additional fields (Figure 11-28).

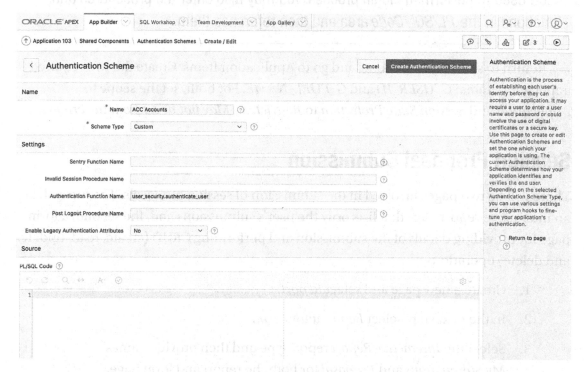

Figure 11-28. *Required information to create a Custom authentication scheme*

4. In the *Authentication Function Name* field, enter the value: user_security.authenticate_user. This function will be called whenever users submit their credentials to sign in.

5.   Scroll further down, and then in the *Post-Authentication Procedure Name* field, enter the value: user_security.post_login. This procedure will be called after each successful login. It is responsible for obtaining additional information about the user and then set the *Application Items G_USER_ID* and *G_FULL_NAME*.

6.   Finally, click the button *Create Authentication Scheme*. This will not only create the authentication scheme but also set it as the current/active scheme.

Note   The authentication scheme does not require developers to package the code used to perform the login process. You may also enter the procedures and functions in the *PL/SQL Code* area and then reference them.

Return to shared components and go to Application Items. Create the two required application items: *G_USER_ID* and *G_FULL_NAME*. For both, set the scope to *Application* and *Session State Protection* to *Restricted - May not be set from the browser*.

Session Proposal Submission

There will be two pages involved in the submission of session proposals. The first will be an interactive report page that lists **only** the user's submissions and, the second, a form page for providing details of the submission and performing CRUD (create, read, update, and delete) operations.

1.   Create a new page and select *Report*.

2.   In the next step, select *Report with Form*.

3.   Select the *Interactive Report* report type and then provide names *My Submissions* and *Proposal* for both the report and form page, respectively. The page numbers should be "3" and "4," and for the *Form Page Mode*, select *Modal Dialog*.

4.   On the next page, select *Create a new navigation menu entry* for the *Navigation Preference*. We want a link to the report page displayed on the top navigation bar.

5. The next step involves selecting a Data Source for the interactive report. Choose *Local Database* and then select the PROPOSALS table. Only choose the following columns to render:

   a. PROPOSAL_ID

   b. TITLE

   c. ABSTRACT

   d. CREATED_ON

   e. UPDATED_ON

6. You will also need to specify the columns to be displayed as fields on the form page. Choose only the following:

   a. SPEAKER_ID

   b. TITLE

   c. ABSTRACT

   d. ADDITIONAL_DETAILS

   e. SPEAKER_BIO

7. Finally, select the primary key column PROPOSAL_ID and then click *Create*.

We will need to tweak these pages. For the My Submissions report page, we should hide the *PROPOSAL_ID* column as it is used only for navigating to the form page and setting the requested primary key on the form page. Search for the column on the left pane, under the Rendering tab. You may have to expand the tree nodes to reveal the columns. Click *PROPOSAL_ID* to display its attributes on the right pane, and then change the value of *Type* to *Hidden Column*. Save your changes when done.

Since this page should only show the authenticated user's submissions, we should add a filter to restrict the rows returned. We can do that by setting the report's *Where Clause* attribute. You will find it under the *Source* attribute group. Add the following code:

```
speaker_id = :G_USER_ID
```

When creating a proposal, the `speaker_id` column value is set to the application item *G_USER_ID* value. *G_USER_ID* was set during the post-login process.

Next, go to Page 4, the *Proposal* form page. Tweak the page items as desired. For example, APEX may have selected the page item type *Textarea* based on the database column size. We might change that to *Text Field* instead. And the other item that needs to be modified is *P4_SPEAKER_ID*. When creating a proposal, the session state for all page items on this page is cleared. We should set the default value of *P4_SPEAKER_ID* to *G_USER_ID*. We can do that by setting the attributes under *Default*. Change the *Type* to *Item*, and for the *Item* value, set it to *G_USER_ID*.

When a proposal is accepted, it will be assigned a session slot, and this is recorded in the SLOTS table, by storing the proposal's primary key in the column SESSION_ID. Once accepted, we do not want the author to modify any of the fields. We can make use of the relationship between tables to restrict further edits.

In APEX, pages can be specified as *Read Only*. For our use case, select the *Rows returned* type and then provide the following SQL query:

```
select null
from slots
where session_id = :P4_PROPOSAL_ID
```

When the condition is met, all page items are immediately "disabled," regardless of any page item–level conditions. For example, a *Text Field* will be rendered as a *Display Only* page item. However, we will also want to ensure that the *SAVE* and *DELETE* buttons are not displayed. Select both items by clicking one, and then clicking the other with the *Shift* key pressed. Both buttons should appear as selected (Figure 11-29).

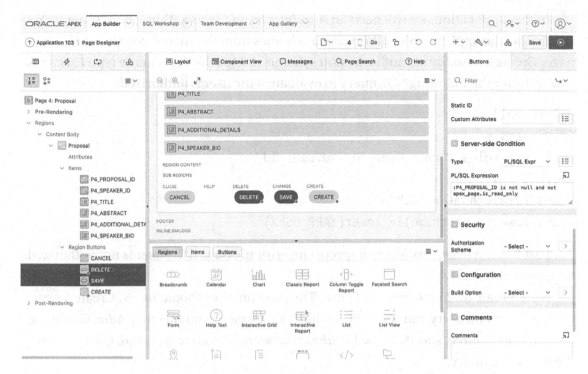

Figure 11-29. *Select multiple page items to edit common attributes*

On the right pane, either scroll down or filter to find the *Server-side Condition* attributes. Choose the type *PL/SQL Expression* and then enter the following code:

```
:P4_PROPOSAL_ID is not null and not apex_page.is_read_only
```

The APEX_PAGE.IS_READ_ONLY function returns true if the page is marked read only, based on the conditions we specified earlier.

Session Scheduler

The final use case that we need to implement is to allow the application's administrators to assign session proposals to available timeslots. First, we will need to define who these administrators are. We did not create a UI component to perform the assignments, but you may do so with the PL/SQL procedure USER_ADMIN.MAKE_ADMIN.

In this application, we will need an *Administration Rights* authorization scheme. You can access the application's authorization schemes from the shared components home page. Create or modify the authorization scheme and specify the scheme type *Exists SQL Query*. Enter the following SQL query to evaluate if the user is authorized:

```
select null
from users u
join user_roles r on r.user_id = u.user_id
where 1 = 1
  and r.role_name = 'ADMIN'
  and lower(u.username) = lower(:APP_USER)
```

Last but not least, provide an appropriate error message if the user is not authorized. Save your changes.

Next, create an *Interactive Grid* page. The page number should be "5". Create a new navigation menu entry, but this time, assign it to the parent menu entry *Administration*. For the Data Source, specify *Local Database* but with the source type *SQL Query*. Enter the following query:

```
select
  slot_id
  , session_id
  , title
  , description
  , session_start
  , session_end
  , location
from slots
```

Last but not least, set the switch to "On" for the item *Editing Enabled*, and then click the button *Create* to complete the process. Once created, modify the following:

1. Set *SLOT_ID* column type to *Hidden*.

2. Change the *SESSION_ID* type to *Popup LOV*, and under the *List of Values*, set the attributes *Type* to *SQL Query* and provide the following code:

```
select
  p.title || ' submitted by ' || u.first_name
    || ' ' || u.last_name as session_title
  , p.proposal_id
from proposals p
left join users u on u.user_id = p.speaker_id
order by p.title
```

3. In the interactive grid's attributes, set the *Allowed Operations* to only *Update Row*.

4. Save your changes.

This concludes our quick-start tutorial on creating a working APEX application. If you encounter any issues, the application export is also available in the code repository, under the chapter's apex subdirectory. It isn't perfect, and there are certainly much more that can be done to improve the features, usability, and security of the application. Hopefully though, it has touched on enough APEX features to inspire you to learn more.

Summary

APEX is touted as both a low code and rapid application development platform, and it truly is. As software developers, we are often tempted to use the latest web application frameworks, even when they require complex architectural decisions. However, we have to remember that our primary goal should always be concerned with delivering a usable and cost-effective solution for our customers. APEX allows us to create modern web applications quickly and effectively.

However, let's be clear, this platform isn't simply a spreadsheet replacement. Support for industry standards like OAuth2 and REST makes this a compelling tool for creating enterprise-ready applications. There is so much more to learn about APEX, and I sincerely hope that you will check out the wealth of information online, engage the community, and, more importantly, get your hands dirty creating really cool APEX applications with your Always Free Autonomous Database.

CHAPTER 12

Oracle REST Data Services

Since the dawn of distributed computing, there have been many different protocols designed to help disparate systems communicate and interoperate. Some were proprietary, while others were developed through industrial standards bodies. The latter are programming language agnostic but are often slow to develop as they generally consist of members that are otherwise competitors. Older protocols involved heavy use of markup languages, and many popular frameworks required developers to generate client stubs for marshaling data.

In his 2000 doctoral dissertation, Roy Fielding proposed a simple approach for designing interoperable distributed systems that relied on the ubiquitous *Hypertext Transfer Protocol* (HTTP). *Representational State Transfer* (REST) dictated that the state of a web-based entity or resource, located by its *Uniform Resource Identifier* (URI), could be created, retrieved, manipulated, or removed by providing a suitable *request method* in the call. The request may also contain HTTP headers, parameters, and/or content body for server-side processing. A RESTful web service may respond with an appropriate HTTP status code and/or payload in an agreed format. This may be text-based *JavaScript Object Notation* (JSON), XML, or any other formats.

Oracle Application Express (APEX) is a rapid application development environment that relies on PL/SQL to generate dynamic HTML content that then renders on the user's web browser. This powerful PL/SQL engine runs within the Oracle Database and so relies on an additional component to relay browser requests and database responses. Early APEX adopters either used *Oracle HTTP Server* (OHS) with *mod_plsql* or the *Embedded PL/SQL Gateway* that runs in *Oracle XML DB Protocol Server*. To replace these older technologies, Oracle released a *Java Enterprise Edition* (Java EE) solution initially named *APEX Listener*, but later renamed *Oracle REST Data Services* (ORDS) when the third version of the software was released. This new release came with support for RESTful Web Services.

© Adrian Png and Luc Demanche 2020
A. Png and L. Demanche, *Getting Started with Oracle Cloud Free Tier*,
https://doi.org/10.1007/978-1-4842-6011-1_12

Getting Started

ORDS comes preinstalled with every *Autonomous Database* (ADB), so you can create RESTful Web Services from the get-go. However, in order for these services to be created in your schemas, they must first be REST-enabled.

Earlier in Chapter 10, we had already REST-enabled the *OCFTCONF* schema that allowed us to access *SQL Developer Web*. To recap, you may enable the schema using this PL/SQL block statement:

```
declare
  c_schema_name constant varchar2(8) := 'ocftconf';
  c_schema_alias constant varchar2(8) := 'accapi';
begin
  ords_admin.enable_schema(
    p_enabled => true
    , p_schema => c_schema_name
    , p_url_mapping_type => 'BASE_PATH'
    , p_url_mapping_pattern => c_schema_alias
    , p_auto_rest_auth => true
  );
  commit;
end;
/
```

Alternatively, you may do this from the APEX workspace (see Chapter 11 on how to get access). Go to *SQL Workshop* and then click the *RESTful Services* icon. The console will notify you if the schema is not REST-enabled (Figure 12-1).

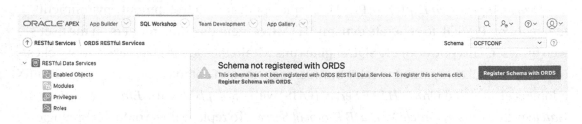

Figure 12-1. *REST-enable a schema from the APEX workspace*

Click Register Schema with ORDS to REST-enable the schema. Provide the required information to proceed (Figure 12-2).

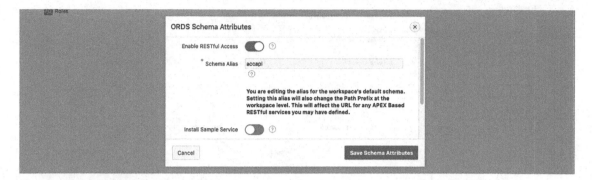

Figure 12-2. *Set the ORDS schema attributes*

Ensure that the field *Enable RESTful Access* is turned on and then provide the *Schema Alias*. You may optionally install the sample services and require authorization for access to the ORDS metadata catalog for the schema. The latter is recommended for securing the schema.

Note   Changing a previously set schema alias also affects access to SQL Developer Web. Update the personalized URL if necessary.

Once enabled, you will have access to the dashboard that provides an overview of the number of modules, privileges, roles, and schema objects that are *autorest-enabled* (Figure 12-3).

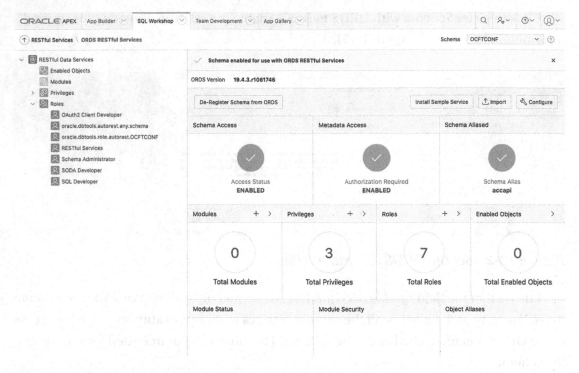

Figure 12-3. *The ORDS RESTful Services dashboard*

The third method for REST-enabling schemas is *via SQL Developer*. Create a connection to the database using the desired schema and then connect to it. Right-click the connection and place the mouse cursor over the menu item REST Services to expose more menu items (Figure 12-4).

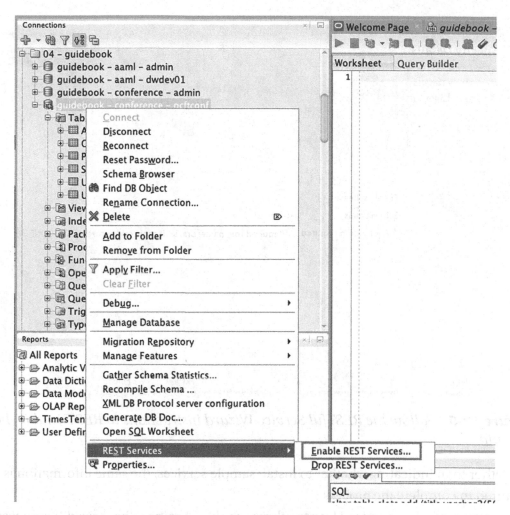

Figure 12-4. *REST-enable a schema using SQL Developer*

Click the *Enable REST Services* menu item to launch the *RESTful Services Wizard* (Figure 12-5).

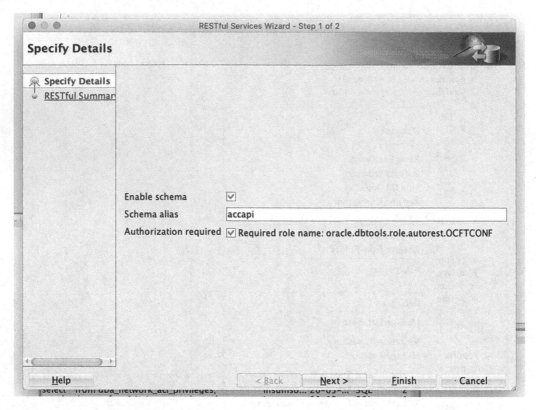

Figure 12-5. *Follow the RESTful Service Wizard instructions to REST-enable the schema*

Other than indicating whether to install sample services, the same information is required to complete the process.

As you might have noticed by now, there are always going to be three different ways to manage ORDS RESTful Services:

1.   Running PL/SQL block statements using a suitable database client

2.   Through a web browser by ORDS RESTful Services console in the APEX workspaces

3.   Using SQL Developer on the desktop

For the rest of the chapter, we will focus on using PL/SQL block statements as it is the best approach for ensuring that code is properly managed using a suitable version control system. However, we will also look at how we can view/manage these services through the APEX workspace.

ORDS RESTful Service

An ORDS REST Service consists of the following components:

- Module

- Resource Template

- Resource Handler

A schema may have zero or more modules defined, but module names must be unique. Each module contains one or more resource templates, and each template has one or more resource handlers.

Before defining the service, create the following database view that we will use to generate the results for the web services:

```
create or replace view vw_sessions
as
  select
    s.slot_id
    , coalesce(p.title, s.description) as title
    , p.abstract
    , u.first_name as speaker_first_name
    , u.last_name as speaker_last_name
    , s.session_start
    , s.session_end
    , cast(s.session_start as timestamp with local time zone)
        at time zone 'UTC' as session_start_utc
    , cast(s.session_end as timestamp with local time zone)
        at time zone 'UTC' as session_end_utc
    , s.location
  from slots s
  left join proposals p on p.proposal_id = s.session_id
  left join users u on u.user_id = p.speaker_id
  order by session_start
;
```

REST Module

After creating the view, define a resource module using the following code:

```
begin
  ords.define_module(
    p_module_name => 'schedule.v1'
    , p_base_path => '/schedule/v1/'
    , p_items_per_page => 25
    , p_status => 'PUBLISHED'
    , p_comments => null
  );

  commit;
end;
/
```

The procedure *DEFINE_MODULE* to create a REST module is defined in the *ORDS_ METADATA* schema, in a package aptly named *ORDS*. It requires a name and base path. Some API developers prefer to introduce a path that contains a semantic version number. The p_items_per_page indicates the number of rows to return when returning the JSON-formatted result set from a SQL query. The default value is *25*. The p_status indicates the module's current publication status. Valid values are PUBLISHED (default) and NOT_PUBLISHED. Comments are optional.

Resource Template

Next, define the templates. We will define two, one for listing all available sessions and another to return a session specified by the primary key in the URI. Execute the following code:

```
begin
  ords.define_template(
    p_module_name => 'schedule.v1'
    , p_pattern => 'session/'
    , p_priority => 0
    , p_etag_type => 'HASH'
```

```
    , p_etag_query => null
    , p_comments => null
);

ords.define_template(
  p_module_name => 'schedule.v1'
  , p_pattern => 'session/:session_id'
  , p_priority => 0
  , p_etag_type => 'HASH'
  , p_etag_query => null
  , p_comments => null
);

commit;
end;
/
```

An entity tag is used in the HTTP protocol to help clients determine the currency of the web resource and it is embedded in the HTTP response header. ORDS provides three options:

- **HASH**: Generate the ETag using a secure digest of the contents returned by the web resource

- **QUERY**: Generate the ETag using a query defined in p_etag_query

- **NONE**: Do not generate an ETag

Resource Handler

One or more handlers can be defined per template. A handler needs to specify a HTTP method that it supports. Valid values are as follows:

- **GET**: Retrieves the attributes about the resource

- **POST**: Either creates a new resource or adds one to a collection

- **PUT**: Updates the attributes of an existing resources

- **DELETE**: Removes an existing resource from the database

Choose a method that aligns with the intent of the handler, for example, a *GET* when retrieving data about the resource and *POST* when creating a resource. Only **one** handler of each HTTP method is allowed per template.

Execute the following code to create a GET handler for the two defined templates, and a module handler parameter for capturing the session identifier:

```
begin
  ords.define_handler(
    p_module_name => 'schedule.v1'
    , p_pattern => 'session/'
    , p_method => 'GET'
    , p_source_type => ords.source_type_collection_feed
    , p_items_per_page => 25
    , p_mimes_allowed => null
    , p_comments => null
    , p_source => q'~
select
  slot_id as session_id
, title
, abstract
, speaker_first_name
, speaker_last_name
, session_start
, session_end
, location
from vw_sessions
    ~'
  );

  ords.define_handler(
    p_module_name => 'schedule.v1'
    , p_pattern => 'session/:session_id'
    , p_method => 'GET'
    , p_source_type => ords.source_type_collection_item
    , p_items_per_page => null
    , p_mimes_allowed => null
```

```
    , p_comments => null
    , p_source => q'~
select
  slot_id as session_id
  , title
  , abstract
  , speaker_first_name
  , speaker_last_name
  , session_start_utc as session_start
  , session_end_utc as session_end
  , location
from vw_sessions
where slot_id = :slot_id
      ~'
  );

  ords.define_parameter(
    p_module_name => 'schedule.v1'
    , p_pattern => 'session/:session_id'
    , p_method => 'GET'
    , p_name => 'session_id'
    , p_bind_variable_name => 'slot_id'
    , p_source_type => 'URI'
    , p_param_type => 'INT'
    , p_access_method => 'IN'
    , p_comments => null
  );

  commit;
end;
/
```

A source type is required when defining a template. Table 12-1 lists the available source types. The source type also determines what other parameters (for the PL/SQL procedure) are necessary for handler to be created successfully.

Table 12-1. *Available source types*

Source Type	HTTP Method	Result Format
source_type_collection_feed	GET	JSON
source_type_collection_item	GET	JSON
source_type_media	GET	Binary (content-type specifies the media type)
source_type_plsql	DELETE, POST, or PUT	JSON

The source types, source_type_collection_feed and source_type_collection_item, used in the defined REST service generate a result set and single row of data in ORDS Standard JSON representation. The following is an edited sample of the output from the first template:

```
{
  "items": [
    {
      "session_id": 21,
      "title": null,
      "abstract": null,
      "speaker_first_name": null,
      "speaker_last_name": null,
      "session_start": "2020-09-21T14:30:00Z",
      "session_end": "2020-09-21T15:15:00Z",
      "location": "Lobby"
    },
    ...
  ],
  "hasMore": false,
  "limit": 50,
  "offset": 0,
  "count": 12,
  "links": [
    {
      "rel": "self",
```

```
      "href": "https://zqbtnc5yxpr941f-conference.adb.us-ashburn-1.
      oraclecloudapps.com/ords/accapi/schedule/v1/session"
    },
    {
      "rel": "describedby",
      "href": "https://zqbtnc5yxpr941f-conference.adb.us-ashburn-1.
      oraclecloudapps.com/ords/accapi/metadata-catalog/schedule/v1/item"
    },
    {
      "rel": "first",
      "href": "https://zqbtnc5yxpr941f-conference.adb.us-ashburn-1.
      oraclecloudapps.com/ords/accapi/schedule/v1/session"
    }
  ]
}
```

The results of the query are returned in an array labeled items. Each table row is encapsulated in a JSON object with the column name as the object's attribute names. Values are rendered based on the columns' data types, with dates returned in ISO 8601 format. The ORDS Standard JSON format also includes attributes that are used for navigation and pagination.

Last but not least, in one of the templates defined, the URL pattern indicates that a parameter session_id is expected. Defining module handler parameters describes the expected data types of values received, and how they may be referenced in the execution code.

This completes the REST service definition task. After the service has been defined, you may view the created objects in the APEX workspace (Figure 12-6).

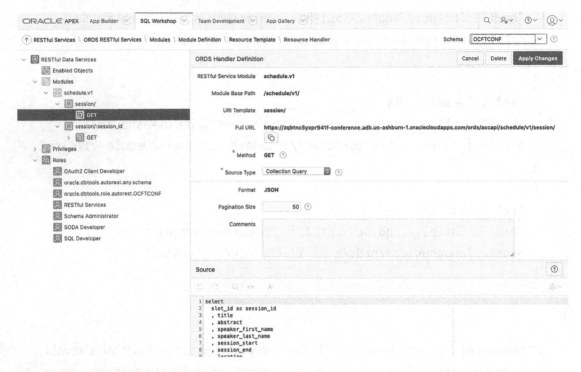

Figure 12-6. Managing ORDS RESTful Services definitions in APEX

Accessing the Endpoint

Accessing the REST services in APEX workspace also provides you the full endpoint URLs to each template. However, you may also derive the URL from the parameters supplied to create these services.

https://<UNIQUE_STRING>-<DATABASE_NAME>.adb.<DATA_REGION>.oraclecloudapps.com/<QUERY_STRING>

Figure 12-7. URL template for accessing ORDS RESTful Services

For my ATP instance, I can determine the following:

- **UNIQUE_STRING**: A random string of alphanumeric characters, for example, *zqbtnc5yxpr941f*.

- **DATABASE_NAME**: This is the database name specified when creating the instance. My database name is called *conference*.

- **DATA_REGION**: This will be the *region identifier* of your Oracle Cloud account's Home Region. You can find a full list of data regions and their identifiers here (*https://bit.ly/oci-docs-regions*). The Home Region for my account is US East (Ashburn) and the region identifier is *us-ashburn-1*.

- **QUERY_STRING**: This placeholder is further expanded in Figure 12-8 to highlight the various components of the URL.

/ords/<SCHEMA_ALIAS>/<MODULE_BASE_PATH>/<URI_TEMPLATE>

Figure 12-8. *ORDS RESTful Services query string template*

- **SCHEMA_ALIAS**: The schema alias was specified when the schema was REST-enabled, for example, *accapi*.

- **MODULE_BASE_PATH**: This value was specified when the module was defined. In the example, the value of `p_base_path` was `/scheduled/v1/`.

- **URI_TEMPLATE**: The URI template for the two templates defined are `schedule/` and `schedule/:session_id`. This value was specified using the parameter `p_pattern` when defining the template.

Securing the Endpoint

OAuth2 is a modern-day standard for authorizing access to web resources. The specification provides several grant types of which ORDS has implemented three:

- Authorization Code

- Implicit Flow

- Client Credentials

In this chapter, we will focus on the using the *Client Credentials* workflow as it is the simplest approach and would cover many usage scenarios, that is, server-to-server interactions.

Suppose we had another REST module for user groups to partner up and submit proposals directly from their websites. The proposal submission endpoint accepts a POST request, with the body containing the required information in a JSON payload. However, we only want authorized partners to access this endpoint. We begin by declaring roles and defining privileges that will be allowed to submit requests.

```
declare
  l_roles owa.vc_arr;
  l_patterns owa.vc_arr;
  l_modules owa.vc_arr;
begin
  l_roles(1) := 'User Group Partners';
  l_modules(1) := 'cfp.v1';
  l_patterns(1) := 'proposal/';

  ords.create_role(
    p_role_name => l_roles(1)
  );

  ords.define_privilege(
    p_privilege_name => 'proposal.contributor'
    , p_roles => l_roles
    , p_patterns => l_patterns
    , p_modules => l_modules
    , p_label => 'Allow user group partners to submit proposals.'
    , p_description => null
    , p_comments => null
  );

  commit;
end;
/
```

The first procedure call creates a role that would be used to assigned users and/or clients to. A privilege is then defined and associated with the role. In a privilege definition, both modules and patterns can be specified and protected.

Next, create a client and assign the client to the role:

```
begin
  oauth.create_client(
    p_name => 'usergroup01'
    , p_grant_type => 'client_credentials'
    , p_owner => 'OCFTCONF'
    , p_support_email => 'support@alwayscloud.guru'
    , p_support_uri => 'https://support.alwayscloud.guru'
    , p_privilege_names => 'proposal.contributor'
  );

  oauth.grant_client_role(
    p_client_name => 'usergroup01'
    , p_role_name => 'User Group Partners'
  );
end;
/
```

Check that the client has been successfully created and take note of the *CLIENT_ID* and *CLIENT_SECRET*:

```
select * from user_ords_clients;
```

And also assigned to the appropriate role:

```
select * from user_ords_client_roles;
```

The following is an example of how the ORDS REST Service can be called from a PL/SQL procedure. The process involves the following:

1. Authenticating with ORDS using OAuth2 client credentials flow

2. Then calling the web service

   ```
   declare
     l_request_payload clob;
     l_response clob;
     l_http_status_code number(3);
   ```

273

```
        l_base_url varchar2(32767) := 'https://zqbtnc5yxpr941f'
          || '-conference.adb.us-ashburn-1.oraclecloudapps.com'
          || '/ords/accapi';
    begin
      apex_web_service.oauth_authenticate(
        p_token_url => l_base_url || '/oauth/token'
        , p_client_id => '************************'
        , p_client_secret => '************************'
        , p_flow_type => apex_web_service.oauth_client_cred
      );

      -- Informational: show the access token and expiry date.
      dbms_output.put_line('Last token '
        || apex_web_service.g_oauth_token.token || ' expires on '
        || to_char(
            apex_web_service.g_oauth_token.expires
            , 'DD-MON-YYYY HH24:MI:SS'
          )
      );

      -- Omitted: code to generate l_request_payload in JSON format.

      l_response := apex_web_service.make_rest_request(
        p_url => l_base_url || '/cfp/v1/proposal/'
        , p_http_method => 'POST'
        , p_body => l_request_payload
        , p_scheme => apex_web_service.oauth_client_cred
      );

      l_http_status_code := apex_web_service.g_status_code;

      case l_http_status_code
        when 200 then dbms_output.put_line(l_response); -- Success!
        else dbms_output.put_line('Proposal submission failed.');
      end case;
    end;
    /
```

RESTful Enabled Objects

There is an even faster way to create RESTful Services to access and manipulate schema objects. Going back to the SQL Workshop in the APEX workspace, access the *Object Browser*, where you will be able to browse the schemas linked to the workspace, along with all the tables, views, and so on. Select the target object, and then on the right panel, click the *REST* tab (Figure 12-9).

Figure 12-9. *Access the target schema object using the Object Browser*

Toggle the switch *REST Enable Object* and then optionally change the *Object Alias*. While not mandatory, it is recommended that the object name and alias are different. *Authorization Required* is enabled by default and recommended. The required *Authorization Role* will be displayed. Client users must belong to this group to have access to the API, regardless of the HTTP method invoked. Click the button *Apply* to complete the process. The page will reload and then display the endpoint URL (*RESTful URI*) for calling the API.

Returning to the ORDS RESTful Services console, you will be able to list all the schema objects that have been REST-enabled (Figure 12-10).

Figure 12-10. *Overview of REST-enabled schema objects using the ORDS RESTful Services console*

Remember, like all other ORDS features, you can also REST-enable objects using SQL Developer, or by using the PL/SQL API:

```
begin
  ords.enable_object(
    p_enabled => true
    , p_schema => 'OCFTCONF'
    , p_object => 'SLOTS'
    , p_object_type => 'TABLE'
    , p_object_alias => 'SESSIONS'
    , p_auto_rest_auth => true
  );

  commit;
end;
/
```

The PL/SQL API also provides greater hints on what type of objects can be REST-enabled using this approach. The parameter p_object_type only accepts the values TABLE (default) or VIEW.

Tip   APEX has strong built-in support for RESTful Services through the *APEX_WEB_SERVICE* PL/SQL API and, in more recent releases, the *Web Source Modules* that allows you to work with these services declaratively.

Summary

ORDS began as a tool to support APEX, a powerful low-code development platform, but has evolved into an important component of the Autonomous Database. By exposing data and its operations as RESTful Services, it has vastly increased the ADB's ability to work with a myriad of software development frameworks and data integration services.

CHAPTER 13

Deploy Multitiered Web Applications

A typical web application would consist of several components or layers. Starting from the bottom of the stack is the data persistence layer. Typically, it involves a relational database system like *Oracle Database* or a *NoSQL* database like *MongoDB*. Next, a business logic layer is implemented with the chosen programming language like *Python*, Java, and so on and then, finally, a presentation layer that renders HTML for display on the user's web browser. This might rely on the same programming language as the business logic layer, or developers might choose a totally different programming framework.

While it is possible to place the entire stack on the same server, it is generally not recommended. Whenever possible, these components and layers should be treated as independent resources and hosted separately. There are several reasons why this is preferred. First, the most obvious reason is the system's resilience to failures. As the old say goes, "Never put all your eggs in the same basket." The same thing could be said for a web application stack.

The other important reason why you might want to keep each layer in a different environment is security. Most web applications would need to be accessible through the Internet to be useful. However, not all the stack's components need to be exposed to the public network. Tiering components in different servers allows administrators to isolate them in different areas of the network, thereby reducing the attack surface area for the more critical components like the database.

Note   In Chapter 11, we looked at the *Oracle Application Express* (APEX) web development platform. While it appears that APEX runs its entire stack on an Oracle Database, it actually does not. The database runs on servers that are separate from the infrastructure supporting *Oracle REST Data Services* (ORDS).

© Adrian Png and Luc Demanche 2020
A. Png and L. Demanche, *Getting Started with Oracle Cloud Free Tier*,
https://doi.org/10.1007/978-1-4842-6011-1_13

The *Oracle Cloud Free Tier* offering provides us the necessary components to build multitier applications for free! We start with the two *Always Free Autonomous Databases* (ADB) for storing application data. Next, we have two Always Free micro-shaped *compute* instances for running your favorite programming language to translate data into meaningful web content. Last but not least, a free *Load Balancer* (LB) for managing Internet traffic to the backend web servers hosted on the instances.

In this chapter, we will look at two different solutions for creating a web front end to display the Always Cloud Conference (ACC) agenda. Each will use a different programming language, namely, Python and *Node.js*. The method of interfacing with the database will also be different, but our approach to deploying the applications will be the same, as *Docker* containers.

Architecture

With the goal to create a multitiered architecture for our ACC agenda website in mind, let us first logically place where each component should reside and how they would reference each other (Figure 13-1).

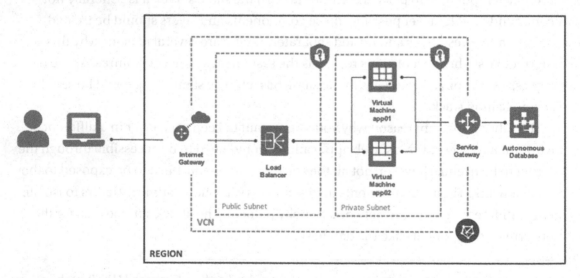

Figure 13-1. *Proposed topology for the ACC agenda website*

In our proposed architecture, we will have three component types in different tiers. Beginning with the persistence layer, we will use an Always Free ADB to provide database services. Next, the applications will be running on Always Free, micro-shaped instances. We will use two of them for scalability and failover. Each server would be provisioned with the same software and use the same deployment strategy to run our code. Last but not least, we will use a micro (10 Mbps bandwidth) LB to manage the traffic received, to and from our application.

Our objective is to keep each component isolated in separate network divisions and avoid access from and to the public network, whenever possible. In the proposal, the ADB lives in a separate network compartment that is managed by Oracle. We do not have the ability to set or change which network or subnet it runs in. The instances are placed in a private subnet, and depending on the amount of isolation desired, access in and out of the subnet is only possible within the *Virtual Cloud Network* (VCN). To access external resources, you will have to create either an *Internet Gateway*, *NAT Gateway*, or for Oracle Cloud services, a *Service Gateway*. In the diagram, the instances, or *virtual machines* (VMs), access to the Internet would be completely walled off. The service gateway, though, would continue to allow access to the Autonomous Database, without traffic routing through the public networks. The LB will be placed in the public subnet as the conference attendees are coming from all over the world and will need access to the website over the Internet.

While ideal, this proposal cannot be implemented as is due to service limits imposed on Free Tier. Both network and service gateways are Oracle Cloud services available at no cost. However, if you have not upgraded to a paid account, then the service limits for these are zero. In which case, the alternative would be to implement a modified topology by swapping the service gateway and using an Internet gateway instead (Figure 13-2).

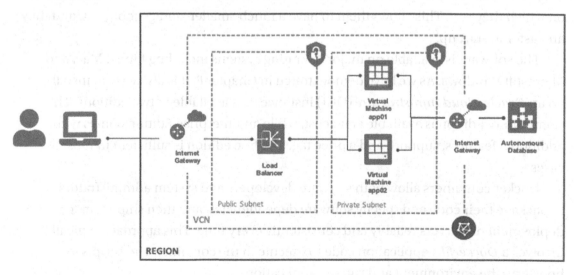

Figure 13-2. *Alternate topology for accounts that have not been upgraded to paid*

Note that while the diagram shows two Internet gateways, there is only a need for one and egress traffic to the ADB can be routed to it. Then, assign public IP addresses to both VMs. I would recommend using *reserved*, as opposed to *ephemeral* public IP addresses. The reason is, we have the option of locking down access to the ADB using the *Access Control List* and can be maintained better with IP addresses that have a more manageable lifetime. However, doing so will block access to other tools like APEX and *SQL Developer Web*.

Note   It is also possible to place the LB and VMs in the same subnet; however, placing them in separate subnets will make it easier to swap the Internet gateway with a service gateway should you choose to upgrade your account later.

Docker

In Chapter 8, we used Docker containers to deploy our demonstration application with load balancers. We will do the same for the next Python and Node.js implementation of the ACC agenda website. Why Docker though?

Docker is an open source containerization technology that shares system resources by means of isolating them. However, unlike virtual machines, Docker containers do not have their own copy of an operating system; rather, they share the kernel with the host on which they run. This allows them to have a much smaller storage footprint, and they are faster to start up.

The software is available on major operating systems including Linux, Mac, and Microsoft Windows. As we have demonstrated in Chapter 8, it is also easy to install on an *Oracle Cloud Infrastructure* (OCI) instance. It is available in two editions. The Community Edition is available at no cost, while an Enterprise Edition comes with additional features, support, and a price tag. The free edition is sufficient in most use cases.

Docker containers allow both software developers and system administrators to package their code and specify software dependencies, and then ship them for deployment on servers reliably and consistently every time. This approach typically involves a *Dockerfile*, application code to execute in the container, and scripts to bootstrap the environment and run the application.

With Docker, we do not have to start by installing an operating system in the container. The Dockerfile is a text file that provides instructions on how to build the container, including referencing an existing image to build on top of. It also contains instructions to perform many operations like setting environment variables, running operating system commands, copy files, and so on.

To demonstrate this simply, let's begin with a simple "helloworld" shell script that greets you. First, create a directory for your application and in it, a file named helloworld.sh, containing the following code:

```
#!/usr/bin/env bash

echo "Hello ${NAME:-Anonymous}"
```

This shell script will attempt to use the environment variable NAME, failing which, it will simply print the word "Anonymous".

Next, create the Dockerfile with the following contents:

```
FROM ubuntu:latest

ENV NAME=John

COPY helloworld.sh /usr/local/bin/

RUN chmod a+x /usr/local/bin/helloworld.sh

CMD ["sh", "-c", "/usr/local/bin/helloworld.sh"]
```

There are five instructions in this Dockerfile. The first (FROM) instruction informs the Docker engine that this image will be layered on top of the latest *Ubuntu* image found in the default, public *Docker Registry* (*https://hub.docker.com*). It then sets (using ENV) the environment variable NAME that we will use in the shell script. The third instruction (COPY) makes a copy of the shell script and places it in the container's directory /usr/local/bin. Next, it changes, using the RUN instruction to execute an OS command to change the file attributes, making the file executable. The final instruction, CMD, defines the command and parameters to execute when the container runs.

Note Unless otherwise specified using the USER instruction, or by means of using scripts, all the instructions will be executed as the superuser. In the case of Linux-based images, this will be the *root* user.

In your project directory, there should now be two files:

```
helloworld $ ls
Dockerfile          helloworld.sh
```

Create the Docker image using the following command:

```
helloworld $ docker build -t helloworld .
Sending build context to Docker daemon  3.072kB
Step 1/5 : FROM ubuntu:latest
 ---> 1d622ef86b13
Step 2/5 : ENV NAME=John
 ---> Using cache
 ---> 0b3d3f6749d8
Step 3/5 : COPY helloworld.sh /usr/local/bin/
 ---> eb75dfa75867
Step 4/5 : RUN chmod a+x /usr/local/bin/helloworld.sh
 ---> Running in 450d5eb01bb5
Removing intermediate container 450d5eb01bb5
 ---> e3ae5b3393d1
Step 5/5 : CMD ["sh", "-c", "/usr/local/bin/helloworld.sh"]
 ---> Running in 2d4f2cd85b14
Removing intermediate container 2d4f2cd85b14
 ---> 032cd5396123
Successfully built 032cd5396123
Successfully tagged helloworld:latest
```

This command builds the image tagged helloworld:latest, using the Dockerfile found in the current directory. As you will recall from the Dockerfile breakdown, the FROM instruction tells the Docker engine to use the image tagged ubuntu:latest from the Docker Registry. If this image isn't already available on your system, then Docker will pull a copy from the Registry, forming the base image layer. It then proceeds to invoke every line of instruction, each time writing a new layer on top of the previous one. The final image is then tagged, and the process ends. Note that the tag consists of two parts, divided by the delimiter :. On the left-hand side is the name of the image, and on the right, the version. It does not have to be numeric, but if you leave it out, Docker automatically assigns it the version latest.

To run the container, execute the following command:

```
Helloworld $ docker run --rm helloworld
Hello John
```

This creates and runs a new container using the image tagged `helloworld:latest` in the foreground. The parameter `--rm` indicates that the Docker engine should remove/delete the container as soon as the command is specified by a `CMD` (or `ENTRYPOINT`) instruction. Do not use it in situations where you would want the container to simply enter a "stop" state and not destroy any data persisted in the container.

In the Dockerfile, we had also declared an environment variable that we can change at "runtime". To do that, add a -e parameter with a name/value pair as a value, for example:

```
helloworld $ docker run -e NAME=April --rm helloworld
Hello April
```

Also, typically, when hosting server-type applications, we expect the application to be always running, listening, and responding to requests. In such scenarios, we can run the container in the background and then let the Docker command exit without stopping or destroying the container. To run the container as a daemon, add the parameter `-d` anywhere between the `run` command and the image's tag.

There are many more parameters that can be used to configure your Docker `build` and `run` commands, and I strongly recommend reading up the official documentation (*https://docs.docker.com/*).

Python Implementation

We laid most of the groundwork in Chapter 8, when we set up a load balancer, two instances, and installed Docker. If you have not completed the tasks in that chapter, I strongly encourage you to follow the instructions to do the following:

- Create two instances and attach them as backend servers. Use the *cloud-init* script that will install Docker and set up the parent directory /opt/docker where we will deploy our code to.

- Create the load balancer and required network configuration to support the infrastructure. The backend servers will both be listening to port 8000.

For this chapter, we will focus instead on how to create a Python web application that will access data from an Autonomous Database and render the results. Package them as Docker containers, and guarantee and maintain the exact same application is deployed on both backend servers.

Connecting to an Autonomous Database

Software Requirements

Oracle provides a Python extension module for connecting to an Oracle Database. It is called *cx_Oracle* (*https://oracle.github.io/python-cx_Oracle/*) and is available to anyone without cost.

At the time of writing, cx_Oracle continues to support both Python 2.7 or 3.5 and later. This application was developed with Python version 3.6, which is the current version provided through Oracle's public *Yum* repositories. cx_Oracle does require the Oracle client libraries that are available with each database installation. Or, you can get the libraries by installing the *Oracle Instant Client*. Binaries are available for Linux, Windows, and macOS, but be sure to download the appropriate version for your database. The libraries are backward compatible only.

After installing both Python module and Oracle Instant Client, you will also have to ensure that the required environment variables are set, or the Oracle client libraries are in the expected search paths. If the environment is not set up correctly, cx_Oracle will fail to connect to the database.

Client Credentials (Wallet)

Next, in order to connect to the ADB, not only do we need the schema/username and password, the wallet file has to be downloaded from the ADB's *Service Console*. These steps were outlined in Chapter 7 on Autonomous Databases. You will need to choose between a region and an instance wallet depending on your needs, but the latter is preferred if your application requires access to only one ADB.

The Python Web Application

Before we begin, I'd like to confess that I am very much a novice Python programmer, having focused the past few years on my career working on the *Oracle Application Express* (APEX). To be more productive in creating a Python web application within a short time frame, I opted to use a popular web framework called Flask (*https://flask.palletsprojects.com/*).

Flask provides an easy-to-learn Python platform for creating a web application, simply by mapping routes to functions that return content for the HTTP response. I will also use its templating feature that allows developers to abstract the user interface design, away from the plumbing code that provides the data-driven content. In our use case, that is the schedule of events.

Flask also comes with an embedded server runtime that allows developers to run their code and preview their web applications. For the purpose of showcasing how Python can work seamlessly with ADBs, it was a great solution. Bear in mind though that it is clear in the documentation that for production rollouts, there are definitely more robust and performant approaches, and you are encouraged to consider them.

The code that I am about to share is available at the book's GitHub repository (*https://github.com/Apress/getting-started-w-oracle-cloud-free-tier/ch13/python-app/*). First, let us examine the directory structure of the code repository. In the preceding URL, you will find the following:

```
python-app $ tree
.
├── Dockerfile
├── app
│   ├── main.py
│   ├── requirements.txt
│   ├── static
│   │   └── css
│   │       └── core.css
│   └── templates
│       ├── base.html
│       └── home.html
├── buildImage.sh
├── runContainer.sh
└── scripts
    └── installCredentialsWallet.sh
```

The Python code, along with its dependencies, is self-contained in the subdirectory app. The main application file is appropriately named main.py and it contains the following Python code. The requirements.txt is a simple text file where we can list module dependencies – a line for each module that will then be installed by *PIP*, Python's package manager.

To keep our database details and credentials away from the code repository, we will make use of the *ConfigParser* module.

```
# Read the configuration file for database connection properties
config = configparser.ConfigParser()
config.read_file(open("/etc/app/db.properties"))
db_username = config["DB_CONFIG"]["db_username"]
db_password = config["DB_CONFIG"]["db_password"]
db_service_name = config["DB_CONFIG"]["db_service_name"]
```

Later, we will look at how to ensure the file db.properties is accessible to the application. For now, ensure that you have a file with that name, in the root directory, with the following details:

```
[DB_CONFIG]
db_username = ocftconf
db_password = supersecret
db_service_name = conference_tp
```

You should of course substitute the values with information about your ADB connection. This information is then used to create a database pool as shown in the following:

```
# Set up the database pool
pool = cx_Oracle.SessionPool(db_username, db_password, db_service_name
    , min=2, max=5, increment=1, encoding="UTF-8")
```

Keep in mind that the Always Free ADB has a cap of **20** parallel database sessions. Make sure the limits used here take into consideration other applications and services that might require access to the database as well. If anyone of them creates a connection at a time when the threshold is reached, the attempt will fail. Be diligent in your code as well and close or release any unused connections.

Traffic and out of an Always Free ADB will always be made using a public endpoint. It is, therefore, very important that the communication channel between your client application and the database is secured. It is, fortunately, not complex to set up with your ADB. The wallet file contains everything that you need, including the necessary certificates to negotiate this connection. It also contains a `tnsnames.ora` file, in which you will find the network service names that can be used to make the secure database connection. The following is an example of the database service name that we will use in our Python application:

```
conference_tp = (description= (retry_count=20)(retry_delay=3)
(address=(protocol=tcps)(port=1522)(host=adb.us-ashburn-1.oraclecloud.
com))(connect_data=(service_name= zqbtnc5yxpr941f.conference_tp.atp.
oraclecloud.com))(security=(ssl_server_cert_dn="CN=adwc.uscom-east-1.
oraclecloud.com,OU=Oracle BMCS US,O=Oracle Corporation,L=Redwood
City,ST=California,C=US")))
```

Deploying with Docker

With these requirements in mind, and a brief overview of how the Python code works, let us know look at how we can streamline the installation and set up procedures, needed to support our web application.

Place the wallet file in the project's root directory, and also create another configuration file named `.env` that will be used by the shell scripts to set environment variables. It requires two variables, and the following is an example of its contents:

```
APP_NAME=acc-web
CREDENTIALS_WALLET=wallet_CONFERENCE.zip
```

At this point, you should have the following files and directories in your project:

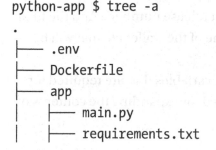

```
python-app $ tree -a
.
├── .env
├── Dockerfile
├── app
│   ├── main.py
│   ├── requirements.txt
```

```
|       ├── static
|       |     └── css
|       |           └── core.css
|       └── templates
|             ├── base.html
|             └── home.html
├── buildImage.sh
├── db.properties
├── runContainer.sh
├── scripts
|       └── installCredentialsWallet.sh
└── wallet_CONFERENCE.zip
```

Let's break down and review the Dockerfile in detail, beginning with the first line:

```
FROM oraclelinux:7-slim
```

One advantage of building Docker images using Oracle Linux as a base is the access to Oracle's Yum repositories. As specified by the tag, this contains a minimal installation of release 7 of the operating system.

It then specifies a list of arguments that can be set to change the build characteristics:

```
ARG USERNAME=appuser
ARG USER_UID=1000
ARG USER_GID=$USER_UID
ARG RELEASE=19
ARG UPDATE=3
ARG CREDENTIALS_WALLET
```

When we run these containers, we want to avoid the use of a privilege user. The first three arguments allow us to specify and run the Python application as the preferred user and group. The next two specify the Oracle Instant Client release numbers. And the final argument CREDENTIALS_WALLET is for specifying the name of the wallet file that will be consumed during the build.

The ENV instruction sets a few required environment variables that are required for the container, including ORACLE_HOME that will be required for expanding the contents of the wallet file.

Next, using the COPY instruction, we will need to stage some of the files required during the build phase:

- The requirements.txt file containing the Python module dependencies.

- A Bash script installCredentialsWallet.sh that will unpack the contents of the wallet file and place them in the $ORACLE_HOME/ network/admin directory.

- Last but not least, we will need the wallet file.

The next stage of the build involves running a sequence of operations, briefly:

1. Install dependencies using the package manager. This includes Python, Oracle Instant Client, and other supporting software utilities.

2. Create the OS user for running the web application.

3. Run the installCredentialsWallet.sh script to set up the client credentials required by cx_Oracle.

Note that by chaining the OS commands and executing them in a single RUN instruction, we reduce the number of layers needed to create the final image. This is generally a good practice that will also reduce the size of the images.

While we near the end of the build, we will need to change the current user, run PIP to install the required Python modules, and then set the working directory to /app, where we will reference the Python code.

Note   Rather than copy the contents of the app directory, we will be attaching it to the Docker container using a bind mount. This helps during the development of the application as we do not have to rebuild the image each time the code changed. Similarly, we can opt to do the PIP installations during a Docker run command rather than during the build phase.

A helper script (buildImage.sh) is provided in the code repository to help perform the build. It loads the environment variables from .env and then executes the command:

```
docker build -t ${APP_NAME} \
  --build-arg CREDENTIALS_WALLET=${CREDENTIALS_WALLET} .
```

The `--build-arg` parameter allows you to override any predefined `ARG` variables specified in the Dockerfile. In this case, it would be the name of the wallet file.

To run a container, we have again a helper script to set the environment variables, remove any existing container with the same name, and then spin one up using the following Docker run command:

```
docker run -d --name=${APP_NAME} \
    -e DOCKER_HOST=$(hostname) \
    -p 8000:5000 \
    -v ${PWD}/app:/app:z \
    -v ${PWD}/db.properties:/etc/app/db.properties:z \
    ${APP_NAME}
```

The parameters used in this command perform the following tasks:

- Run the container in the background.

- Set the container name to the value of the environment variable `APP_NAME`.

- Set the container's environment variable `DOCKER_HOST` to the hostname of the host system.

- Expose the port 8000 and map it to the container's port 5000, the port number used by Flask to serve up web pages.

- Mount the directory/`app` and the file `db.properties` found in the current working directory as volumes in the container, using the paths specified.

Just like that, you will have a Python web application up and running, serving data-driven content over the network.

When you are ready to deploy your code to the servers, upload the python-app directory to the server. You may do this with secure tools like *SCP* (secure copy) or *rsync* over *SSH*.

Using SCP:

```
python-app $ scp -r ../python-app opc@192.0.2.100:/opt/docker/
```

However, using rsync over SSH has its advantages. When running the Python web application, you may have observed that the directory app/__pycache__ was created. If we wanted to exclude these files, rsync might just do the trick. For example:

```
python-app $ rsync -a -e ssh --exclude='__pycache__*' \
> ../python-app opc@192.0.2.100:/opt/docker/
```

Note   To use SCP or SSH, your public key must already be added to the *opc* user's $HOME/.ssh/authorized_keys. You would have done this when the instance was provisioned. If the private key is not in the default file and path, be sure to specify its location using the -i parameter.

Once the servers and containers are up and running, wait a while for the load balancer's health checks to update their metrics and statuses, and beginning channeling requests. If all goes well, exciting lineup of sessions for the Always Cloud Conference will be displayed (Figure 13-3).

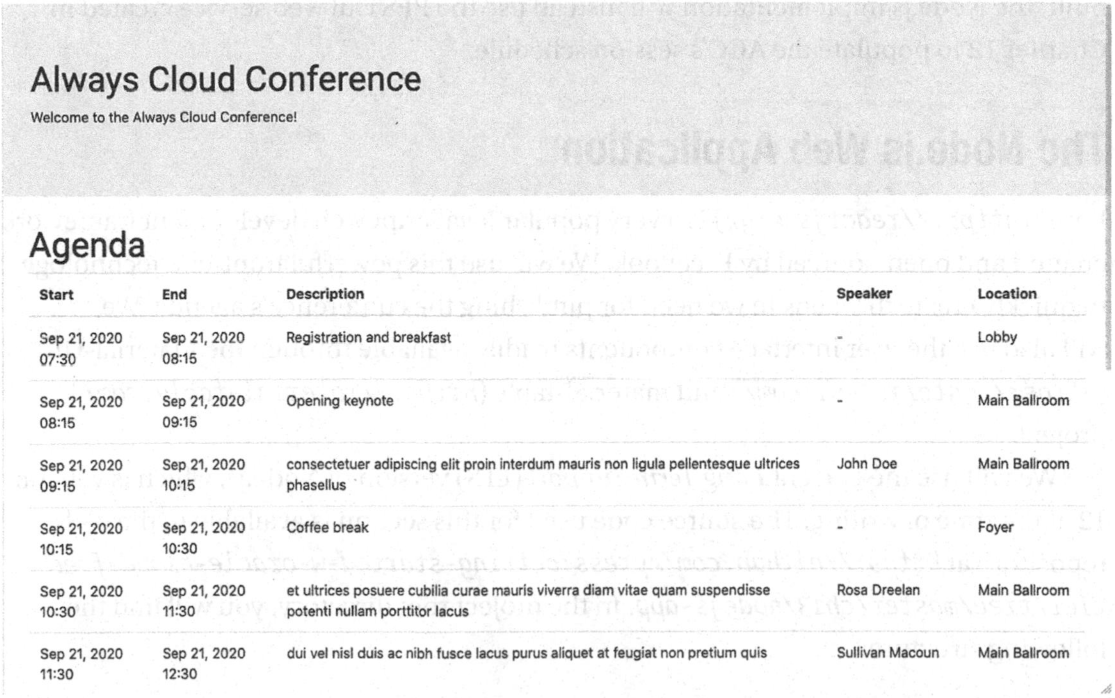

Always Cloud Conference

Welcome to the Always Cloud Conference!

Agenda

Start	End	Description	Speaker	Location
Sep 21, 2020 07:30	Sep 21, 2020 08:15	Registration and breakfast	-	Lobby
Sep 21, 2020 08:15	Sep 21, 2020 09:15	Opening keynote	-	Main Ballroom
Sep 21, 2020 09:15	Sep 21, 2020 10:15	consectetuer adipiscing elit proin interdum mauris non ligula pellentesque ultrices phasellus	John Doe	Main Ballroom
Sep 21, 2020 10:15	Sep 21, 2020 10:30	Coffee break	-	Foyer
Sep 21, 2020 10:30	Sep 21, 2020 11:30	et ultrices posuere cubilia curae mauris viverra diam vitae quam suspendisse potenti nullam porttitor lacus	Rosa Dreelan	Main Ballroom
Sep 21, 2020 11:30	Sep 21, 2020 12:30	dui vel nisl duis ac nibh fusce lacus purus aliquet at feugiat non pretium quis	Sullivan Macoun	Main Ballroom

Figure 13-3. *The Always Cloud Conference Agenda website developed using Python*

Node.js Implementation

Node.js is a popular web development framework based on JavaScript. It can be used to build a great variety of application types including web applications, REST APIs, and even desktop applications.

For this application, we will use the same infrastructure and follow the same deployment approach used with the Python implementation. You will simply need to "swap" the Docker image and container used in the final deployment.

Connecting to an Autonomous Database

Oracle provides database support for Node.js through the *node-oracledb* (*http://oracle.github.io/node-oracledb/*) project. Like cx_Oracle, you can easily install and add this module as a project dependency. It does also require the Oracle client libraries and will have to be installed as well.

Connecting to the ADB with Node.js follows a very similar process used in Python. However, rather than take the same approach as the Python web application we had just built, the Node.js implementation will instead use the RESTful web service created in Chapter 12 to populate the ACC's session schedule.

The Node.js Web Application

React (*https://reactjs.org/*) is a very popular JavaScript web development framework created and open-sourced by Facebook. We will use this powerful front-end technology to quickly create the website we need for publishing the conference's agenda. We will also use the user interface components readily available through the Material-UI (*https://material-ui.com/*) and material-table (*https://material-table.com/*) project.

We will use the current *Long Term Support* (LTS) version of Node.js, which is version 12 at the time of writing. The source code used for this section is available in the code repository at *https://github.com/Apress/getting-started-w-oracle-cloud-free-tier/tree/master/ch13/nodejs-app*. In the project root directory, you will find the following structure:

```
nodejs-app $ tree
.
├── Dockerfile
├── app
│   ├── README.md
│   ├── package-lock.json
│   ├── package.json
│   ├── public
│   │   ├── favicon.ico
│   │   ├── index.html
│   │   ├── logo192.png
│   │   ├── logo512.png
│   │   ├── manifest.json
│   │   └── robots.txt
│   ├── serve.sh
│   └── src
│       ├── components
│       │   ├── Agenda.js
│       │   ├── App.js
│       │   ├── App.test.js
│       │   ├── ButtonAppBar.js
│       │   ├── logo.svg
│       │   └── serviceWorker.js
│       ├── index.css
│       ├── index.js
│       └── setupTests.js
├── buildImage.sh
└── runContainer.sh
```

All the React code for the web application is placed in the subdirectory app. The
application's scaffolding code was initially generated by using the command:

```
npx create-react-app app
```

The required Node.js packages for the UI components were then added to the project using the Node.js Package Manager (npm) utility. Run the following command from the app subdirectory:

```
npm install @material-ui/core @material-ui/icons \
  material-table –save
```

This will install the required packages and save the dependencies in the app/ package.json file.

Since this book isn't about React, I will not delve deep into the fundamentals of React but rather focus on how the code integrates with what the Autonomous Database provides and how we are going to deploy the application on an Always Free instance. If you wish to learn more about React, I highly recommend taking a look at some of the books published by Apress that covers the framework in detail.

One custom React component that I would like to examine further though is the Agenda component (app/src/components/Agenda.js). This component contains the *MaterialTable* component provided by the material-table project. It is able to use a statically defined *JSON* data source, or from remote source. In our scenario, the remote data source would be the RESTful web service module created in Chapter 12, which returns the list of sessions, times, and location as an array of JSON objects.

First, we declare a constant that contains the column definitions:

```
const [state] = React.useState({
  columns: [
    { title: 'Start', field: 'session_start', type: 'datetime' },
    { title: 'End', field: 'session_end', type: 'datetime' },
    { title: 'Description', field: 'title' },
    {
      title: 'Speaker',
      render: rowData => rowData.speaker_first_name ?
        rowData.speaker_first_name + ' ' +
        rowData.speaker_last_name : '-'
    },
    { title: 'Location', field: 'location' },
  ]
});
```

This definition states that the rendered table will contain five columns. The first two will contain data with date and time information. The remaining columns are text-based columns. However, for the fourth column, it should display, if any, the speaker's full name that is composed of his/her first and last names.

With the columns defined, we then return the MaterialTable with the following attributes:

```
<MaterialTable
  title="Agenda"
  columns={state.columns}
  data={query =>
    new Promise((resolve, reject) => {
      let url = window.env.ACC_SCHEDULE_URL;
      fetch(url)
        .then(response => response.json())
        .then(result => {
          resolve({
            data: result.items
          });
        });
    })
  }
  options={{
    paging: false,
    search: false
  }}
/>
```

Most of the attributes are rather self-explanatory, and you can find documentation on all available properties of the component that can be customized to meet your needs. The data attribute, however, warrants a bit more details on what we are attempting to do here. As mentioned earlier, the component's table rows are populated by an array of JSON objects that can either be statically defined or sourced from a remote endpoint. The endpoint URL is specified by a variable (window.env.ACC_SCHEDULE_URL) and that allows us to set this in a configuration file that is required for our deployment strategy to be successful.

When this page loads, the browser will fetch the data using an asynchronous call. The data returned by our RESTful service should look like this:

```
{
  "items": [
    {
      "session_id": 1,
      "title": "Registration and breakfast",
      "abstract": null,
      "speaker_first_name": null,
      "speaker_last_name": null,
      "session_start": "2020-09-21T14:30:00Z",
      "session_end": "2020-09-21T15:15:00Z",
      "location": "Lobby"
    },
    {
      "session_id": 2,
      "title": "Opening keynote",
      "abstract": null,
      "speaker_first_name": null,
      "speaker_last_name": null,
      "session_start": "2020-09-21T15:15:00Z",
      "session_end": "2020-09-21T16:15:00Z",
      "location": "Main Ballroom"
    },
    ...
  ]
}
```

The JSON array that we need to return as the data source is contained in the attribute items and that's what we will return to the component to render in HTML.

In the absence of any endpoint security requirements, this appears to be a relatively simple, no-frills approach to use the data persisted in the ADB. There are no wallets to download, database connection credentials to share, or additional software to install. If, however, the endpoints are protected, it is still possible to use RESTful web services as data sources for your Node.js applications. It just requires additional strategies on ensuring any credentials used are stored and used securely.

Deploying with Docker

Deploying this Node.js web application is mostly similar to the approach we used for the Python implementation. In the project's code repository, you will also find the Dockerfile and two helper shell scripts. Like in the earlier approach, you will need to provide a .env file containing some environment variables that we require, for example:

```
APP_NAME=acc-web
EXPRESS_PORT=3000
ACC_SCHEDULE_URL="https://zqbtnc5yxpr941f-conference.adb.us-ashburn-1.
oraclecloudapps.com/ords/accapi/schedule/v1/session/"
```

We will continue to use the latest Oracle Linux "slim" image as a base and, also, continue with the strategy of not running the application as *root*.

The RUN instruction avoids installing any unnecessary software components to keep the image size small. Unlike the previous example, we will be copying the application code to the image. More on that later, but first, we install our software dependencies, the Node.js runtime:

```
RUN curl -sL https://rpm.nodesource.com/setup_12.x | bash - && \
  yum install -y \
      nodejs \
      gcc-c++ \
      make \
      && \
  rm -rf /var/cache/yum && \
  npm install -g serve && \
  groupadd --gid $USER_GID $USERNAME && \
  useradd -m -d /home/${USERNAME} -s /bin/bash --uid $USER_UID \
    --gid $USER_GID $USERNAME && \
  mkdir -p /app && \
  chown $USER_UID:$USER_GID /app
```

In addition to the runtime, we will also install the Node.js package *serve* (*https://github.com/zeit/serve*), a simple web server for hosting static web content. This package is not a project dependency and will be installed globally.

Once the OS software installation and setup has completed, we will proceed to copy everything contained in the project's app directory, onto the container's /app directory. The directories and files copied will also concurrently have its ownership updated.

The Dockerfile has a second RUN instruction that is executed after the current user and working directory are changed:

```
RUN npm install && npm run build
```

The *npm* commands executed here will perform the following:

1. Install all packages listed as dependencies in the package.json file. You will find these downloaded artifacts in the container, in the path /app/node_modules.

2. Execute the build script defined in the package.json file. This is when React generates the stand-alone files that will be hosted by the server application. These files are placed in the path /app/build on the container.

Note   As an alternative, some might choose to perform the build process only when the Docker container runs. There are pros and cons to either approach, like build and run times, and you will have to weigh these carefully when deciding the approach that you will to take for your projects.

The last instruction is CMD, and for our Node.js web application, we will not call the application directly. Instead, we will run a shell script /app/serve.sh that was staged by the COPY instruction earlier. This is the script that we will run:

```
#!/usr/bin/env bash

cat << EOF > build/server.js
window.env = {
  "DOCKER_HOST": "${DOCKER_HOST}",
  "ACC_SCHEDULE_URL": "${ACC_SCHEDULE_URL}"
}
EOF

serve -s /app/build -l ${EXPRESS_PORT:-3000}
```

There are two tasks performed in this script. The first creates the file `/app/build/server.js` in the container. The second runs the *serve* command, specifying the `/app/build` as the directory for serving the web content, and the port to using the environment variable `EXPRESS_PORT`.

The `server.js` file is necessary to specify a new object in the JavaScript runtime when it runs in the client browser. This populates the object with values of the environment variables `DOCKER_HOST` and `ACC_SCHEDULE_URL` when the container run. The first is used in the footer, and it indicates to the user which host the code is running on. The latter, `window.env.ACC_SCHEDULE_URL`, is used in the Agenda component to specify the RESTful web service URL to call. These are necessary as it is important to point out that this website has not server-side code that we can use to dynamically set and retrieve these values.

To stage the files, we use the same approach as we did earlier with the Python application:

```
nodejs-app $ rsync -a -e ssh
> ../nodejs-app opc@192.0.2.100:/opt/docker/
```

Note   React provides a built-in server that reloads live during development. From the app subdirectory, you may run commands `npm install`, followed by `npm start`. You will also need to add the same `server.js` configuration file in the app/`public` subdirectory with the appropriate values replacing the placeholders.

If you do, however, use this approach for development, be sure to remove the subdirectories app/`node_modules` before uploading the files to the server. It is not critical but will save you network bandwidth and time.

Once the files have been uploaded to the server, change the working directory and then run the scripts `buildImage.sh` and `runContainer.sh` in that order. Before running the scripts though, be sure that the `.env` file has been created and updated with the correct values. If the name of the `APP_NAME` is the same as the Python application's, it would simply swap the containers, and you should see the results (Figure 13-4) almost immediately.

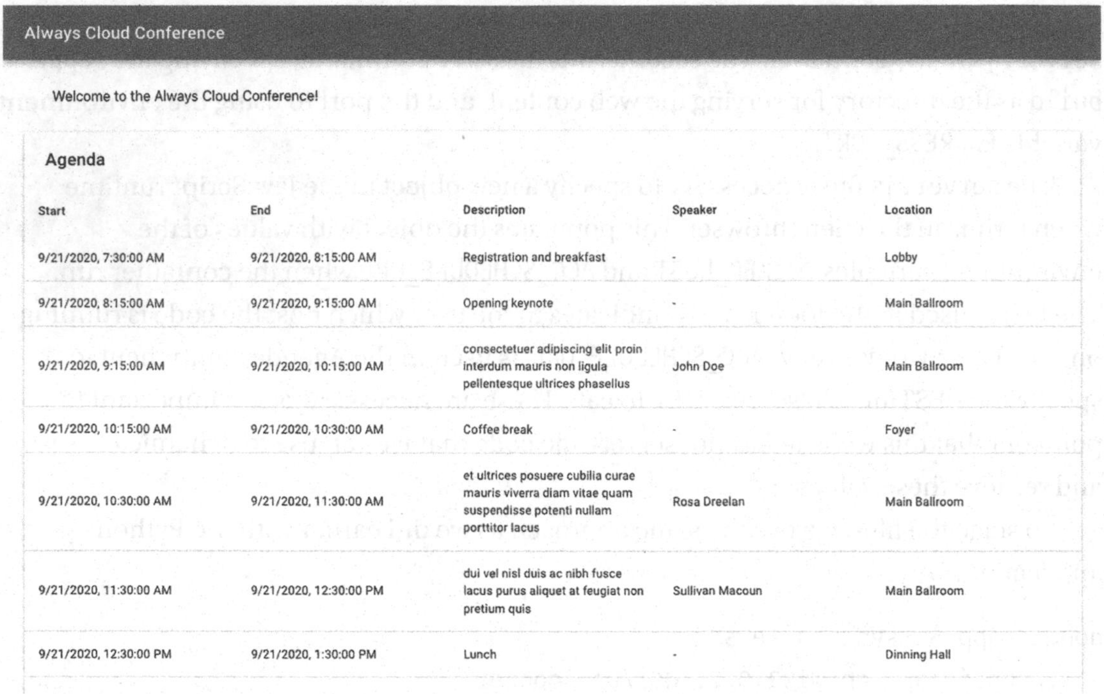

Figure 13-4. *The Always Cloud Conference Agenda website developed using Nodejs*

Summary

In this chapter, we have examined two different programming languages and how they can consume data from an Autonomous Database to create useful web applications. Taking advantage of the two Always Free instances and single load balancer, we are able to create a scalable infrastructure to host the application. Using Docker as a deployment strategy, we are able to create self-contained, consistent environments for running the application. With Docker, we are also able to define the configuration in code and be able to maintain it with version control.

The Always Free resources provide a comprehensive infrastructure platform for just about any programming flavor that you choose. While Oracle has provided database connection drivers for a wide variety of programming languages, we can also interact with the data using RESTful web services hosted through Oracle REST Data Services, and as evident in Chapter 12, it is not a difficult process to create them. The possibilities are endless.

CHAPTER 14

Oracle Machine Learning Notebooks

Over the last few decades, the costs of storage and computational power have decreased, while capacity and performance have increased exponentially. Network availability and bandwidth too are much faster, and we are seeing a huge proliferation of network-connected sensors and devices. Together, these factors have played a significant role in the modern-day data deluge.

In Computer Science, *Artificial Intelligence* (AI) and *Machine Learning* (ML) are fields of study that have been with us since the 1950s. However, back then, applications of AI and ML were often met with suspicion, fear, and skepticism. While there were early applications of the technology, most were either sidelined or kept under a low profile so as not to solicit negative reactions.

Today, the landscape for AI/ML professionals has changed vastly. Someone had to make sense and take advantage of *Big Data*, and data analytics and predictive modeling show a lot of promise. Coupled with cheaper computing resources to perform the number crunching, it is no wonder that today these specialists are highly sought after. Do you aspire to be one of them?

Oracle is now giving us a chance to partake of this future of work with the Oracle Cloud Free Tier offering and Always Free resources. As explained earlier in the book, these include the ability to provision two Autonomous Databases. They can either be provisioned for transactional or data warehouse workloads. You could, for example, run your ecommerce shop using Oracle Application Express (APEX), backed by an Autonomous Transaction Processing (ATP) database, and then offload sales data to a second Autonomous Data Warehouse (ADW) database to analyze sales, create predictive models, and then improve your marketing strategy to gain higher returns. Best of all, these can all be done for free!

© Adrian Png and Luc Demanche 2020
A. Png and L. Demanche, *Getting Started with Oracle Cloud Free Tier*,
https://doi.org/10.1007/978-1-4842-6011-1_14

Overview of Oracle Machine Learning Notebooks

Every Autonomous Database comes with free toolsets and we have looked at some of these in the preceding chapters. To recap, we have SQL Developer Web for allowing database developers to work with schema objects using only a web browser; APEX, a low-code platform for the rapid development of web applications; and finally Oracle REST Data Services (ORDS) for creating secure web-based interfaces to the data stored in the database. In this chapter, we will learn more about the Oracle Machine Learning (OML) Notebooks.

Based on Apache Zeppelin, OML Notebooks is a web-based application that allows data analysts to collaborate and develop insightful visualizations and predictive models that will help operations and discovery. Apache Zeppelin supports multiple programming languages through *interpreters*; unfortunately, at the time of writing this chapter, OML Notebooks currently only supports SQL and PL/SQL. It is anticipated that both Python and R will be supported very soon.

Manage Access

For this chapter, a separate Always Free Autonomous Database was provisioned with a data warehouse workload in mind. Once created, one of the first tasks is to allow users to have access to the OML Notebooks application. There are two ways to manage users: either access the OML User Administration from the ADB's *Tools* tab (Figure 14-1) or through the *Service Console*, on the *Development* page.

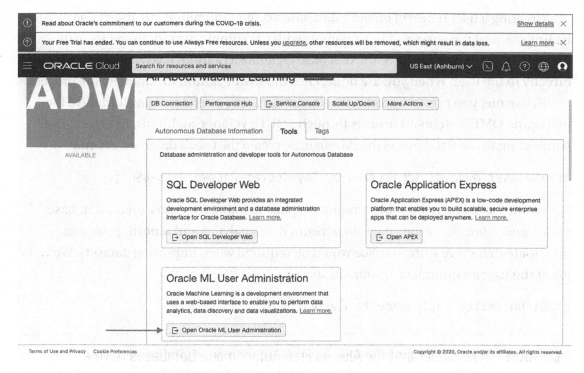

Figure 14-1. *Access OML Notebook's User Administration from the Tools tab*

Log in to the OML Notebooks User Administration using the *admin* credentials. Click the *Create* button and then provide the required values (Figure 14-2).

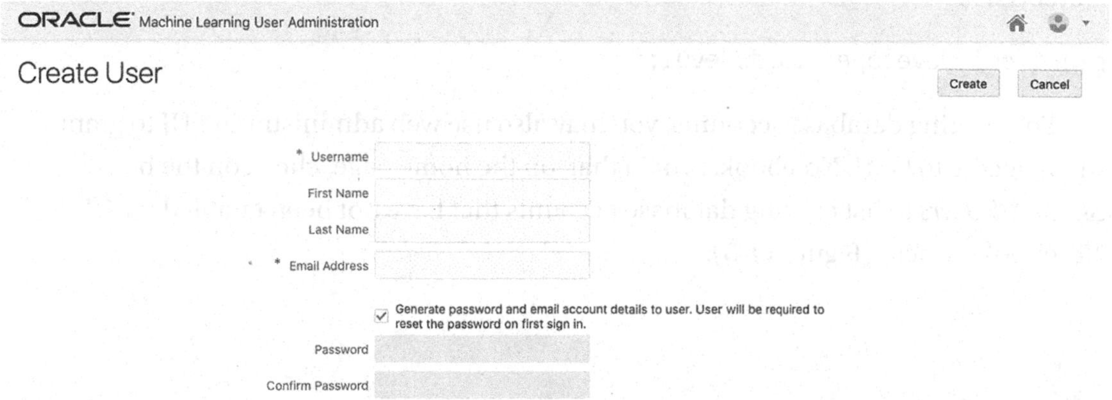

Figure 14-2. *Information requested about OML Notebooks users*

Creating a user here will create a database account; therefore, the username must be unique, and the password must comply with the complexity requirements of the database. You may opt to have the database generate a random password and email that directly to the user. When you are done, click the *Create* button to complete the process.

If, like me, you prefer to work with a command-line interface, one alternative for managing OML Notebooks users is through SQL Developer, SQL*Plus, or SQLcl. After connecting to the database as the *admin* user, create the user's database account:

```
create user dwdev01 identified by "my-secret-Password-is-456";
```

Grant the user a reasonable amount of space to import datasets, create database views, and more. Since the goal is to perform data analytics and reporting, we can anticipate that more storage space would be required when importing datasets. We will grant the user an unlimited amount of space:

```
grant unlimited tablespace to dwdev01;
```

Caution   A reminder that the Always Free Autonomous Databases have a maximum 20 GB of storage available. While convenient, giving users an unlimited amount of storage quota could very quickly consume all available space.

Next, grant the necessary database role that will allow the user access to the OML Notebooks:

```
grant oml_developer to dwdev01;
```

For existing database accounts, you may also use web administration UI to grant them access to OML Notebooks. To do that, on the home page, check on the box *Show All Users* to list existing database accounts that have not been enabled for OML Notebooks access (Figure 14-3).

Figure 14-3. *Show All Users to select existing database accounts for enabling access to OML Notebooks*

You will need to provide an email address and, optionally, the users' first and last names. Do not change the password if not necessary. Once the user information updates are saved, the system will grant the *OML_DEVELOPER* database role to the user.

To access OML Notebooks, the most obvious path to navigate is through the ADB's Service Console (Figure 14-4).

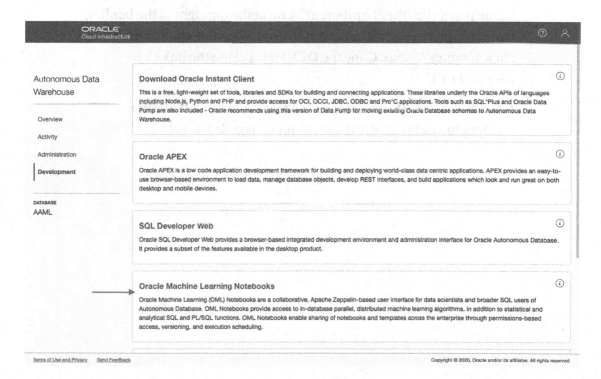

Figure 14-4. *Accessing OML Notebooks from the ADB's Service Console*

However, it is usually not practical to give every OML Notebooks user access to the Service Console as it will require an Oracle Cloud Infrastructure (OCI) account. Fortunately, like the SQL Developer Web, we can access the application directly by understanding and providing the information needed to create the link (Figure 14-5).

https://adb.<DATA_REGION>.oraclecloud.com/oml/tenants/<TENANT_OCID>/databases/<DATABASE_NAME>/

Figure 14-5. *URL template for accessing OML Notebooks*

For the ADW created for this chapter, I can determine the following:

- **DATA_REGION:** This will be the *region identifier* of your Oracle Cloud account's Home Region. You can find a full list of data regions and their identifiers here (`https://bit.ly/oci-docs-regions`). The Home Region for my account is US East (Ashburn) and the region identifier is *us-ashburn-1*.

- **TENANT_OCID:** Obtain this value from the OCI console. From the home page, click the "hamburger" icon at the top right of the landing page (≡), place your mouse over the item Administration, and then click *Tenancy Details*. Copy the OCID by clicking the link *Copy* (Figure 14-6).

- **DATABASE_NAME:** This is the database name specified when creating the instance. My database name is called *aaml*.

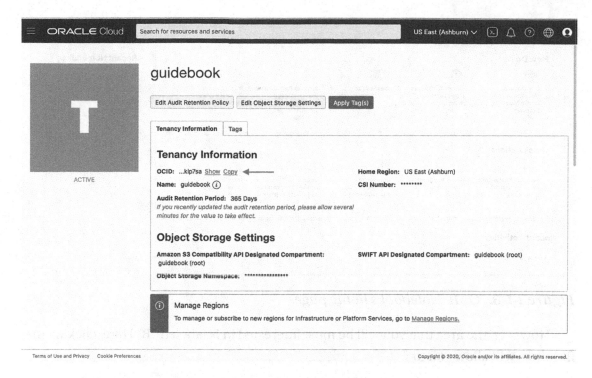

Figure 14-6. *Obtain the tenant's OCID from the OCI console*

Using the values gather, we can derive that the URL for accessing OML for *aaml* is as shown in Figure 14-7. Note that the tenant's OCID is typically a very long string and it is truncated in the example.

https://adb.us-ashburn-1.oraclecloud.com/oml/tenants/ocid1.tenancy.oc1..aaaaaaaa.../databases/aaml/

Figure 14-7. *Example OML Notebooks URL for ADW aaml*

When working with notebooks, do not use the admin account as there are usage limitations. Only use it for managing user accounts.

Using OML Notebooks

Upon successful login, users are redirected to the application's home page (Figure 14-8) where you will find links to read documentation and access tutorials (region labeled "A"). If you have been using the application actively, the notebooks and actions recently accessed and performed recently will be displayed in regions "C" and "D", respectively.

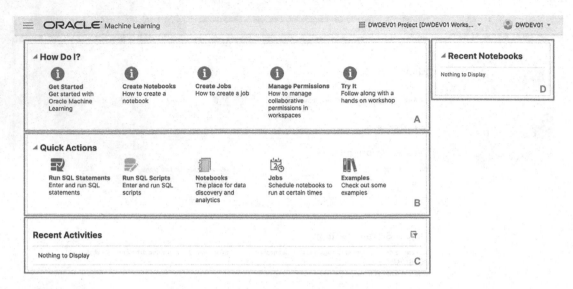

Figure 14-8. *OML Notebooks home page*

However, the area that you will be most interested in is labeled "B". Here, clicking the five links will allow you to

1. Access the SQL Query Scratchpad to run SQL statements

2. Access the SQL Script Scratchpad to run SQL or PL/SQL statements

3. Manage notebooks

4. Manage jobs

5. Access example notebooks

Items 1–3 are fundamentally centered around the notebook concept. While jobs are a method of scheduling notebook executions at preset intervals, we can manage these with item 4. Last but not least, item 5 is a catalog of predefined notebooks from Oracle that are useful templates (or quick-start guides) for creating your own notebooks.

Before using any of these functions, let's first examine the typical notebook user interface. The key areas of the UI are broken out in several regions in Figure 14-9.

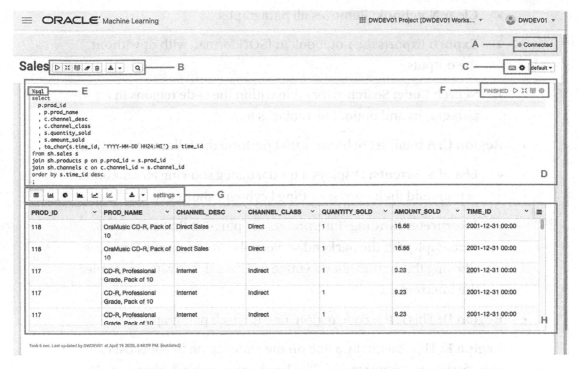

Figure 14-9. A breakdown of the notebook user interface

- **Region A:** Notebooks sessions are executed on Apache Zeppelin servers that are managed by Oracle. This is an indicator that you have connected the notebook successfully and are ready to create some magic.

- **Region B:** Notebooks have quite a few toolbars containing one or more buttons to help us perform tasks. Here are the buttons in detail, starting from the left:

  - **Run All Paragraphs:** A notebook contains one or more paragraphs. This button executes all of them in sequential order.

  - **Show/Hide Code:** Shows or hides all code regions in the notebook.

  - **Show/Hide Output:** Shows or hides all output regions in the notebook.

  - **Clear Output:** Clears all output regions in the notebook.

- **Clear Notebook:** Removes all paragraphs.

- **Export:** Exports the notebook in JSON format, with or without the outputs.

- **Search Code:** Searches for code within the code regions in all paragraphs and optionally replaces text.

- **Region C:** A small set of buttons that perform the following functions:

  - **List of Shortcuts:** Displays a modal dialog showing all notebook actions and their corresponding keyboard shortcuts.

  - **Interpreter Binding:** Interpreters are plug-ins that connect a paragraph with the backend servers, the Autonomous Database. Clicking this button allows you to activate, deactivate, or reorder the interpreters.

- **Region D:** This is the code region, one for each paragraph.

- **Region E:** This is actually a line on the code region to allow users to specify the interpreter to use. The line begins with a % character. **Do not** remove this. Valid values will be discussed later in this chapter.

- **Region F:** Like region B, it contains several buttons to perform the following tasks:

  - **Run This Paragraph:** Execute only the code contained in the paragraph.

  - **Show/Hide Code:** Shows or hides the code region in the paragraph.

  - **Show/Hide Output:** Shows or hides the output region in the paragraph.

  - Clicking the last button in this region allows users to customize how code is displayed, remove the paragraph, and so on.

- **Region G:** This toolbar is for the paragraph's output region.

  - The first set of button allows users to switch the output to be viewed as a table, bar chart, pie chart, area chart, line chart, and scatter chart.

- Next, the drop-down menu allows users to download the data in either CSV or TSV formats.

- Clicking the *settings* drop-down menu exposes additional options, depending on the output type selected.

- **Region H:** The output region for a paragraph.

Note   Oracle provides sample datasets found in the schema *SH* that you can use to familiarize yourself with the various features of the OML Notebooks, as well as the many available data mining algorithms included with the Autonomous Database.

Interpreters

Interpreters are an integral part of OML Notebooks. As mentioned earlier, they act as a bridge between notebooks and the backend servers that perform the computational workload. At this time, Oracle supports SQL, PL/SQL, and Markdown interpreters.

Note   Markdown (*https://daringfireball.net/projects/markdown//*) is a markup language designed for readability but sufficiently structured to allow markup processing software to translate into HTML or other formats.

Clicking the *Interpreter binding* button in region "C" (Figure 14-9) will reveal the current selection and order of interpreters (Figure 14-10).

Figure 14-10. *Managing interpreters' state and order*

Active interpreters are colored blue, while inactive interpreters are white. By default, they are ordered to use the ADB's lowest to highest predefined service names that specify the different levels of performance and concurrency for SQL execution.

Specifying the SQL and script interpreter bindings using the text `%sql` and `%script`, respectively, will use the low ADB service name. You may specify a different binding for any paragraph, by including the service name. For example, to use the high service name for running scripts, specify the binding:

```
%aaml_high.script
```

Organizing Notebooks

OML Notebooks have a hierarchical structure consisting of workspaces, projects, and notebooks (Figure 14-11).

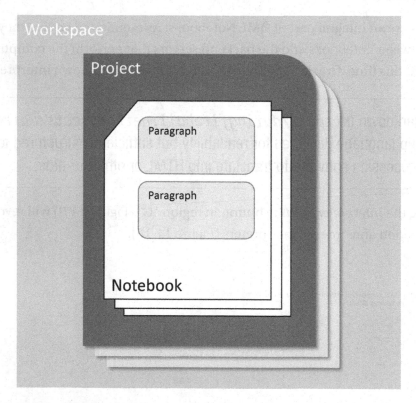

Figure 14-11. *Hierarchical structure of workspaces, projects, and notebooks in OML Notebooks*

All notebooks may only exist within a project, and a project inside a workspace. A workspace and project are automatically created for each OML user. A workspace may have more than one project, and likewise, a project may contain more than one notebook. While users may not create additional workspaces, they can certainly be granted permission to access other workspaces.

Manage Workspace and Projects

To manage workspace access rights and projects, click the second drop-down menu at the top right of any page (Figure 14-12).

Figure 14-12. *Workspace and project administration tasks*

Click the *Workspace Permissions...* menu item to manage access to your workspace. A modal dialog will open that allows you to select users with the *OML_DEVELOPER* role (Figure 14-13).

Figure 14-13. *Manage workspace permissions*

Select the role to assign to the user and then click *Add*. The user will show up in the following table. The permissions and actions available to them are listed in Table 14-1.

Table 14-1. *Permission types and allowable actions*

Permission Type	Workspace	Project	Notebook	Jobs
Manager	View only	Create, update, and delete	Create update, delete, and run	Schedule
Developer	View only	View only	Create, update, and run. Delete owned notebooks.	View and run only
Viewer	View only	View only	View only	View and run only

To remove any user, simply select the user and then click the *Delete* button. When you are done with managing user permissions, click *OK* to apply the changes and close the dialog.

A workspace manager may create additional projects to organize notebooks. Clicking *Select Project...* (Figure 14-12) opens a modal dialog displaying the workspace collapsed (Figure 14-14).

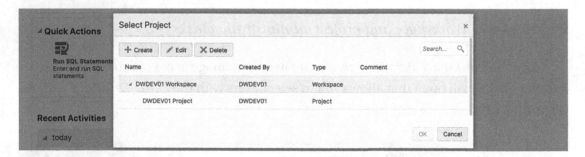

Figure 14-14. *Create, edit, or delete projects in the workspace*

Expand the workspace to list its projects. Besides creating new projects, users may select existing projects to either modify or remove. Click *OK* to persist changes.

Data Visualization

Generating useful graphical representations of data is an important step in understanding the information in your databases. Charts, graphs, and other visual formats can help discovery trends and patterns more easily than a regular data table. OML Notebooks facilitates the discovery process by providing these visual tools at your fingertips.

When using the SQL interpreter binding, the output region in a notebook paragraph will render query results in a table when the query is executed. Apart from sorting the data, there isn't very much you can do with the table. More often than not, you will find it more useful to look at your data columns, pick a suitable chart type, and visualize your data instead. For example, given the query:

```
select
  p.prod_id
  , p.prod_name
  , c.channel_desc
  , c.channel_class
  , s.quantity_sold
  , s.amount_sold
  , to_char(s.time_id, 'YYYY-MM-DD HH24:MI') as time_id
from sh.sales s
join sh.products p on p.prod_id = s.prod_id
join sh.channels c on c.channel_id = s.channel_id
where extract(year from s.time_id) = 2001;
```

Let's generate a chart that can tell us which channels (channel_desc) generated the greatest number of products sold (quantity_sold) in the year 2001. I find a pie chart useful in situations where we wanted to visualize distribution in a dataset. First, click the pie chart button (labeled "A" in Figure 14-15).

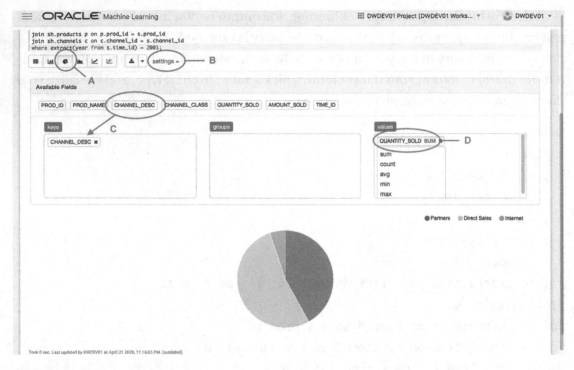

Figure 14-15. *Visualize your data*

Expand the settings by clicking the link *settings* (labeled "B"). The down-pointing chevron will point up instead and a subregion will display between the toolbar and chart. Here you will find the list of columns/fields defined and returned in your query. To add fields to the chart, drag and drop them in the respective boxes. Fields can be assigned to keys, groups, or values. For the pie chart, drag the CHANNEL_DESC field (labeled "C") and place it in the box under *keys*. Remove any other fields already added to *keys* by clicking the *x*, next to the field name.

Next, drag the field QUANTITY_SOLD and place it in the box under *values*. Remove any other fields in this box. You might also have noticed that the field is now suffixed with the word *SUM*. OML Notebooks automatically detects that an aggregate function needs to be applied to the column you have selected, so as to render the pie chart correctly. Click the field (labeled "D") to select a different aggregate function. You may choose between sum, count, average (avg), minimum (min), and maximum (max) values.

Scheduling Jobs

Workspace managers can create and schedule notebooks to run based on a predefined schedule. A scheduled job that was executed successfully can be viewed as a read-only notebook. This is a great feature if you had, for example, time-sensitive queries and reports to generate. Create the report before creating your job.

After the target report is created, head over to the Jobs page where you can create, schedule, and monitor jobs. To create a job, you will need to specify an appropriate name, select the job, and specify the frequency/interval and any additional conditions, for example, the maximum number of runs (Figure 14-16).

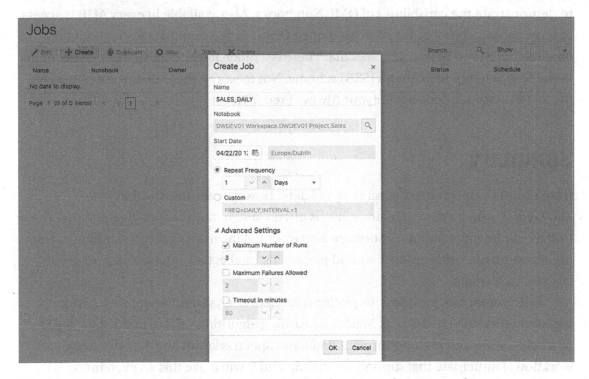

Figure 14-16. *Create a job to execute notebooks at regular intervals*

Machine Learning

Oracle Machine Learning (formerly known as Oracle Advanced Analytics) was previously an option Oracle Database Enterprise Edition Database Option that could be purchased to provide database developers access to data mining PL/SQL. A strong proposition to run Machine Learning algorithms where the data resides is performance, as there are no network or data marshaling overheads to contend with.

These APIs are built into the Autonomous Database offering, and data scientists can gain access to these advanced algorithms through OML Notebooks, such as decision trees, random forest, artificial neural networks, and k-means clustering. You may perform various mining functions like feature extraction, solve classification functions, or generate clusters inferred from your datasets.

Examples and Datasets

Whether you are an experienced data scientist, or someone seeking to learn some of these techniques, you will be pleased to know that Oracle does provide several examples to demonstrate the capabilities of OML Notebooks. Also available in every ADB is access to large sample datasets. We have used one of these in the examples throughout this chapter, the Sales History (SH) schema. There is a much larger dataset that can be found in the Star Schema Benchmark (SSB) schema. Not to worry, these do not count toward the 20 GB storage allocation for your Always Free ADBs.

Summary

It isn't hard to collect massive amounts of data. However, turning the data into knowledge, which creates greater value, is often a much more challenging process. Collaboration and communication are also essential in ensuring the best minds in your organization are working together and preserving intellectual assets in easy-to-read structured formats.

OML Notebooks provides this platform for data analysts and scientists to work together efficiently. It also puts Machine Learning algorithms closer to the data, backed by a self-tuning and high-performant database. Speed is key in any data discovery workflow. I anticipate that support for Python and R will make this an even more compelling solution when they become available in the near future.

PART 4

Next Steps

CHAPTER 15

Infrastructure as Code

We are always trying to be more efficient and more optimal in our IT operations. We are looking for ways to standardize our infrastructure, to accomplish the same work and the same operations with less time, and also to minimize the risk of error. Automation becomes our friend in order to accomplish things quicker, less expensively, with less risk of error and also to ensure our infrastructure is built the same way. To help us in this process, a new concept became very interesting, *Infrastructure as a Code* (IaC). IaC build and manage an infrastructure using machine-readable configuration files. The purpose of this chapter is to provide a basic understanding of an IaC tool called *Terraform*.

Terraform by HashiCorp

HashiCorp offers an *Infrastructure as a Code* tool called Terraform. Using this tool, we can build and maintain your cloud infrastructure components, not only on *Oracle Cloud Infrastructure* (OCI) but also on AWS, Azure, Google Cloud Platform, and so on. HashiCorp partnered with major cloud providers to offer the APIs in order to interact with them. This component that interacts with the infrastructure is called *Provider*.

In this chapter, we will use Terraform to build and maintain a cloud infrastructure including Virtual Cloud Network (VCN), Internet Gateway, Security List, Route Table, Subnet, one Compute Instance, and one Always Free Autonomous Transaction Processing. Figure 15-1 shows the topology that will be totally created and managed using *IaC*.

323

© Adrian Png and Luc Demanche 2020
A. Png and L. Demanche, *Getting Started with Oracle Cloud Free Tier*,
https://doi.org/10.1007/978-1-4842-6011-1_15

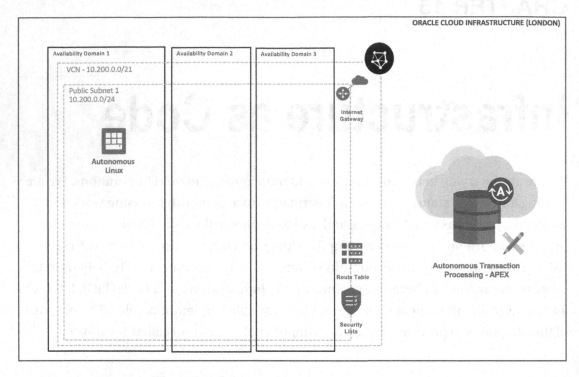

Figure 15-1. *Topology managed by IaC*

Installation of Terraform

Terraform is a single binary file that you can download from the Terraform website at
www.terraform.io/downloads.html. From this page, depending of you operating system
on which you will run Terraform, locate the link and copy the hyperlink. In my demo, we
want to run Terraform from a Compute Instance on OCI, so right-click the Linux 64-bit
link and select *Copy Link Location.*

Make sure your Compute Instance has access to the Internet, because the wget
command that follows will attempt to get the zip file from the HashiCorp website. The
wget command will fail if your Compute Instance lacks Internet access.

Log in now to your Compute Instance where you will deploy Terraform with the root
user. Perform the following commands:

```
# mkdir ~/stage && cd ~/stage
# wget <paste the link here>
# unzip terraform_0.12.26_linux_amd64.zip -d /usr/local/bin
```

Note   We extract the binary in */usr/local/bin.* This path is already in the PATH variable of the user root. You will be able to run the binary from any folder on the compute.

The installation of Terraform is now completed and you can launch it from the command line using the following command:

```
# terraform
```

The sections in this chapter show some of what can be done using Terraform now that you have it installed.

Provider

HashiCorp is using *GitHub* to share all their plug-ins and scripts. This link *https://github.com/terraform-providers* will list all the available providers Terraform is able to use. In this chapter, we will use the *Oracle Cloud Infrastructure* provider called *terraform-provider-oci.*

To download and configure the provider, we have to initialize the working folder where you will run Terraform from. Create your first script and add the block identifying the provider you would like to use. Let's create our first script called *01-vcn.tf* with the following content:

```
provider "oci" {
}
```

Note   Every Terraform script has to have the file extension *tf.*

From the command line, execute the following command:

```
# terraform init -upgrade
```

This command will initialize Terraform for the specific working folder that is current and will create a subfolder called *.terraform.* In this subfolder you will find the information for the provider you have mentioned in the script. Terraform is now ready to be used.

State File

After the creation of the first cloud component by Terraform, you will notice a new file in the working folder. The file *terraform.tfstate* stores the state of the current infrastructure. This file will be used by Terraform to map the current infrastructure with the configuration files. It will then be possible to compare and come up with required changes in order to get to the desired configuration. This file is crucial and needs to be in a secure location to make sure it will not be deleted and altered. The default location for this file is the working folder.

Authentication

The provider needs to interact with *Oracle Cloud Infrastructure* in order to manage OCI components, so it needs to use an authentication process. There are two ways to do this authentication with OCI:

- **API Key Authentication**: You have to provide the Tenancy OCID, OCID of the user, private key path, the fingerprint for the key pair, and the region. You can follow the instructions provided in this link https://docs.cloud.oracle.com/en-us/iaas/Content/API/Concepts/apisigningkey.htm.

  Your configuration file will have to have the following details in the provider block:

  ```
  provider "oci" {
    tenancy_ocid = var.tenancy_ocid
    user_ocid = var.user_ocid
    fingerprint = var.fingerprint
    private_key_path = var.private_key_path
    region = var.region
  }
  ```

- **Instance Principal Authentication**: The *Instance Principal* IAM service authorized a compute to perform actions on service resources. Here are the steps to enable an instance to call services:

1. Create a Dynamic Group and Matching Rules.

    From the navigation menu, click Identity, Dynamic Groups, and Create Dynamic Group. Provide a name, a description, and a matching rule like this one:

    ```
    ALL {instance.id = '<OCID of the compute instance>'}
    ```

2. Write Policies for Dynamic Group.

    You have to create a policy in the root compartment like this one:

    ```
    Allow dynamic-group <dynamic_group_name> to manage
    all-resources in tenancy
    ```

3. Configure Terraform.

    In the Terraform script, we will use this block:

    ```
    provider "oci" {
      auth    = "InstancePrincipal"
      region = var.region
    }
    ```

Building the Infrastructure

It is now time to build the infrastructure. Terraform has its own language, describing the desired infrastructure. We will use Terraform's resource to define each piece of the infrastructure. Examples of resources are *oci_core_vcn* to manage VCN, *oci_core_instance* to manage Compute Instance, and *oci_database_autonomous_database* to manage ADB. The code will be written in a regular text files with extension *.tf* and they will all be loaded from the working folder to create the execution plan or to apply the changes. We will also use a *variable definition* file with an extension *.tfvars*. This file will contain only variables and values. Instead of having the variable definition file, we can have variables and values in every .tf configuration files, but personally I prefer having all of them in a single variable definition file. That eases the preparation for a new deployment as I only have to modify the value in the variable definition file with the respective new values rather than going through each and every .tf configuration file.

In the next section, I will describe every resource I will create in the demo. To ease the management of the resources and the configuration files, I prefer having one resource block (oc_core_vnc, oci_core_instance, etc.) or related resource blocks into their own configuration files. For this demo, we will have six configuration files and a variable definition file:

- **01-vnc.tf**: Creation of the virtual cloud network and internet gateway

- **02-security-list.tf**: Creation of the security list

- **03-route-table.tf**: Creation of the route table

- **04-subnets.tf**: Creation of the subnet

- **05-compute.tf**: Creation of the compute

- **06-freeatp.tf**: Creation of the Autonomous Database

- **terraform.tfvars**: Variable definition file

The code that I am about to share is available at the book's GitHub repository (*https://github.com/Apress/getting-started-w-oracle-cloud-free-tier/tree/master/ch15*).

I will start by explaining in detail the content of the first configuration file *01-vcn.tf*. The other configuration files have the same exact structure, so I will only explain the main sections of each file.

Note   We have used the examples provided by HashiCorp on *GitHub* to build my demo. You can find a lot more examples at *https://github.com/terraform-providers/terraform-provider-oci/tree/master/examples*.

Virtual Cloud Network

This section shows the entire content of the file *01-vcn.tf*. This configuration file is separated in four sections:

- **Variables**: Each variable used in the configuration file must be declared in this section. The values of these variables are in the file *terraform.tfvars*.

- **Authentication**: Authentication method used by the provider. In this case we are using *Instance Principal*.

- **Virtual Cloud Network**: Resource block for the creation of the VCN. We need at least the *CIDR Block* and the *compartment_ocid*. The display name and DNS label are optional information.

- **Internet Gateway**: Resource block for the creation of the Internet Gateway. The required information are *compartment_ocid* and *vcn_id* of the virtual cloud network you want to assign the internet gateway to. Display name is optional.

The following is the actual code from the file, showing the four sections just described:

```
variable compartment_ocid {}
variable region {}
variable vcn_cidr {}
variable vcn_display_name {}
variable vcn_dns_label {}
variable internetgateway1_display_name {}

# Authentication
provider "oci" {
  auth    = "InstancePrincipal"
  region = var.region
}

# Virtual Cloud Network
resource "oci_core_vcn" "vcn1" {
  # Required
  cidr_block      = var.vcn_cidr
  compartment_id = var.compartment_ocid

  # Optional
  display_name    = var.vcn_display_name
  dns_label       = var.vcn_dns_label
}
```

```
# Internet Gateway
resource "oci_core_internet_gateway" "internetgateway1" {
  # Required
  compartment_id = var.compartment_ocid
  vcn_id         = oci_core_vcn.vcn1.id

  # Optional
  display_name   = var.internetgateway1_display_name
}
```

In the .tfvars file, we have these related variables:

```
#
# Common variables
#
region="uk-london-1"
compartment_ocid="ocid1.compartment.oc1..
aaaaaaaaucqsaxg3ejrnddtalaqdt342ic6c4wknz4vn7idnjq2ydse5j4xq"

#
# Used in 01-vcn.tf
#
vcn_cidr="10.200.0.0/21"
vcn_display_name="VirtualCloudNetwork_Book"
vcn_dns_label="vcnbook1"
internetgateway1_display_name="InternetGateway01_VirtualCloudNetwork_Book"
```

The first section of the variable definition file is used by every configuration file. Information like *region* is necessary for the authentication, and *compartment_ocid* is necessary for the creation of every cloud component.

The second section of the file is related to the configuration file *01-vcn.tf*, for the creation of the virtual cloud network and internet gateway. We have the values of every required or optional variable.

Now that we have created the configuration file for the creation of the VCN, internet gateway, and provided the values of the variables in the variable definition file, it's now time to use the Terraform binary. We will use two Terraform actions:

- **Plan**: Used to create the execution plan. It determines the required actions to get to the desired infrastructure defined in the configuration files.

- **Apply**: Used to apply the changes.

We have, at that moment, two files in our working folder, *01-vcn.tf* and *terraform. tfvars*. The command *terraform plan* will propose the required actions by comparing with the existing infrastructure. In this case, the infrastructure doesn't exist, and so the state file. Let's execute the command *terraform plan*.

```
# terraform plan
Refreshing Terraform state in-memory prior to plan...
The refreshed state will be used to calculate this plan, but will not be
persisted to local or remote state storage.

-----------------------------------------------------------------------

An execution plan has been generated and is shown below.
Resource actions are indicated with the following symbols:
  + create

Terraform will perform the following actions:

  # oci_core_internet_gateway.internetgateway1 will be created
  + resource "oci_core_internet_gateway" "internetgateway1" {
      + compartment_id = "ocid1.compartment.oc1..
aaaaaaaaucqsaxg3ejrnddtalaqdt342ic6c4wknz4vn7idnjq2ydse5j4xq"
      + defined_tags   = (known after apply)
      + display_name   = "InternetGateway01_VirtualCloudNetwork_Book"
      + enabled        = true
      + freeform_tags  = (known after apply)
      + id             = (known after apply)
      + state          = (known after apply)
      + time_created   = (known after apply)
      + vcn_id         = (known after apply)
    }
```

```
# oci_core_vcn.vcn1 will be created
+ resource "oci_core_vcn" "vcn1" {
    + cidr_block               = "10.200.0.0/21"
    + compartment_id           = "ocid1.compartment.oc1..
      aaaaaaaaucqsaxg3ejrnddtalaqdt342ic6c4wknz4vn7idnjq2ydse5j4xq"
    + default_dhcp_options_id  = (known after apply)
    + default_route_table_id   = (known after apply)
    + default_security_list_id = (known after apply)
    + defined_tags             = (known after apply)
    + display_name             = "VirtualCloudNetwork_Book"
    + dns_label                = "vcnbook1"
    + freeform_tags            = (known after apply)
    + id                       = (known after apply)
    + ipv6cidr_block           = (known after apply)
    + ipv6public_cidr_block    = (known after apply)
    + is_ipv6enabled           = (known after apply)
    + state                    = (known after apply)
    + time_created             = (known after apply)
    + vcn_domain_name          = (known after apply)
  }
```

Plan: 2 to add, 0 to change, 0 to destroy.

In this example, as we can see in red, the plan is to create two components, the *virtual cloud network* and the *internet gateway*.

If you are OK with this plan, the next operation will be to apply these changes, using the command *terraform apply*. I did remove some output as it's the same as for the execution plan.

```
# terraform apply
```

```
An execution plan has been generated and is shown below.
Resource actions are indicated with the following symbols:
  + create
```

```
Terraform will perform the following actions:
```

--- I have removed some output here

Plan: 2 to add, 0 to change, 0 to destroy.

Do you want to perform these actions?
  Terraform will perform the actions described above.
  Only 'yes' will be accepted to approve.

  Enter a value: yes

By confirming with **yes**, Terraform will perform the required operations in Oracle Cloud Infrastructure. In this case, Terraform will create the *virtual cloud network* and the *internet gateway*.

Here is an excerpt of the output from the creation of these components:

oci_core_vcn.vcn1: Creating...
oci_core_vcn.vcn1: Creation complete after 1s [id=ocid1.vcn.oc1.uk-london-1.amaaaaaav4fcskyao4oftxf7igh7zauflscskjzi63437yk3hrixd6ii6uoa]
oci_core_internet_gateway.internetgateway1: Creating...
oci_core_internet_gateway.internetgateway1: Creation
complete after 0s [id=ocid1.internetgateway.oc1.uk-london-1.
aaaaaaaawclhz7bqrinrtkeeivkgjpsxca7dhd6k7rlcpldvydnsbsyffdoa]

Apply complete! Resources: 2 added, 0 changed, 0 destroyed.

We have successfully created our first two cloud components, the VCN and the Internet Gateway. Now, let's look at the other components.

Security List

To manage the security list, we have created another file called *02-security-list.tf* that contains this main section:

```
# Security List
resource "oci_core_security_list" "subnet1_security_list" {
  # Required
  compartment_id = var.compartment_ocid
  vcn_id         = oci_core_vcn.vcn1.id

  # Optional
  display_name   = var.security_list1_display_name
```

```
# Egress Security Rule
egress_security_rules {
  # Required
  destination = "0.0.0.0/0"
  protocol    = "6"

  # Optional
  description = var.security_list1_egress_security_rules_description
}

# Ingress Security Rule that allows incoming TCP connections using port 22
ingress_security_rules {
  # Required
  protocol = "6"
  source   = "0.0.0.0/0"

  # Optional
  description = var.security_list1_ingress_security_rules_22_description
  stateless = false

  tcp_options {
    min = 22
    max = 22
  }
}

# Ingress Security Rule that allows incoming TCP connections using port 80
ingress_security_rules {
  # Required
  protocol = "6"
  source   = "0.0.0.0/0"

  # Optional
  description = var.security_list1_ingress_security_rules_80_description
  stateless = false
```

```
  tcp_options {
    min = 80
    max = 80
  }
 }
}
```

The required information for the creation of the *security list* are the *compartment_ocid* and the *vcn_id* on which you want to assign the security list. You will also see in red the information about the *egress* (outbound traffic) and *ingress* (inbound traffic) rules.

Note   Protocol = "6" in the definition of the egress and ingress rules refer to TCP.

I have also added the values of the variables in the *terraform.tfvars* file required for the creation of the *security list*. Here is an excerpt of the output of the command *terraform plan*:

```
# terraform plan
Refreshing Terraform state in-memory prior to plan...
The refreshed state will be used to calculate this plan, but will not be
persisted to local or remote state storage.

oci_core_vcn.vcn1: Refreshing state... [id=ocid1.vcn.oc1.uk-london-1.
amaaaaaav4fcskyao4oftxf7igh7zauflscskjzi63437yk3hrixd6ii6uoa]
oci_core_internet_gateway.internetgateway1: Refreshing
state... [id=ocid1.internetgateway.oc1.uk-london-1.
aaaaaaaawclhz7bqrinrtkeeivkgjpsxca7dhd6k7rlcpldvydnsbsyffdoa]

------------------------------------------------------------------------

An execution plan has been generated and is shown below.
Resource actions are indicated with the following symbols:
  + create

Terraform will perform the following actions:

  # oci_core_security_list.subnet1_security_list will be created
  + resource "oci_core_security_list" "subnet1_security_list" {
```

```
    + compartment_id = "ocid1.compartment.oc1..
      aaaaaaaaucqsaxg3ejrnddtalaqdt342ic6c4wknz4vn7idnjq2ydse5j4xq"
--- I have removed some output here

Plan: 1 to add, 0 to change, 0 to destroy.

-------------------------------------------------------------------------
```

The first action performed by *terraform plan* is the *refreshing state* where it compares with the current state using the *terraform.tfstate* file and the configuration files. Terraform notices the existence of the *virtual cloud network* and the *internet gateway*. The proposed plan is, as we can see in red, the creation of one component, the *security list*. Let's execute the *terraform apply* now. Here is the last section of the output:

```
Do you want to perform these actions?
  Terraform will perform the actions described above.
  Only 'yes' will be accepted to approve.

  Enter a value: yes


oci_core_security_list.subnet1_security_list: Creating...
oci_core_security_list.subnet1_security_list: Creation
complete after 1s [id=ocid1.securitylist.oc1.uk-london-1.
aaaaaaaapexej7hgx6hylxagiwjxsubvjbpih22un355po2moqcrcwjbclea]

Apply complete! Resources: 1 added, 0 changed, 0 destroyed.
```

Terraform apply did create one new component which is the *security list*.

Route Table

We have a file called *03-route-table.tf* that contains the information for the creation of the route table. The file contains the following:

```
# Route Table
resource "oci_core_route_table" "subnet1_route_table" {
  # Required
  compartment_id = var.compartment_ocid
  vcn_id         = oci_core_vcn.vcn1.id
```

```
# Optional
display_name    = var.subnet1_route_table_display_name

# Route Rule to route traffic to the Internet
route_rules {
  # Required
  network_entity_id = oci_core_internet_gateway.internetgateway1.id

  # Optional
  description = var.route_rule1_internet_gateway_description
  destination        = "0.0.0.0/0"

  }
}
```

The required information for the creation of the *route table* are the compartment_ocid and the vcn_id. The required information for the creation of the *route rule* is the entity ID used in this rule which is the *Internet Gateway*. I have also added the values of the variables in the *terraform.tfvars* file required for the creation of the *route table and rule*.

The execution of *terraform apply* creates one route table with one route rule. Here is an excerpt of the output.

```
Terraform will perform the following actions:

  # oci_core_route_table.subnet1_route_table will be created
  + resource "oci_core_route_table" "subnet1_route_table" {

--- I have removed some output here

Plan: 1 to add, 0 to change, 0 to destroy.

Do you want to perform these actions?
  Terraform will perform the actions described above.
  Only 'yes' will be accepted to approve.

  Enter a value: yes

oci_core_route_table.subnet1_route_table: Creating...
```

```
oci_core_route_table.subnet1_route_table: Creation
complete after 0s [id=ocid1.routetable.oc1.uk-london-1.
aaaaaaaatbohuogn7t6ddzomomgdcq2tmtpqe4ag54gyichthyz6llvzdz3a]
```

Apply complete! Resources: 1 added, 0 changed, 0 destroyed.

Subnet

We have a file called *04-subnets.tf* that contains the information for the creation of the subnet. The file contains the following:

```
# Subnet
resource "oci_core_subnet" "subnet1" {
  # Required
  vcn_id             = oci_core_vcn.vcn1.id
  compartment_id     = var.compartment_ocid
  cidr_block         = var.subnet1_cidr

  # Optional
  display_name       = var.subnet1_display_name
  dns_label          = var.subnet1_dns_label
  security_list_ids  = [oci_core_security_list.subnet1_security_list.id]
  route_table_id     = oci_core_route_table.subnet1_route_table.id
  dhcp_options_id    = oci_core_vcn.vcn1.default_dhcp_options_id
}
```

The required pieces of information for the creation of the subnet are the *compartment_ocid*, the *vcn_id,* as well as the *CIDR block* used by the subnet. I have also added the values of the variables in the *terraform.tfvars* file required for the creation of the *subnet.*

Here is an excerpt of the *terraform apply* output:

```
Terraform will perform the following actions:

  # oci_core_subnet.subnet1 will be created
  + resource "oci_core_subnet" "subnet1" {

--- I have removed some output here

Plan: 1 to add, 0 to change, 0 to destroy.
```

Do you want to perform these actions?
  Terraform will perform the actions described above.
  Only 'yes' will be accepted to approve.

  Enter a value: yes

oci_core_subnet.subnet1: Creating...
oci_core_subnet.subnet1: Creation complete after 0s [id=ocid1.subnet.oc1.
uk-london-1.aaaaaaaa5stwgizbmlnr7ji7qm4u4mmtj4weph6qfokpuzio6jffutsvugtq]

Apply complete! Resources: 1 added, 0 changed, 0 destroyed.

Compute

We have a file called *05-compute.tf* that contains the information for the creation of the compute. The file contains the following:

```
# Compute
resource "oci_core_instance" "instance01" {
  # Required
  availability_domain = lookup(data.oci_identity_availability_domains.ADs.
  availability_domains[count.index%3],"name")
  compartment_id       = var.compartment_ocid
  shape                = var.instance01_shape

  # Optional
  count = "1"
  display_name         = var.instance01_name
  shape_config {
    ocpus = "1"
  }

  create_vnic_details {
    # Required
    subnet_id          = oci_core_subnet.subnet1.id

    # Optional
    display_name    = "Primaryvnic"
    assign_public_ip = true
```

```
  hostname_label    = var.instance01_name
}

source_details {
  # Required
  source_type = "image"
  source_id   = "ocid1.image.oc1.uk-london-1.aaaaaaaaz57okycdlykwzwegouf
                 6p4fl6leo3mf7zs2setxxbls26hctpkgq"
}

metadata = {
  ssh_authorized_keys = var.ssh_public_key
  user_data = base64encode(file(var.instance01_script))
}
}
```

The required pieces of information are the following:

- Availability Domain in which the compute will be created

- Compartment_ocid

- Desired shape which is for this demo "VM.Standard.E2.1.Micro"

- Subnet ID required for the VNIC

- Source image ID

- SSH authorized key which is your public ssh key

As for the other resources, I have also added the values of the variables in the *terraform.tfvars* file required for the creation of the *compute*. Here is an excerpt of the *terraform apply* output:

```
Terraform will perform the following actions:

  # oci_core_instance.instance01[0] will be created
  + resource "oci_core_instance" "instance01" {
--- I have removed some output here

Plan: 1 to add, 0 to change, 0 to destroy.
```

```
Do you want to perform these actions?
  Terraform will perform the actions described above.
  Only 'yes' will be accepted to approve.

  Enter a value: yes
```

```
oci_core_instance.instance01[0]: Creating...
oci_core_instance.instance01[0]: Still creating... [10s elapsed]
oci_core_instance.instance01[0]: Still creating... [20s elapsed]
oci_core_instance.instance01[0]: Still creating... [30s elapsed]
oci_core_instance.instance01[0]: Still creating... [40s elapsed]
oci_core_instance.instance01[0]: Still creating... [50s elapsed]
oci_core_instance.instance01[0]: Still creating... [1m0s elapsed]
oci_core_instance.instance01[0]: Still creating... [1m10s elapsed]
oci_core_instance.instance01[0]: Creation complete
after 1m15s [id=ocid1.instance.oc1.uk-london-1.
anwgiljtv4fcskycwxai4z6sdl2focs5t5kgkcaelgsrlrhutmr6dtktntra]
```

Apply complete! Resources: 1 added, 0 changed, 0 destroyed.

As you can see in the Compute configuration file, I'm also using *the user_data parameter, refering to a script that will be executed during the provisioning process of the Compute.* This script contains the following:

```
#!/bin/bash

echo "The time is now $(date -R)!" | tee /tmp/cloud-init_start.txt
sudo mkdir /root/wallets
sudo yum -y update
sudo yum -y install sqlcl
sudo yum -y install httpd
sudo su -c "systemctl start httpd"
sudo su -c "systemctl enable httpd.service"
sudo su -c "systemctl stop firewalld"
sudo echo 'My First WebApp using Oracle Cloud Free Tier' > /var/www/html/
index.html
echo "The time is now $(date -R)!" | tee /tmp/cloud-init_end.txt
```

In order to follow the execution of the script, the first operation is creating the file /
tmp/cloud-init_start.txt and the last operation is creating the file */tmp/cloud-init_end.txt*.
I'm using this *cloud-init* script to perform important tasks like *yum update* to apply the
latest operating system patches. I also install the utilities *sqlcl* and *Apache HTTP Server*.
You can follow the *yum update* process by using the comment *tail -f /var/log/yum.log*.
Once the provisioning process is completed, as I have installed and configured *Apache
HTTP Server,* you can validate the deployment by using this URL in your preferred
browser, *http://<ComputeIPAddress>/index.html*.

At this point, the last element we would like Terraform to create is the *Always Free
Autonomous Database*.

Free Autonomous Database

We have a file called *06-freeatp.tf* that contains the information for the creation of the
Always Free Autonomous Transaction Processing. The file contains the following:

```
# Always Free Autonomous Transaction Processing
resource "oci_database_autonomous_database" "freeatp01" {
  # Required
  admin_password          = var.adb_password
  compartment_id          = var.compartment_ocid
  cpu_core_count          = "1"
  data_storage_size_in_tbs = "1"
  db_name                 = var.adb_name

  # Optional
  db_workload  = "OLTP"
  display_name = var.adb_display_name
  is_auto_scaling_enabled = "false"
  license_model           = "LICENSE_INCLUDED"
  is_free_tier            = "true"
}
```

The required pieces of information for the creation of the ATP are the following:

- Admin password

- Compartment_OCID

- CPU Count

- Size of data storage

- Database Name

Again, as for the other resources, I have also added the values of the variables in the *terraform.tfvars* file required for the creation of the *ADB*. Here is the excerpt of the *terraform apply* output:

```
Terraform will perform the following actions:

  # oci_database_autonomous_database.freeatp01 will be created
  + resource "oci_database_autonomous_database" "freeatp01" {
--- I have removed some output here

Plan: 1 to add, 0 to change, 0 to destroy.

Do you want to perform these actions?
  Terraform will perform the actions described above.
  Only 'yes' will be accepted to approve.

  Enter a value: yes

oci_database_autonomous_database.freeatp01: Creating...
oci_database_autonomous_database.freeatp01: Still creating... [10s elapsed]
oci_database_autonomous_database.freeatp01: Still creating... [20s elapsed]
oci_database_autonomous_database.freeatp01: Still creating... [30s elapsed]
oci_database_autonomous_database.freeatp01: Still creating... [40s elapsed]
oci_database_autonomous_database.freeatp01: Still creating... [50s elapsed]
oci_database_autonomous_database.freeatp01: Still creating... [1m0s elapsed]
oci_database_autonomous_database.freeatp01: Still creating... [1m10s elapsed]
oci_database_autonomous_database.freeatp01: Still creating... [1m20s elapsed]
oci_database_autonomous_database.freeatp01: Still creating... [1m30s elapsed]
oci_database_autonomous_database.freeatp01: Creation complete
after 1m36s [id=ocid1.autonomousdatabase.oc1.uk-london-1.
abwgiljtmxp55fsipzgkfv7axsthefpflk3qtsvvqaskswrlcvxjvyg22tba]

Apply complete! Resources: 1 added, 0 changed, 0 destroyed.
```

At the end of the provisioning, you can go in the OCI console and validate the creation of the ADB. You can refer to Chapter 7 to download the credential wallet, transferring it to the previously created compute, and to use *sqlcl* to connect to this new ADB.

Modifying the Infrastructure

We have seen how we can use Terraform to build a new infrastructure. Now we will see how Terraform can maintain this infrastructure. Imagine you would like to add one security list rule. You would like to use SSL certificates and you need to add a rule for the port 443 in the current security list.

You will add this block in the file 02-security-list.tf.

```
# Ingress Security Rule that allows incoming TCP connections using port 443
ingress_security_rules {
  # Required
  protocol = "6"
  source   = "0.0.0.0/0"

  # Optional
  description = var.security_list1_ingress_security_rules_80_description
  stateless = false

  tcp_options {
    min = 443
    max = 443
  }
}
```

As you can see, this block adds the rule to open the port 443 for the protocol TCP. Now you will execute the command *terraform plan*. After comparing the current infrastructure using the *terraform.tfstate* file, terraform will display the execution plan. Here is an excerpt of the output:

```
An execution plan has been generated and is shown below.
Resource actions are indicated with the following symbols:
  ~ update in-place
```

Terraform will perform the following actions:

 # oci_core_security_list.subnet1_security_list will be updated in-place
--- I have removed some output here

```
    + ingress_security_rules {
        + description = "Allow ingress connection from Internet on port 80"
        + protocol    = "6"
        + source      = "0.0.0.0/0"
        + source_type = (known after apply)
        + stateless   = false

        + tcp_options {
            + max = 443
            + min = 443
        }
    }
}
```

Plan: 0 to add, 1 to change, 0 to destroy.

Terraform is proposing to do an update in-place of the current security list. If you are in agreement with this plan of changing the current security list to add this new rule, you can perform the command *terraform apply*. At the end of this process, your infrastructure will be modified, and you will have two security list rules.

If you decide to use Terraform or any *IaC*, it would become the only way to maintain your infrastructure. You must not manually modify the infrastructure without using Terraform as the current state in the *terraform.tfstate* will be out of sync. For any change you would like to do, change the configuration files, and then Terraform will compare the configuration files with the current infrastructure using the *terraform.tfstate* and come up with an execution plan. If you don't agree with the plan, modify the configuration files again until you are in agreement, and then run the command *terraform apply*.

Summary

In this chapter we have explored the *Infrastructure as a Code* concept using Terraform, provided by HashiCorp. Using an *IaC* tool, we would be more effective in our IT operations, more secure and low cost. Terraform uses configuration files to define the desired infrastructure. Once defined, terraform will compare with the current (if any) infrastructure and will then come up with actions to bring the infrastructure as defined in the configuration file. If you decide to use an *IaC* tool like Terraform, you have to use it for the creation, changes, and destruction of your cloud resources.

CHAPTER 16

Account Management

As we have mentioned already, the *Oracle Cloud Free Tier* is giving you access to a subset of cloud services. But you might have extra needs that would require some services not part of the *Free Tier*. For example, you want your *APEX* application to send emails; you would like to use *Functions*; you would like to leverage other great services like *Streaming, Integration Cloud, Data Safe, Analytic Cloud,* and so on. So you would need to upgrade your account. The first section of this chapter will explain the options you have in regard to upgrading your account to a paid account.

Since the beginning of this book, we are talking about and explaining what we are able to accomplish using *Oracle Cloud Free Tier* and *Always Free* resources. With this offering, we are able to build a cloud infrastructure and run a multitiered application including the best data management product from Oracle, the Autonomous Database. The next section of this chapter will discuss about the estimated value of this offering and the *Cost Analysis* utility.

We will conclude this chapter by describing the *Compartment Explorer* feature and how it ease the exploration of compartments across the tenancy.

Upgrading to Paid Account

One very important point that we really have to understand is even though you upgrade your account to a paid account, you will still have the *Always Free* cloud resources available. Each and every OCI account, either a *Free Tier* or a *paid account*, will always have the *Always Free* resources that we have explored in this book. To upgrade your account, click the navigation menu, Account Management ➤ Payment Method. Once on this page, you will see two options:

© Adrian Png and Luc Demanche 2020
A. Png and L. Demanche, *Getting Started with Oracle Cloud Free Tier,*
https://doi.org/10.1007/978-1-4842-6011-1_16

- **Pay As You Go (PAYG)**: PAYG account type will allow you to use all OCI Services. This account type doesn't require any minimum commitment, and it is ideal for less than USD $1000 of cloud usage per month.

- **Request a Sales Call**: If you are estimating a higher usage than $1000, we would recommend contacting the Oracle sales team.

Figure 16-1 shows the page with these options.

Payment Method

Select an account type and confirm your payment method to begin your paid Oracle Cloud account.

Account Type   Estimate your costs [↗]

Pay As You Go

Access all of our Oracle Cloud Infrastructure services

- **No minimum term**
- **No prepayment required**

Pay As You Go is for accounts where the monthly spend is up to a few thousand dollars. For larger accounts, we recommend discussing options with our sales team.

Request a Sales Call

We have a global Oracle sales team available to assist you in a variety of topics including new orders, activation, and managing your subscription.

Select

Payment Method

Credit Card	Name on card	Expires
No credit cards found. You can add a credit card by clicking on the "Add a credit card" button below.		

Add a credit card

☐ I agree to the terms and conditions of the Cloud Services Agreement for Oracle Canada ULC (also available here) and this Order including Service Description for B88206 - Oracle PaaS and IaaS Universal Credits.

Start Paid Account

Figure 16-1. *Upgrading your account*

Once you have selected *Pay As You Go*, you will have to provide your credit card information. Once completed, you have to accept the terms and conditions and you will be able to click *Start Paid Account*. You will be notified when your account has been upgraded, and you will see the other cloud services become available.

If you select the second option, you will be asked to provide a phone number or email address in order for an Oracle representative to contact you.

Cost Analysis

The *Free Tier* has some limitations, but what would be the cost of my application if I needed to pay for the Load Balancer, two computes with the storage, as well as the Autonomous Database. Here is a table that lists the free resources included in the Oracle Cloud Free Tier and the estimated monthly cost.

Table 16-1. *Monthly cost*

Cloud Resource	Description	Estimated Monthly Cost (USD)
Load Balancer	One Always Free 10 Mbps Load Balancer	16
Computes	Two Always Free Computes with the VM.Standard. E2.1.Micro shape	6
Storage for Computes	A total of 100 GB of Always Free	4
Autonomous Databases	Two Always Free Oracle Autonomous Databases	2800
Storage for ADBs	20 GB of storage per ADB, for a total of 40 GB of storage	60
Object Storage	20 GB of storage	1

Based on this table, the *Oracle Cloud Free Tier* offering is giving you more than USD $2800 worth of cloud credits per month.

One day, you will most probably upgrade your account to a paid account. As we were saying, this will give you access to all of the other cloud services. Once you would start using paid cloud services, the first thing you would be worried about is the cost of using these services, and this is totally normal. The *Cost Analysis* page is providing you this information. Click the navigation menu, Account Management and Cost Analysis. As we are writing this book, two versions of this page exist. I will provide details on both of them. You will see in Figure 16-2 the old version page with the default values.

Cost Analysis

ⓘ Free Trial   Trial Credits Used   CA$3.02 / CA$400.00   Total Days Used   65 / 30

Upgrade account

Filters

START DATE	END DATE	COMPARTMENT	TAG KEY
Jun 1, 2020	Jun 5, 2020	Filter by Compartment	Filter by Tag

TAG VALUE

Apply Filters

Jun 1, 2020 - Jun 5, 2020

Total Usage Charges
CA$0.60

Service	Total Cost	Total Cost Trend (Jun 1, 2020 - Jun 5, 2020)
› Compute	CA$0.00	
› Block Storage	CA$0.60	

Figure 16-2. *Cost Analysis page*

First of all, you have the information of your Free Trial and also you can launch the upgrade process by clicking *Upgrade Account*. The consumption is always based on filters, and by default, we are seeing the consumption for the current period and for the entire tenancy. Personally, I like having compartments per project or department, so I always use compartment in my filters. Filtering by compartment is a great approach, but some customers would like to have deeper information, for example, having cost information per servers. In that case, as we have explained in Chapter 7, we can use predefined *Oracle-Tags* or create our own *Cost Tracking Tag Key Definition*. Using cost tracking tags, attached to the compute instances, these tags can be used as filters to extract consumption information per Compute Instance.

Oracle Cloud is in the process of rolling out a new version of the Cost Analysis page. If you click *Switch to Latest Version*, you will get to the new version. This version brings new features and improves the way we can use filters. Using a mix of filters would allow you to create more detailed cost information. To add a filter, click Add filter, and you will be able to add multiple filters (which was not the case before). An example could be having a tag to filter on the compartment (using its name, OCID, or the path) and the tag *Oracle-Tags.CreatedBy*. You will then get the cost, per compartment and per OCI users that created cloud components during that period. I encourage you to create tags that would allow you to get the fine-grained detail you would require. A common example is having tags for project, environment, and server name. This way you would be able to generate cost information for a specific project, for an environment, and even for a specific server.

The first example of using the new version (Figure 16-3) is the simplest report using one filter on a specific compartment.

Figure 16-3. *Cost report by compartment*

We have a basic report showing the day-to-day cost of the cloud usage for the specific period. At the bottom of the page, we have the same data in a table format.

A new feature in this release is the ability to group the information using the *Grouping Dimension*. In my next example, I grouped the information by *Service,* and Figure 16-4 shows the output.

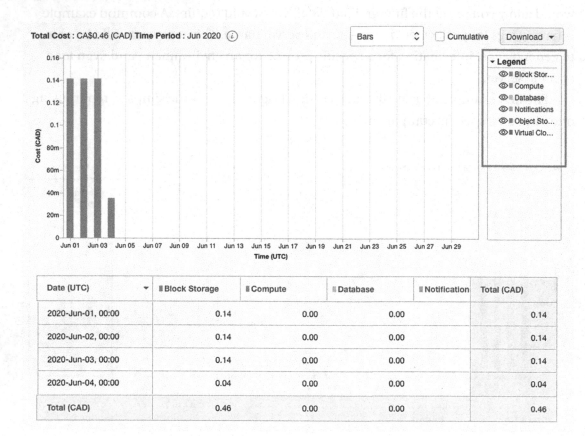

Date (UTC)	▼	▮ Block Storage	▮ Compute	▮ Database	▮ Notification	Total (CAD)
2020-Jun-01, 00:00		0.14	0.00	0.00		0.14
2020-Jun-02, 00:00		0.14	0.00	0.00		0.14
2020-Jun-03, 00:00		0.14	0.00	0.00		0.14
2020-Jun-04, 00:00		0.04	0.00	0.00		0.04
Total (CAD)		0.46	0.00	0.00		0.46

Figure 16-4. *Cost report by services*

I have highlighted in the table legend the *Services* that appear in the graph. We can see, day after day, the total cost of cloud usage. The same data is also presented in a table format.

Another new feature is the *Download* button to download in CSV format the data represented in the table. You can either keep the CSV files for reference or consolidate the information in a centralized location and perform more complex reports.

As for every other cloud service, this section is evolving very rapidly, and I'm sure they will include a lot of new capabilities in the future. For example, at this moment, we are not able to use a calendar to identify a start and end date. We should select the time period between five specific time periods, which doesn't provide a lot of flexibility.

Compartment Explorer

Someday, or you might be there already, you will have a lot of cloud components, in different compartments, and soon, using multiple regions. The page *Compartment Explorer* will help you explore your compartments and help locate your components across your tenancy. Let's have a look (Figure 16-5) at the *Compartment Explorer* page and its content.

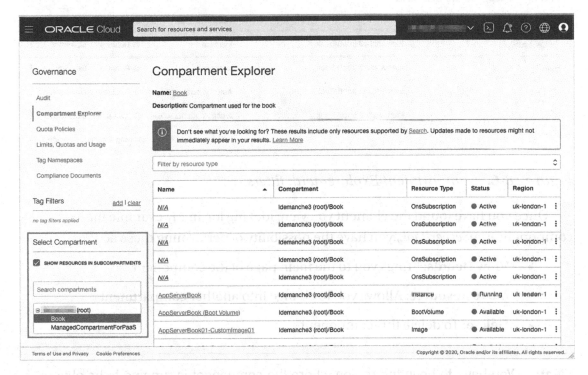

Figure 16-5. Compartment Explorer

On the left side of the page, under Select Compartment, you have to select the compartment you want to look into. If you use subcompartments, I recommend to check the *SHOW RESOURCES IN SUBCOMPARTMENTS* box. When you select or change the compartment, the result will appear automatically. You also have the possibility to use filters. For example, you can view all the *Autonomous Database* and *Instance* for the compartment Book. Figure 16-6 shows the results with these filters.

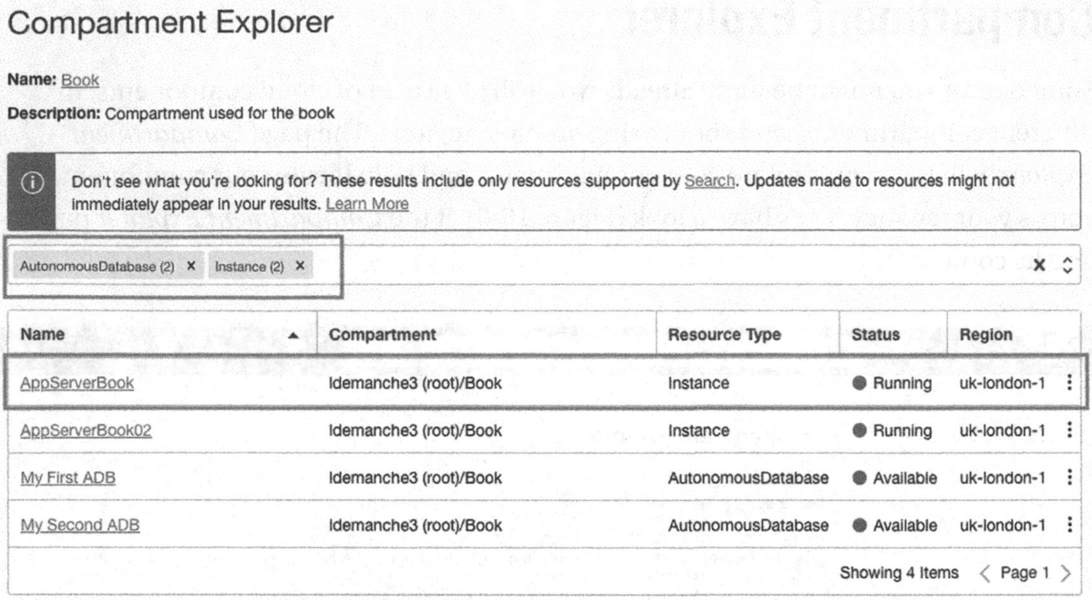

Compartment Explorer

Name: Book

Description: Compartment used for the book

> ⓘ   Don't see what you're looking for? These results include only resources supported by Search. Updates made to resources might not immediately appear in your results. Learn More

AutonomousDatabase (2) ✕   Instance (2) ✕   ✕ ⌄

Name ▲	Compartment	Resource Type	Status	Region	
AppServerBook	Idemanche3 (root)/Book	Instance	● Running	uk-london-1	⋮
AppServerBook02	Idemanche3 (root)/Book	Instance	● Running	uk-london-1	⋮
My First ADB	Idemanche3 (root)/Book	AutonomousDatabase	● Available	uk-london-1	⋮
My Second ADB	Idemanche3 (root)/Book	AutonomousDatabase	● Available	uk-london-1	⋮

Showing 4 Items   ⟨ Page 1 ⟩

Figure 16-6. *Compartment Explorer with filters*

Once you have found the element you were looking for, in my example the component *AppServerBook*, you have the possibility of performing these actions:

- **View Details**: Brings you to the main page of the component

- **Move Resource**: Allows you to change into another compartment

- **Delete**: To delete this component

Note   You have to be in the region where the component is running to be able to use these options.

Be aware that if you create or modify a component, it might not show up immediately.

Summary

One day, you will probably want to upgrade your Free Tier to a paid account, so we have explained the way to accomplish this.

We have also discussed about cost and how we can get your historical or current cloud usage cost across your tenancy. This topic is important as the concept of "paying for what you are using" could end up with surprising bills. I encourage you to regularly look at your current cloud usage cost.

The last item we have looked at is the *Compartment Explorer* and how it is easy to explore the content of the compartments. We will be at a point where you will have multiple compartments, across multiple regions, and it easily becomes complicated locating resources that you are looking for.

Index

© Adrian Png and Luc Demanche 2020
A. Png and L. Demanche, *Getting Started with Oracle Cloud Free Tier*,
https://doi.org/10.1007/978-1-4842-6011-1

U

V

W, X, Y, Z

Printed in the United States
By Bookmasters